Language typology and syntactic description

Volume II

Complex constructions

Language typology and syntactic description is published under the auspices of the Center for Applied Linguistics.

Volume I: *Clause structure*
Volume II: *Complex constructions*
Volume III: *Grammatical categories and the lexicon*

Language typology and syntactic description

Volume II
Complex constructions

Edited by
TIMOTHY SHOPEN
Australian National University

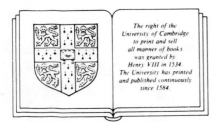

The right of the
University of Cambridge
to print and sell
all manner of books
was granted by
Henry VIII in 1534.
The University has printed
and published continuously
since 1584.

CAMBRIDGE UNIVERSITY PRESS

Cambridge

New York   Port Chester   Melbourne   Sydney

Published by the Press Syndicate of the University of Cambridge
The Pitt Building, Trumpington Street, Cambridge CB2 1RP
40 West 20th Street, New York, NY 10011, USA
10 Stamford Road, Oakleigh, Melbourne 3166, Australia

First published 1985
Reprinted 1987, 1990

Printed by the Athenaeum Press Ltd, Newcastle upon Tyne

Library of Congress catalogue card number: 84-20028

British Library cataloguing in publication data

Language typology and syntactic description.
Vol. 2. Complex constructions
1. Grammar, Comparative and general – Syntax
I. Shopen, Timothy
415   P291

ISBN 0 521 26858 3 hard covers
ISBN 0 521 31898 X paperback

Contents

3 Relative clauses

EDWARD L. KEENAN

University of California, Los Angeles

4 Adverbial clauses

SANDRA A. THOMPSON

University of California, Los Angeles
and

ROBERT E. LONGACRE

University of Texas at Arlington

5 Sentences as combinations of clauses

ROBERT E. LONGACRE
University of Texas at Arlington

Acknowledgements

This work began at a conference on field work questionnaires initiated by Rudolph Troike at the Center for Applied Linguistics (CAL). The participants agreed that the best way to prepare for field work is to develop an idea of what to look for, and this led to the idea of a typological survey that could serve as a reference manual and a textbook for students.

Many people have helped us in the work that we now present. I will name only a few here. Rudolph Troike and John Hammer of CAL, and Alan Bell of the National Science Foundation did much to help in the organization of the project, and the National Science Foundation provided generous financial support without which the work would not have been possible. Diana Riehl of CAL was a reliable and capable intermediary in the complex administration of the project. Carmen Silva-Corvalan and Sandra Thompson deserve special thanks for their work at UCLA, while here in Australia many people provided help. The Australian National University has been very generous in its support of my work. I am grateful to Penny Carter and Julia Harding of Cambridge University Press for the careful work in the production of our books. Three people that have been especially helpful to me in the final stages of the editing are Edith Bavin, Jean Harkins, and above all, Rosemary Butt. My thanks to all.

Timothy Shopen
Canberra, Australia
February 1984

Abbreviations for grammatical terms

The following are abbreviations for grammatical terms used frequently in the glosses for example. Other abbreviations are explained as they are presented.

ABS	Absolutive	IO	Indirect object
ACC	Accusative	IRR	Irrealis
ACT	Actor	LOC	Locative
AG	Agent	NOM	Nominative
ART	Article	NZN	Nominalization
ASP	Aspect	NZR	Nominalizer
ASSOC	Associative	OBJ	Object
AUX	Auxiliary	OBL	Oblique
BEN	Benefactive	PART	Participle
CL	Classifier	PASS	Passive
COMP	Complementizer	PCL	Particle
COMPL	Completive	PERF	Perfective
COND	Conditional	PL	Plural
DAT	Dative	PREP	Preposition
DECLAR	Declarative	PRES	Present
DEF	Definite	PRO	Pro form
DEM	Demonstrative	PROG	Progressive
DET	Determiner	Q	Question marker
DO	Direct object	REFL	Reflexive
DU	Dual	REL	Relativizer
EMPH	Emphasis	RPRO	Relative pronoun
ERG	Ergative	SG	Singular
FUT	Future	SJNCT	Subjunctive
GEN	Genitive	SUBJ	Subject
HABIT	Habitual	TNS	Tense
IMP	Imperative	TOP	Topic
IMPERS	Impersonal	VN	Verbal noun
INCOMPL	Incompletive	I	First person
INDIC	Indicative	2	Second person
INF	Infinitive	3	Third person
INSTR	Instrumental		

Introduction

Complex constructions is the second of three volumes comprising the work *Language typology and syntactic description*. The first volume is *Clause structure* and the third is *Grammatical categories and the lexicon*. Our purpose has been to do a cross-linguistic survey of syntactic and morphological structure that can serve as a manual for field workers, and for anyone interested in relating observations about particular languages to a general theory of language.

There are five chapters in this volume. The first is by John Payne on complex phrases and complex sentences. He examines the notion of co-ordination in phrases, especially in noun phrases, and in sentences. He establishes a semantic typology for types of co-ordination and illustrates their use in a variety of languages.

The second chapter is by Michael Noonan on complementation. He looks at the morphology and syntax of complementation with concern for such notions as equi-deletion, raising, parataxis and serialization, with the view that a good deal in the form of complements follows from the semantics of the complement-taking predicate.

The third chapter is by Edward Keenan on relative clauses. He defines the major types of relative clauses and describes the ways in which various languages give formal realization to these types. Included in his discussion is concern for the interaction of relative clause formation and other syntactic operations.

The fourth chapter is by Sandra Thompson and Robert Longacre on adverbial clauses. They show that the meanings expressed in adverbial clauses can always be expressed in other ways, but are presented as they are for reasons of discourse structure. The first half of the chapter presents a typology of adverbial clauses and the second provides a set of notions for understanding the function of these clauses in discourse.

The last chapter of the volume is by Robert Longacre with the title 'Sentences as combinations of clauses'. Looking at complex sentences from this point of view he develops a typology for the way in which various languages combine clauses into larger structures, with sketches of some representative languages.

Note: References to chapters in all three volumes of *Language typology and syntactic description* are preceded by the volume number. For example: chapter II.1 (chapter 1, this volume), chapter I.3 (chapter 3, Volume I).

1 Complex phrases and complex sentences

JOHN R. PAYNE

0 Preliminaries

0.1 *Types of co-ordination*

All languages, seemingly without exception, possess strategies which permit various types of co-ordination to occur at the phrasal as well as the sentential level, thereby forming complex phrases of various grammatical categories.

From a logical point of view, it is possible to distinguish five basic co-ordination types which are realized linguistically both at phrasal and sentential levels: these are *conjunction* (p and q), *postsection* (p and not q), *presection* (not p and q), *disjunction* (p or q), and *rejection* (not p and not q; not ... p or q).

In most languages, postsection and presection are treated analytically as a combination of conjunction and negation, but rarely they may be realized by a distinct synthetic form. Similarly, rejection may be treated analytically as a combination of conjunction and negation, or of disjunction and negation; alternatively, there may be a distinct synthetic form, as with English *neither ... nor*. Other co-ordination types (like English *for*) occur only at the sentential level, and will not be considered in this chapter.

On the basis of this primarily logical division (though the logical connectives, of course, do not exhaust the meanings of the corresponding linguistic ones, particularly at phrasal levels when no sentential paraphrase is available), further semantic subdivisions may be made. The ones we shall adopt are in most cases similar to those suggested by Dik (1972:279). They may be expressed in feature form, with attribution of markedness (in the Praguian sense) to the plus-valued member: [±Adversative], [±Separate] and [±Emphatic]. Table 1.1 illustrates the most usual occurrences using adjectival co-ordinations from English.

The feature [±Adversative], which specifies whether or not the conjuncts are to be contrasted, subdivides all the basic types except disjunction, with which it appears to be incompatible. In general, the marked value is realized in English by the co-ordinating conjunction

Table 1.1 *Co-ordination types*

(i) Conjunction (p.q)	±Adversative	±Separate	±Emphatic: rich, happy, and wise
			+Emphatic: rich, and happy, and wise
		+Separate	±Emphatic: both rich, happy, and wise
			+Emphatic: both rich, and happy, and wise
	+Adversative: rich, but happy		
(ii) Postsection (p.q̄)	±Adversative		±Emphatic: rich, happy, and not wise
			+Emphatic: rich, and happy, and not wise
	+Adversative: rich, but not happy		
(iii) Presection (p̄.q)	±Adversative:		±Emphatic: not rich, happy, and wise
			+Emphatic: not rich, and happy, and wise
	+Adversative: not rich, but happy		
(iv) Disjunction (pvq)	±Separate		±Emphatic: rich, happy, or wise
			+Emphatic: rich, or happy, or wise
	+Separate		±Emphatic: either rich, happy, or wise
			+Emphatic: either rich, or happy, or wise
(v) Rejection (p̄.q̄) = (p̄v̄q̄)	±Adversative		±Emphatic: neither rich, happy, nor wise
			+Emphatic: neither rich, nor happy, nor wise
	+Adversative: not rich, but not happy		

but. While '[$_{AP}$ rich *but* happy]' always has an adversative sense, the corresponding unmarked form '[$_{AP}$ rich *and* happy]' may perhaps in context require an adversative reading, but is essentially vague.

The feature [±Separate], which specifies that emphasis is to be placed on the separateness of the conjuncts, and in the case of phrasal co-ordination implies the existence of a sentential paraphrase, is realized in English by the addition of *both* in the case of conjunction and *either* in the case of disjunction. While '[$_{NP}$ *both* John *and* Mary] got married' always implies that John and Mary should be considered as separate individuals undertaking marriage (and therefore most probably not with each other), the corresponding unmarked '[$_{NP}$ John *and* Mary] got married' is neutral and equally likely to imply a reciprocal interpretation. The feature [+Separate] does not co-occur with the feature [+Adversative], as is evidenced by the impossibility of *'[AP *both* rich *but* happy]'. In combination with negation, as in presection, postsection or rejection, it results in at least some degree of awkwardness or deviance. This deviance is particularly evident with NP co-ordinations: compare the acceptable '[NP John *and not* Mary]' with the unacceptable *'[NP *both* John *and not* Mary]'.

The feature [±Emphatic], which in its marked form specifies that the co-ordination itself is to be emphasized, is realized in English by the repetition of a co-ordinating conjunction between three or more conjuncts. Such repetition is clearly impossible with only two conjuncts, which provides an explanation for the incompatibility of the features [+Emphatic] and [+Adversative].

Whereas individual languages may lack the strategies which enable these marked forms of co-ordination to achieve distinct expression in any simple way, it can be predicted that all languages possess some strategy for each unmarked form, even if that strategy is merely simple juxtaposition of the conjuncts. Table 1.1 therefore presents a universal schema as far as the unmarked co-ordination types are concerned, and covers the marked types which are most likely to be found. Further marked types are found in isolated languages, and a survey of these is given in section 1.5. This section, I expect, is far from any pretension to completeness.

Corresponding to their theoretical status, the marked forms of co-ordination are discussed first, in section 1 of this chapter. Section 2 is then devoted to the unmarked realization of each basic type of co-ordination.

0.2 *A putative category hierarchy*

One major focus of concern in this chapter is the extent to which essentially sentential co-ordination strategies are permitted at phrasal levels. For example, English *and* is used ubiquitously to conjoin sentences ('[S John left *and* Mary left]'), verb phrases ('John [VP got up *and* left]'), adjectival phrases ('John is [AP rich *and* famous]'), prepositional phrases ('John spoke [PP to me *and* to Mary]') and noun phrases ('[NP John *and* Mary] left') plus a variety of subphrasal categories. Such a pattern is widespread, recurring for example in French *et*, Welsh *a*, Russian *i* and Tagalog *at*, but is by no means universal. The Fijian conjunction *ka* for instance may conjoin sentences, verb phrases, adjectival phrases and prepositional phrases, but *not* noun phrases, where a distinct form *kei* is used (cf. section 2.1).

In general, the phrasal categories appear to form a hierarchy: **S – VP –**

AP – PP – NP. Individual strategies are used to cover contiguous categories, so that for instance Fijian *ka* covers the categories s to PP, and *kei* solely the category NP. It is claimed therefore that a language will not use one strategy for s and NP alone unless the intervening categories also permit the same strategy. Numerous examples of the operation of the hierarchy are given throughout the chapter.

To some extent the hierarchy itself is probably too weak a constraint on the possible forms of co-ordination at phrasal levels. Is there any language which uses one strategy for s and VP conjunction, a separate strategy for AP and PP conjunction, and yet a third strategy for NP conjunction? In general the patterns observed are the following: for postsection, presection, rejection and disjunction, and also for the marked co-ordination types [+Adversative] and [+Separate], the sentential strategy may be permitted at some or all phrasal levels, or none at all. The extent to which the sentential strategy 'reaches down' is subject to the category hierarchy. Unmarked conjunction may behave somewhat differently: because of the greater semantic discrepancies between phrasal (particularly NP) and sentential levels, phrasal strategies may arise independently of the sentential ones. A notable example of this is the frequent use of a comitative form for NP conjunction (independently of any comitative meaning). This strategy may then spread in the opposite direction 'up' the category hierarchy.

1 Marked forms of conjunction

1.1 *The feature 'adversative'*
Co-ordinations with the marked feature [+Adversative] differ from the unmarked ones by specifying that a contrast exists between the conjuncts, or between the implications of the conjuncts. The most general realization in English is with the co-ordinating conjunction *but*. Because of the very nature of contrast, the number of conjuncts is almost universally restricted to two, and we very rarely find the iterated co-ordinators which frequently occur in other co-ordination types. Compare '[AP rich *and* happy *and* wise]' with the unacceptable *'[AP rich *but* happy *but* wise]'.

From a notional point of view, at least three varieties of adversative conjunction may be distinguished:

1.1.1 *Semantic opposition*
Semantic opposition (the term is taken from Lakoff 1971) implies that the relationship between the conjuncts is simply one of contrast or opposition, uncomplicated by further presuppositions or dependencies.

At the sentential level, the conjuncts are similar in topic and structure, but different in lexical content:

(1)   a. [s John is rich *but* I am poor]

     b. [s In France it rains, *but* in England the sun shines]

                                              (Conjunction)

(2)   a. [s John *isn't* rich *but* he is handsome]

     b. [s In France it *doesn't* rain, *but* in England it does (rain)]

                                              (Presection)

(3)   a. [s John is rich *but* he *isn't* handsome]

     b. [s In France it rains, *but* in England it *doesn't* (rain)]

                                           (Postsection)

(4)   a. [s John is*n't* rich *but* he *isn't* poor (*either*)]
      [s John is*n't* rich *but neither* is he poor]

     b. [s In France it *doesn't* rain, *but* in England it *doesn't* rain (*either*)]
      [s In France it *doesn't* rain, *but neither* does it rain in England]

                                              (Rejection)

Note the existence of a dual strategy for rejection in English at the sentential level.

1.1.2 *Denial of expectation*
Denial of expectation (this term is also taken from Lakoff 1971) implies a contrast which is pragmatically based. A co-ordination of this type with the form 'A *but* B' is taken to mean: given A, it might be expected that *not* B, nevertheless B holds. Contrary to semantic opposition, there is no need for any similarity in general topic or structure between the conjuncts themselves, for example:

(5)   a. [s John is rich, *but* the party will take place]

     b. [s John *isn't* rich, *but* the party will take place]

     c. [s John is rich, *but* the party *won't* take place]

     d. [s John *isn't* rich, *but* the party *won't* take place]

The meaning of (5a) is: John is rich, and therefore it might have been expected that the party would not take place (perhaps the guest list is restricted to the poor, but John, who is rich, turns up); nevertheless, the party will take place. Similar interpretations may be given to the other examples. Note that in the case of rejection, (5d), a version with *neither* (or *either*) is unacceptable under this interpretation:

(6)   a. ?[s John *isn't* rich, *but* the party *won't* take place *either*]

       b. ?[s John *isn't* rich, *but neither* will the party take place]

From the semantic point of view, sentences involving denial of expectation with the co-ordinating conjunction *but* are similar to sentences with the subordinating conjunction *although*. Sentence (5a) may be paraphrased:

(7)   Although John is rich, the party will take place

1.1.3 *Preventative*

Preventative forms of adversative involve a hypothetical first conjunct. In general, a co-ordination of this type with the form 'A *but* B' has the following meaning: A, which otherwise would take place, will fail to take place on account of B:

(8)   a. [s I would go, *but* Bill has the money]

       b. [s I *wouldn't* go, *but* Bill has the money]

       c. [s I would go, *but* Bill *hasn't* the money]

       d. [s I *wouldn't* go, *but* Bill *hasn't* the money]

In (8a), for example, the interpretation is that Bill's possession of the money prevents me from going, and similarly in (8b), Bill's possession of the money prevents me from *not* going, hence I most probably will go.

The preventative form of adversative is similar to the denial of expectation form in that for rejection the *neither* (or *not ... either*) strategy is not permitted:

(9)   a. *[s I *wouldn't* go, but Bill *hasn't* the money *either*]

       b. *[s I *wouldn't* go, but *neither* has Bill the money]

It differs from both denial of expectation and semantic opposition adversatives, however, in the requirement that the first conjunct be hypothetical. This has the important consequence that phrasal forms lower on the category hierarchy than verb phrase are automatically excluded.

The English co-ordinating conjunction *but* may be used in all the three forms of adversative discussed, and possibly more. Indeed, this seems to be a very common strategy: many languages likewise employ a single co-ordinating conjunction with a variety of functions. In Latin we have, for example:

(10)   a. [s *Non* ego erus   tibi   *sed* servus sum]
                not I   master to you but slave I am
                'I am not a master to you but (I am) a slave'

                                                    (Plaut. Capt. 2,1,44)

         b. [s Difficile factu est *sed* conabor tamen]
                difficult do   is but I will try nevertheless
                'It is difficult to do but I will try nevertheless'

                                                    (Cic. Rep. 1,43,66)

The first sentence is clearly a case of semantic opposition, and the second a case of denial of expectation, reinforced by co-occurrence with the adverb *tamen*.

As in English, the adversative co-ordinating conjunction may contrast with a conjunction unmarked for that feature. In German, for instance, the adversative *aber* contrasts with the unmarked *und* (example (11)); and in Tagalog (example (12)) the adversative *pero* contrasts with the unmarked *at* (Schachter and Otanes 1972:544):

(11)   [s Ich rief dich an, *aber* du   kamst *nicht*]
                I   rang you up but   you came not
                'I rang you up but you didn't come'

(12)   [s *Hindi* namin magagawa ngayon, *pero* gagawin namin
                not   we   can do   today   but will do   we
                bukas]
                tomorrow
                'We can't do it today, but we will do it tomorrow'

In languages like Vietnamese, (13) (Thompson 1965:262) and Japanese, (14) (Dunn and Yanada 1958:69) however, a co-ordinating conjunction is used for the adversative even though in non-adversatives the strategy involves simple juxtaposition of the conjuncts with no intervening conjunction (cf. section 2.1):

(13)   [s Tôi chờ nó, *song le* nó *không* dên]
                I   wait him but   he not   come
                'I waited for him but he didn't come'

(14)   [s Niwa   ni neko wa imasu *ga* inu wa *imasen*]
                garden in cat TOP be   but dog TOP not be
                'In the garden there's a cat but not a dog'

It is further possible for a language to possess two (or more) adversative co-ordinating conjunctions with distinct nuances of meaning. For example, Russian possesses *a* (a more general conjunction which is used for all cases of adversative) and *no* (which is specifically excluded from cases of semantic opposition, (15a), but may express denial of expectation, (15b), or preventative adversatives, (15c)):

(15)   a. [s Utrom   my spešili na rabotu, *a*   večerom my sideli
             morning we hurried to work   but evening we sat
             doma]
             at home
             'In the morning we hurried to work but in the evening we
             sat at home'   (Semantic opposition)

        b. [s On postupil pravil'no, *a/no* otec   nedovolen im]
           he acted   correctly but father dissatisfied with him
           'He acted correctly but father was dissatisfied with him'
                              (Denial of expectation)

        c. [s Ja uexal by,   *a/no* ne bylo deneg]
           I   leave COND but   not was money
           'I would have left, but there was no money'
                                   (Preventative)

A detailed description of the functions of *a* and *no* may be found in Švedova (1970:667–74) and Yokoyama (1981).

As well as being situated between the conjuncts, co-ordinating conjunctions may be cliticized to the first word of the second conjunct (cf. Latin *que*). I am aware of at least one adversative conjunction which may be cliticized in this way, namely Russian *že* which is used to express semantic opposition (Švedova 1970:670):

(16)   [s My živem na dače   tol'ko letom,   sosedi
        we live   in summer-house only   summer neighbours
        že kruglyj god]
        but round   year
        'We live in a summer-house only in summer, but our neighbours (live in one) the year round'

Despite the fact that adversative co-ordinating conjunctions are probably the most frequent strategy, the similarity of denial of expectation adversatives to concessives with a form like *although* means that a language may use an overt concessive as its sole strategy in such cases. Fijian, for example, appears to treat semantic opposition with the unmarked co-ordinator *ka* ('and', cf. example (67)), whilst employing a concessive construction for denial of expectation (Milner 1967:29, 91):

(17) a. [S E katakata ko Viti *ka* batabatā ke Toga]
DECLAR hot ART Fiji and cold ART Tonga
'Fiji is hot, and/but Tonga is cold'

b. [S E *dina gā* ni ratou ā rogoca, *ia*
DECLAR although COMP they(TRIAL) PAST hear yet
eratou ā sega ni vakabauta]
they(DECLAR TRIAL) PAST not COMP believe
'Although they heard it, yet they did not believe it'

In such constructions as (17b), the distinction between co-ordination and subordination may become blurred. The Russian particle *no*, for example, which is usually considered to be a co-ordinating conjunction on the basis of its fixed position between the two conjuncts and its non-combinability with other co-ordinating conjunctions, may also occur in a concessive construction exactly parallel to the Fijian one, as in (18):

(18) [S *Xotja* on postupil pravil'no, *no* otec nedovolen im]
although he acted correctly but father dissatisfied him

'Although he acted correctly, {*but / yet} father was dissatisfied with him'

English permits *yet* to combine with *although* in such a construction, but not *but*. However in English, *yet* must be considered an adverbial, rather than a co-ordinating, conjunction. Of the two tests which help to distinguish these categories (co-occurrence with co-ordinating conjunctions and/or relative freedom of movement within the conjunct for adverbials), *yet* satisfies the first in its combinability with *and* or *but*, but has a fixed position. Many languages possess a system of adverbials which can express the adversative relation, or refined nuances of it, in tandem with or apart from the standard co-ordinating conjunction. Further examples from English are *however* and *nevertheless*, and from Latin we have *tamen* (cf. example (10b)), *enim*, *enimvero* and *autem*.

More interestingly, it is possible for a language to possess no adversative co-ordinating conjunctions as such, but to permit the expression of adversatives by means of adverbials. Such a strategy is an alternative to the Fijian one in such a situation, namely using the unmarked co-ordinator except when the concessive is appropriate. It occurs for instance in standard Arabic:

(19) a. [S ɣaadara jon *wa lakin* meri *lam* tuɣaadir]
left John and Mary not left
'John left but Mary didn't leave'

b. [s ɣaadara jon   *wa   'amma* meri *fa-lam* tuɣaadir]
   left   John and   Mary not   left
   'John left but Mary didn't leave'

The adversative forms *lakin* and *'amma* may both co-occur with the unmarked co-ordinating conjunction *wa*, or alternatively *wa* may be omitted.

1.2 *Phrasal adversatives*

The strategies used for phrasal adversatives mirror very closely those used at the sentential level, and indeed, it is clear why this should be so, since in many cases it is hard to tell whether a given string should be analysed as a phrasal co-ordination or as a sentential co-ordination with omitted material (omitted material will be placed in parentheses):

(20)   a. John is [AP rich *but not* handsome]

        b. [s John is rich *but* (John is) *not* handsome]

There are perhaps two reasons for wanting to set up a separate category of phrasal adversative at all. Firstly, when complex scopes are involved, the phrasal adversative may not be so simply reanalysed as a sentential one, if at all. Compare (21a) and (21b), which differ in meaning:

(21)   a. Many men are [AP rich *but not* handsome]

        b. [s Many men are rich *but* (many men are) *not* handsome]

Secondly, the position of negation in a phrasal adversative may differ from the position of negation in the corresponding sentential adversative, thus suggesting an independent structure. Contrast (22a) with (22b):

(22)   a. I saw [NP *not* John *but* Bill]

        b. *[s I saw *not* John *but* (I saw) Bill]

On the other hand, sentences like (23) are perhaps best analysed in a sentential manner:

(23)   [s I *didn't* see John, *but* (I did see) Bill]

At the phrasal level in English, we find the following patterns:

Conjunction

(24)   a. John [VP is rich *but* has good taste]

        b. John is [AP rich *but* handsome]

        c. *It's raining [PP in France *but* in England]

        d. *I saw [NP John *but* Bill]

Note first that (24a) and (24b) may be given either semantic opposition or denial of expectation interpretations. A preventative interpretation is however only possible at the VP level, since the conjuncts must be assigned distinct modalities:

(25)   John [VP would go at once *but* has a cold]

Secondly, the bare adversative is unacceptable at the PP and NP levels, as illustrated by (24c) and (24d). This unacceptability is partially mirrored in the corresponding sentential adversatives:

(26)   a. ? [S It's raining in France *but* it's raining in England]

       b. ? [S I saw John *but* I saw Bill]

It would seem that (26a) and (26b) cannot be given semantic opposition readings; at best, they can be interpreted as denial of expectation. However, the comparative acceptability of the denial of expectation interpretation is not reflected at the NP and PP levels. In other words, the VP co-ordination corresponds most closely to sentential co-ordination, followed by AP co-ordination and then NP and PP co-ordination.

Presection

(27)   a. John [VP is *not* rich *but* has good taste]

       b. John is [AP *not* rich *but* handsome]

       c. It's raining [PP *not* in France *but* in England]

       d. I saw [NP *not* John *but* Bill]

Note that the PP and NP forms are acceptable (as are the corresponding sentential adversatives).

   A particularly interesting variant of adversative presection is *not only ... but also*, in which the negative bears on the adverb *only*:

(28)   a. John is [VP *not only* rich *but also* has good taste]

       b. John is [AP *not only* rich *but also* handsome]

       c. It's raining [PP *not only* in France *but also* in England]

       d. I saw [NP *not only* Fred *but also* Bill]

Postsection

(29)   a. John [VP is rich *but* does *not* have good taste]

       b. John is [AP rich *but not* handsome]

       c. It's raining [PP in France *but not* in England]

       d. I saw [NP John *but not* Bill]

The PP and NP forms are again acceptable.

Rejection

(30) a. John [$_{VP}$ is *not* rich, *but* doesn'*t* have good taste (*either*)]

  b. John is [$_{AP}$ *not* rich *but not* handsome (*either*)]

  c. *It's raining [$_{PP}$ *not* in France *but not* in England (*either*)]

  d. *I saw [$_{NP}$ *not* John *but not* Bill (*either*)]

Note that the PP and NP versions have acceptable parallel forms at the sentential level:

(31) a. [$_S$ It's *not* raining in France, *but* it's *not* raining in England (*either*)]

  b. [$_S$ I did*n't* see John, *but* I did*n't* see Bill (*either*)]

The restriction involved here seems to parallel the one involved in the conjunction examples. The *neither* strategy, acceptable at the sentential level (cf. example (4b)), is not permitted at any phrasal level:

(32) a. *John [$_{VP}$ is *not* rich, *but neither* has good taste]

  b. *John is [$_{AP}$ *not* rich *but neither* handsome]

  c. *It's raining [$_{PP}$ *not* in France *but neither* in England]

  d. *I saw [$_{NP}$ *not* John *but neither* Fred]

This may be due to the requirement of subject–auxiliary inversion imposed by this occurrence of *neither*, since the corresponding Latin *nec ... sed nec ...* does appear to be permitted at least at the VP level (Kühner and Stegmann 1955:49). Here, as elsewhere in these paradigms based on English, the operation of the category hierarchy may be observed. The blocking of all phrasal levels gives the pattern S – *VP – *AP – *PP – *NP for the *not ... but neither ...* strategy, whilst the other rejection forms *not ... but not ...* and *not ... but not ... either* give the pattern S – VP – AP – *PP – *NP. This same pattern occurs in the case of the simple conjunction with *but*, whereas presection and postsection provide examples of a given strategy operating over the whole hierarchy: S – VP – AP – PP – NP. The category hierarchy corresponds to the overall semantic proximity of adversatives at different phrasal levels to adversatives at the sentential level. Nevertheless, the hierarchy appears to operate syntactically since the existence of an acceptable sentential paraphrase does not guarantee the acceptability of the corresponding phrasal adversative.

As the English paradigm suggests, strategies for phrasal adversatives are invariably identical to strategies for sentential adversatives, with the proviso that not all sentential strategies are necessarily permitted at phrasal levels, and that those strategies which are used phrasally do not necessarily occur at all phrasal levels. Languages therefore differ primarily not with respect to the distinctness of phrasal and sentential strategies (as in unmarked conjunction, section 2.1), but with respect to the extent to which sentential strategies may be used at the phrasal level.

Examples of complete restriction to the sentential level appear to be the Japanese conjunction *ga* (14), the Fijian construction *e dina gā . . . ia* (17) and the English *not . . . but neither* (for rejection). Russian *a* and *no* (and *xotja . . . no*) behave similarly to English *but* with restrictions at the PP and NP levels for conjunction (but not postsection and presection). The Russian clitic *že* (16) on the other hand is permitted at sentential and VP levels, giving the pattern: S – VP – *AP – *PP – *NP.

When making a detailed analysis of phrasal adversatives in individual languages, it is essential to give separate consideration to the various co-ordination types (conjunction, presection, postsection and rejection), since these do not necessarily behave identically even when the same basic conjunction (like English *but*) is used throughout. Constraints on the forms of negation may be one of the factors which contribute to the patterns observed. Consider for instance the following (postsection) paradigm from standard Arabic:

(33) a. [s ɣaadara jon   *wa   lakin* meri *lam* tuɣaadir]
            left   John and but   Mary not left(FEM)
            'John left but Mary didn't leave'

     b. *Kaana jon [AP ɣaniyyan *wa   lakin lam* mašhuuran]
            was   John   rich   and but   not famous
            'John was rich but not famous'

     c. *ɣaadara jon [PP maʻa meri *wa   lakin lam* maʻa fred]
            left   John with Mary and but   not with Fred
            'John left with Mary but not with Fred'

     d. *ɣaadara [NP jon   *wa   lakin lam* fred]
            left   John and but   not Fred
            'John but not Fred left'

The absence of a VP example is due to the absence (at surface levels) of a VP node in Arabic (the basic word order being VSO). Co-ordinations of the type VSO + VO are best interpreted as sentential, with omitted subject in the second conjunct. The restriction of *wa lakin lam* to the sentential level may be attributed to the status of *lam*, which acts as a verbal negator and can only occur preverbally, rather than to the operation of the category hierarchy (though the two do not conflict in this case). In order to express (33b–d) correctly in Arabic, a sentential strategy must be used, employing the verb form *laysa*, a negative form of the copula:

(34)   a. [$_S$ Kaana jon ɣaniyyan *wa lakin laysa*
           was   John rich   and but   was not (he)
           mašhuuran]
           famous
           'John was rich but not famous'

       b. [$_S$ ɣaadara jon ma'a meri *wa lakin laysa*   ma'a fred]
           left   John with Mary and but   was not with Fred
           'John left with Mary but not with Fred'

In the case of NP co-ordination, the simplest sentential paraphrase
involves full repetition of the verb as in (33a).

   One major typological variation in the treatment of phrasal adversatives is however the existence in many languages of a separate strategy
for presection. Whereas languages like English use the negative *not* in
conjunction with the standard adversative *but*, these languages possess a
distinct co-ordinator which may be used solely after a negation of the
first conjunct. An Indo-European example, shown in (35), is the
German *nicht . . . sondern*, where the adversative used elsewhere is *aber*
(although forms like *zwar nicht . . . aber* and *nicht . . . wohl aber* exist
side by side with *nicht . . . sondern*):

(35)   Er hat [$_{NP}$ *nicht* meinen Vetter *sondern* meinen Bruder]
        he has   not   my   cousin but   my   brother
        getötet
        killed
        'He killed not my cousin but my brother'

Non-Indo-European examples are Hungarian, (36), *nem . . . hanem*
(where the standard adversative is *de*) and Tagalog *hindi . . . kundi*
(where the standard adversative is *pero*). It is interesting to note the
etymology of Hungarian *hanem*, which itself consists of the conjunction
ha (=*if*) and the negator *nem* (Majtinskaja 1960:258). Such forms (like
German *sondern*) tend to be used only when the two conjuncts are
mutually exclusive (i.e. in cases of semantic opposition), with the result
that combinations like *nem . . . de . . .* are not impossible, and indeed
favoured when such a direct opposition does not exist:

(36)   a. [$_S$ *Nem* is   Trudenak hívják, *hanem* Marinak]
              not also Trude to they call but   Mary to
              'They don't call her Trude, but Mary'

       b. A lakás [$_{AP}$ *nem* nagy, *de* kényelmes]
          the flat   not big   but comfortable
          'The flat is not big, but comfortable'

In (36a) the names 'Trude' and 'Mary' are clearly in opposition and the form *hanem* is the one used, whilst in (36b) the two adjectives are not mutually exclusive, the most natural interpretation being one of denial of expectation rather than of semantic opposition.

1.3 *The feature 'separate'*

Many languages possess a strategy (or strategies) whose function is to stress that the conjuncts in a phrasal co-ordination are to be considered as separate units, despite their syntactic linking. A phrasal co-ordination may be understood, when it has the marked form [+Separate], as a reduced sentential co-ordination, whereas in the case of the unmarked form no claim is made about the existence of a conjoined sentence paraphrase. In English the marked form for conjunction is *both . . . and*, and for disjunction *either . . . or*.

The force of such strategies is particularly evident in the case of NP conjunction, which is from a semantic point of view furthest removed from sentential conjunction. Firstly, many unmarked NP conjunctions cannot in any circumstances be reduced to sentential ones, for example in combination with predicates like *are a motley crew* (Dougherty 1970:871), *are a happy couple* (Gleitman 1965:290), *are 3000 miles apart* (Lakoff and Peters 1969:131); or with prepositions like *between* (Dik 1972:88). In such cases, the marked form *both . . . and* is totally impossible:

(37) a. *[NP *Both* John *and* Bill] are a motley crew

b. *[NP *Both* John *and* Mary] are a happy couple

c. *[NP *Both* London *and* New York] are 3000 miles apart

d. *There was fighting between [NP *both* John *and* Bill]

Secondly, many NP conjunctions are ambiguous (or perhaps just vague) between a sentential and a non-sentential interpretation (Smith 1969). In these cases, the marked form *both . . . and* stresses the sentential interpretation:

(38) a. [NP John *and* Mary] got married

b. [NP *Both* John *and* Mary] got married

(39) a. [NP John *and* Mary] bought a new house

b. [NP *Both* John *and* Mary] bought a new house

In (38a) the symmetric predicate *got married* may be understood either as a marriage between John and Mary, or as separate marriages between John and Mary and other unspecified individuals. The *both . . .*

and version, however, stressing the separateness of John's being married and Mary's being married, is more likely (though not absolutely) to imply that they are not marrying each other. Similarly in (39), the *both ... and* version is more likely, though not absolutely, to imply the purchase of two separate new houses. What is important is that the purchasing is attributed to two separate individuals.

It has further been observed, by Lakoff and Peters (1969:113), that in English *both ... and* is incompatible with the adverb *together*:

(40)   *[_{NP} *Both* John *and* Mary] arrived together

This would appear to be due to the non-existence of a sentential paraphrase:

(41)   *[_S John arrived together *and* Mary arrived together]

The unacceptability cannot be attributed however to the specific semantics of the adverb *together*, since *both ... and* is also incompatible with adverbial expressions like *at different times*, at least on the reading which indicates that John and Mary arrived at different times to each other:

(42)   *[_{NP} Both John *and* Mary] arrived at different times

The marked conjunction alone, without further adverbial specification, must be taken to be totally vague as to the relative times of arrival, or whether John and Mary arrived in each other's company. The marked conjunction does however stress that the act of arriving is to be attributed to each individual separately, and it is in this sense that the feature [+Separate] must be understood.

The feature [+Separate] is also in operation in the distinction between the unmarked disjunction *or* and the marked disjunction *either ... or*. The marked form must be understood as stressing the separateness of the conjuncts, and hence implying a sentential paraphrase, even though in this case the discrepancies may not be so great since phrasal disjunctions generally permit sentential paraphrases, even if their existence is not stressed. The difference is however revealed in comparisons like the following, which involve numerals:

(43)   a. He is coming for two *or* three weeks

       b. He is coming for *either* two *or* three weeks

In (43b), the marked disjunction implies a paraphrase: 'Either he is coming for two weeks, or he is coming for three weeks.' While the unmarked disjunction in (43a) also permits this reading, an alternative interpretation is one in which 'two *or* three' expresses an approximation. This interpretation of course has no sentential paraphrase.

A further difference in English between the *or* and *either ... or* forms is that *either ... or* does not occur happily within independent alternative questions. Compare for instance (44a) and (44b):

(44) a. Do you want [$_{NP}$ tea *or* coffee]?

  b. ?? Do you want [$_{NP}$ *either* tea *or* coffee]?

Moravcsik (1971), using a sample of about forty languages, shows that such a distribution of forms is widespread, though by no means universal. For dependent alternative questions, on the other hand, a double form like English *whether ... or* is more common, the first element serving as a complementizer to introduce the question.

Among the strategies which are available to languages for the realization of the feature [+Separate], one of the commonest, especially in languages which use a given co-ordinating particle throughout the category hierarchy, is the repetition of that same particle before the first conjunct (shown here for Latin in (45), Russian in (46) and Romanian in (47)). Thus for conjunction we have:

(45) a. [$_{NP}$ *et* tragoediae *et* comoediae]

  b. [$_{NP}$ tragoediae *et* comoediae]

(46) a. [$_{NP}$ *i* tragedii *i* komedii]

  b. [$_{NP}$ tragedii *i* komedii]

(47) a. [$_{NP}$ *şi* tragedii *şi* comedii]

  b. [$_{NP}$ tragedii *şi* comedii]

The (a) versions correspond to the English '*both* tragedies *and* comedies', whereas the (b) versions are the unmarked [±Separate] forms. Similarly, for disjunction we have Latin *aut ... aut ...* or *vel ... vel ...*, Russian *ili ... ili ...*, French *ou ... ou ...*, Persian *yâ ... yâ ...* and Hungarian *vagy ... vagy ...*.

There are three points to be made about this strategy. Firstly, in cases where there are more than two conjuncts, the co-ordinating particle may generally be repeated between each of them as well as initially before the first conjunct. The effect of such a repetition is, however, emphatic (cf. section 1.4), and does not alter the semantic properties of the co-ordination. Secondly, just as the non-repeated co-ordinator may occur at all levels in the category hierarchy, so may the repeated co-ordinator, including sententially, as in the Latin example in (48).

(48)   [s *Et* in tragoediis comicum vitiosum est *et* in comoediis
        and in tragedies comedy bad   is and in comedies
        turpe tragicum]
        ugly   tragedy
        'Just as in tragedies comedy is bad, so in comedies tragedy is
        ugly'

(Cicero Opt. Gen. 1, cited by
Kühner and Stegmann 1955:34)

Note that the English translation of (48) employs a strategy *just as . . .
so*, which is permitted solely sententially. Thirdly, it is not generally
possible to achieve the same effect by repeating postposed rather than
preposed co-ordinators, since these have a tendency to be obligatorily
repeated in any case, for example Tamil . . . *um* . . . *um* (Beythan
1943:155). Japanese *–to* must also be repeated after each conjunct, but
may be, and usually is, deleted after the final one, again with no
semantic effect.

A variant of this strategy is to maintain the original co-ordinator, but
to attach a second and distinct element to the first conjunct. Thus for
conjunction we have English *both . . . and . . .* and Swedish *både . . . och
. . .*, and for disjunction English *either . . . or . . .*, Swedish *antingen . . .
eller . . .*, Finnish *joko . . . tai . . .* and, with a postposed element,
Tagalog, *. . . man o . . . .* We give examples of these last two (from Olli
1958:161 for Finnish, (49), and Schachter and Otanes 1972:543 for
Tagalog, (50)):

(49)   Poika [vp *joko* menee kouluun *tai* hakee työpäiken]
        boy   either goes   school to or seeks work place
        'The boy is either going to school or is trying to get a job'

(50)   [np Ikaw *man   o* ako] ay maaaring gumawa niyan
        you   either or I   TOP can   do   that
        'Either you or I can do that'

In this case, there may be restrictions on the levels at which the
strategies may be employed. English *both . . . and . . .* for instance does
not occur sententially:

(51)   *[s *Both* John arrived *and* I left]

Whilst maintaining the distinctness of the two co-ordinating elements, it
is possible that both are themselves basic co-ordinators. This is the
pattern found in Latin *et . . . . . . que, . . . que . . . et, et . . . atque . . ., . . .
que atque . . . .* Finally, it is possible for the first element to be a basic

co-ordinator. but the second not. as in the Finnish examples in (52) (Olli 1956:161):

(52)   a. [NP *Sekä* poika *että* tyttö] ovat koulussa
            both boy   and girl   are   school in
            'Both the boy and the girl are in school'

        b. [NP Poika *sekä*   tyttö] ovat koulussa
            boy   and also girl   are   school in
            'The boy and also the girl are in school'

        c. [NP Poika *ja*   tyttö] ovat koulussa
            boy   and girl   are   school in
            'The boy and the girl.are in school'

In this case, the conjunction *sekä* is itself a marked form, meaning 'and also', distinct from the unmarked conjunction *ja*.

In an overwhelming majority of languages, the strategies of the type discussed above involve distinct additional co-ordinating particles for conjunction and disjunction (cf. English *both* and *either*, Swedish *både* and *antingen*). or the strategy is available in only one of the two cases (in Tagalog, for example, only in disjunction). There is however one possible case of the same particle being added. namely Old Provençal *entre*, which according to Lafont (1967:388) occurs with the conjunction *entre* . . . *e* . . . and the disjunction *entre* . . . *o* . . . . *Entre* also has the meaning 'between'.

In languages whose basic co-ordinators do not cover the whole category hierarchy, it seems common for totally distinct repeated particles to be used, generally without restriction to individual categories. Turkish for example may form phrasal conjunctions by means of simple juxtaposition, but also has a postposed suffix *-ile* to enable the conjunction of no more than two NPS, and a suffix *-ip* (varying with vowel harmony) to enable the conjunction of VPS. The co-ordinating particle *ve*, which is of Arabic origin and does occur throughout the hierarchy, is little used. To mark a co-ordination as [+Separate] however, four distinct forms are available, . . . *de* . . . *de*, *hem* . . . *hem(de)* . . . , *ha* . . . *ha* . . . and *gerek* . . . *gerek(se)* . . . , as illustrated in (53) (Lewis 1967:269):

(53)   a. [NP ben *de* sen *de* kardeşin *de*]
            I   you   brother your
            'both I and you and your brother'

        b. [NP *hem* ziyaret *hem* ticaret]
                pilgrimage   trade
            'both pilgrimage and trade'

   c. [_{NP} *ha* bağ,   *ha* bahçe, *ha* tarla]
      orchard   garden   field
    'both orchard, garden and field'

   d. [_{PP} *gerek* Ankara'da *gerekse* Vaşington'da]
      Ankara-in   Washington in
    'both in Ankara and in Washington'

The particles which are used in this way may often also be used singly, in which case they may be equivalent to English 'also', as for example with Turkish ... *de* ... *de*, Japanese ... *mo* ... *mo* and Hungarian *is* ... *is* .... They may also be related to the 'all' quantifier, as with Hungarian *mind* ... *mind* ... and Persian *ham* ... *ham* .... This latter may also be used in tandem with the basic conjunction *va*, thus giving rise to a further type, as illustrated by the Persian example in (54):

(54)   Jân [_{AP} *ham* puldâr *va ham* mašhur] bud
     John   rich   and   famous was
     'John was both rich and famous'

The source of repeated particles indicating disjunction is often the verb 'to be' (compare English *be it* ... *be it* ...). Instances of this are French *soit* ... *soit* ... (alongside *ou* ... *ou* ... and the basic *ou*), Romanian *fie* ... *fie* ... (alongside *sau* ... *sau* ..., *ori* ... *ori* ... and basic *sau* and *ori*), Turkish ... *olsun* ... *olsun* (alongside *ya* ... *veya* ... and the basic *veya*) and Tamil *āvatu* ... *āvatu* ... (alongside the basic *allatu*). Alternatively the source may be the verb 'to want' (as with many basic disjunction particles), for instance in Turkish *ister* ... *ister* ... and Russian *libo* ... *libo* ....

   Finally, it is possible for a language to possess none of these devices for indicating the separateness of the conjuncts within the co-ordination itself. In the case of NP conjunction, an alternative strategy is often the use of an adverb or preverbal particle (like English *each*), as for example in Fijian:

(55)   Erau   sā   *dui*   kania na kona ika
     DECLAR (DU) EMPH each eat   ART his   fish
     [_{NP} ko Jone *kei* Filipe]
        ART Jone and Filipe
     'Jone and Filipe are each eating their own fish'

1.4 *The feature 'emphatic'*
There is little to be said about this feature from a typological point of view. It is designed to handle the optional repetition of co-ordinating particles between conjuncts when these are more than two in number.

The unmarked form will then contain a single occurrence of the particle. This repetition may occur both when the co-ordinating particle is used throughout the category hierarchy, as with English *and*, and when it is restricted, as with Fijian *kei* (see (57)), which also means 'with' and occurs only at the NP level:

(56)   [$_{NP}$ John $\left\{ \begin{matrix} \emptyset \\ and \end{matrix} \right\}$ Bill *and* Mary] are an excellent team

(57)   Au a   raica [$_{NP}$ na   turaga $\left\{ \begin{matrix} \emptyset \\ kei \end{matrix} \right\}$ na   gone kei   na   marama]

        I   PAST see   ART chief $\left\{ \begin{matrix} \emptyset \\ and \end{matrix} \right\}$ ART child and ART lady

        'I saw the chief $\left\{ \begin{matrix} \emptyset \\ and \end{matrix} \right\}$ the child and the lady'

As (56) indicates, the repetition does not require the conjuncts to be considered separately.

However, in many languages there is no distinct [+Emphatic] form. This occurs when the co-ordinator is permitted to link only two conjuncts, as with Turkish *-ile*, or where the co-ordinator is obligatorily repeated in any case, as with Japanese *-to*. We have not discovered a language in which the co-ordinator is obligatorily non-repeatable in the case of more than two conjuncts.

1.5 *Further marked forms of co-ordination*
The following marked forms are handled by basic strategies in isolated languages. All have the feature [+Separate].

A and B (for example)
This co-ordination type is found in Japanese with the co-ordinators *ya*, *yara* and *toka*:

(58)   [$_{NP}$ John $\left\{ \begin{matrix} ya \\ yara \\ toka \end{matrix} \right\}$ Mary ga]   kekkonsita

        John   Mary SUBJ married
        'John and Mary (among others) got married'

According to Kuno (1973:114), and confirmed by my informant, (58) presents John and Mary as typical examples of those who got married.

A and also B
This is found in Finnish *sekä* (as opposed to the unmarked co-ordinator *ja*: compare examples (52b) and (52c)).

A and then B
A single co-ordinator may express temporal succession, as in Malagasy *dia* (Rajemisa-Raolison 1966:147).

A and B and C ...
A language may use a distinct co-ordinator when the conjuncts are understood to represent a list. Usually therefore more than two conjuncts are required, as with Japanese *ni* (Kuno 1973:114–5).

As A so B
The notion that two conjuncts are equally relevant may lead to a marked form of co-ordination involving particles normally used for comparison. Such for example is the Russian *kak ... tak(i) ...*:

(59)   Vremja izmenjaet čeloveka [$_{PP}$ *kak* v fizičeskom *tak i*   v
       time   changes   man   as in physical   so (and) in

       duxovnom otnošenii]
       spiritual   manner

       'Time changes man both in a physical and in a spiritual manner'

Equally we have Vot (Finnic) *mi ... mi ...* (Adler 1966:132) and German *sowohl ... als auch ....*

Not so much A as B
A presection variant of the same notion as in 'As A so B', but with the indication that the two conjuncts are not equally relevant. Again Russian provides a convenient example (Švedova, 1970:64):

(60)   Vinovat [$_{NP}$ *ne stol'ko* ty *skol'ko*   ja]
       guilty   not so-much you as-much-as I
       'It's not so much you who are guilty as I'

A and B (in alternation)
This is generally handled adverbially, as in English 'at one time A *and* at another time B'. In Russian however a basic co-ordinating particle has this meaning (Švedova 1970:639):

(61)   Ja znal ego [$_{AP}$ *to* veselym *to* grustnym *to* zadumčivym]
       I knew him   happy   sad   thoughtful
       'I knew him (alternatingly) happy, sad and thoughtful'

'Open disjunction'
This term is used by Dixon (1972:363) to refer to a kind of disjunction which implies that the listed alternatives do not exhaustively cover all the possibilities (unlike the more standard 'closed' disjunction which generally implies that the alternatives are exhaustive unless a statement is made to the contrary). The particle used in Dyirbal to express this

yamba, which appears to have the meaning 'perhaps'. According to Kuno (1973:122), Japanese *nari* similarly expresses open disjunction, but also implies that the alternatives not stated might be better, and cannot be used in factual statements (compare English *be it*).

Disjunction of identicals

According to Olli (1958:161), Finnish has a special disjunctive particle used when the disjuncts are separate names for identical things, as for example *eli* in *viikon eli seitsamän päivää* ('a week or seven days').

'Good fellowship'

Tarahumara (Mexico) is claimed to possess a co-ordinator *yuga* which is used 'when harmony and/or good fellowship are implied between the conjuncts' (Thord-Gray 1955:516).

2 Unmarked forms of co-ordination

2.1 *Unmarked conjunction*

2.1.1 *Zero strategy.*

The conjuncts are simply juxtaposed, with no additional markers of conjunction. Such a strategy is probably available to all languages, though it may be stylistically marked, as in English. In many languages, however, it is a normal alternative, existing side by side with other strategies at various levels. This is the case for example in Turkish (Lewis 1967:206):

$$(62) \quad [_{NP} \text{ sen, ben } \begin{Bmatrix} ve \\ \emptyset \end{Bmatrix} \text{ kardeşin]}$$

$$\text{you I } \begin{Bmatrix} and \\ \emptyset \end{Bmatrix} \text{ brother your}$$

'you, I and your brother'

Similar examples may be cited from Tatar (Zakijev and Kurbatov 1971:78) and Nogai (Baskakov 1940:123).

The classical languages also widely permit the zero alternative. We have of course the well-known Latin *veni, vidi, vici* ('I came, I saw, I conquered'), and in Sanskrit (example (63)), side by side with a strategy involving the postposition *-ca*, large co-ordinate compounds may be formed by sandhi rules:

(63) a. [_{NP} yajñám havis   ca]
              sacrifice libation and
              'sacrifice and libation'

(RV 1.12.10)

b. [NP devagandharvamānuṣoragarākṣasān]
= deva gandharva   mānuṣa uraga   rākṣasa ān
god heavenly singer man   serpent demon ACC(PL)
'gods, heavenly singers, men, serpents and demons'

More significantly, the zero strategy appears to be the only strategy permitted at certain levels in some languages. A thoroughgoing example of this is Pacoh (a Mon-Khmer mountain language of Vietnam), illustrated in (64), which, according to Watson (1966:170), uses conjunctions in general 'sparingly'. The zero strategy seems to apply at all levels (Watson 1966:176):

(64)   a. Nháng tiráp [NP tilĕt,   callóh, acŏq]
       we   prepare baskets spears knives
       'We prepare baskets, spears and knives'

       b. Do chŏ [PP tŏq cayâq,   tŏq apây]
       she return to   husband to   grandmother
       'She returns to (her) husband and to (her) grandmother'

       c. Do [VP chŏ   tŏq cayâq   chŏ   tŏq apây]
       she   return to   husband return to   grandmother
       'She returns to (her) husband and returns to (her) grandmother'

Vietnamese (as shown in (65) from Thompson 1965:230–1) appears to be similar, despite the availability of a co-ordinator va (at least sententially). The zero strategy is used for unmarked conjunction, but repeated particles vừa ... vừa ... and nào ... nào ... exist for indication of the marked [+Separate] form (Thompson 1965:269–76). Conjoined VPs may form a 'serial verb' construction, such as is found also in certain African languages (for example FeʔFeʔ (Hyman 1971)). This has the syntactic form of a co-ordination of potentially independent verb phrases, but corresponds semantically in other languages to more complex forms involving prepositions and dependent infinitives:

(65)   a. Ông   ấy   [VP ở Sàigòn ra   Hànội]
       gentleman just referred to   be in Saigon go out Hanoi
       thư hai]
       Monday
       'He left Saigon for Hanoi on Monday'

       b. Tôi [VP đi chợ   mua đồ]
       I   go market buy things
       'I'm going to market to buy some things'

In sentence (65a) the forms ở and ra may both occur independently as the verbal nucleus of a simple sentence, whereas the English gloss expresses the same idea by means of a single independent verb followed by a preposition, and in (65b) the English gloss indicates the relation of purpose between the two verbs by giving the second infinitival form, whereas in the Vietnamese again there is no reason for not treating the construction as a conjunction of two verb phrases.

The Vietnamese and Pacoh verbs cited above are not inflected for tense, mood, person or number. In languages which use the zero strategy for VP conjunction and possess inflected verb forms, it is sometimes the case that only one of the conjoined verbs is given the full inflections, though the remainder, in some kind of dependent paradigm, are interpreted as if they were inflected in the same manner. For instance, in Yagnobi, an Iranian language spoken in Soviet Tadzhikistan, the first verb in the conjunction is the only one to undergo person/number agreement in past tenses. The simple past is formed from the verb root by a prefix *a-* and the following suffixes: 1st person singular *-im*, 2nd person singular *-i*, 3rd person singular ϕ, 1st person plural *-óm/-im*, 2nd person plural *-ti/-si*, 3rd person plural *-ór*. The dependent paradigm simply consists of the prefix and root without the suffix. We have then *Man a-šáw-im a-tiraš* ('I went and fell') and *A-tiraš-ór a-únxoy* ('They fell and broke'). In the present tense the full paradigm is: 1st person singular *-omišt*, 2nd person singular *-išt*, 3rd person singular *-tišt/-či*, 1st person plural *-imišt*, 2nd person plural *-tišt/-sišt*, and 3rd person plural *-ošt*. The dependent forms, this time likewise agreeing in person and number, generally omit (except for 3rd person plural *-ór*) the continuous marker *išt* (Xromov 1972). A dependent form in *-ip* is also found in Turkish: instead of, for example *Kalk-ti-k git-ti-k* ('We rose and we went'), the past and person/number markers may be omitted from the first verb to give the equivalent *Kalk-ip gittik* (Lewis 1967:178).

Yagnobi and Turkish both permit strategies other than the zero strategy at the NP level (with the postposed particles *-at* and *-ile* respectively), and both have borrowed more widely applicable co-ordinators from other languages (Yagnobi *u* from Tadzhik, and Turkish *ve* from Arabic). A more general lack of co-ordinating particles on the Pacoh model is however reported in Samoyed languages of the northern USSR, for example Nenets (Tereščenko 1966a:391–3) and Enets (Tereščenko 1966b:455). It appears however that in Nenets at least, especially in the speech of the younger generation, various adverbial and pronominal elements may be used to emphasize the conjunctive link, for example *tădikexed* ('then'), or a borrowing is made from Russian (Tereščenko 1973:17).

2.1.2 'And' strategy

The 'and' strategy is the familiar Indo-European strategy in which the co-ordinating particle used for sentential conjunction is also used for phrasal conjunction. In Indo-European, indeed, the same particle generally extends over the entire category hierarchy, as for example with Persian *va* in example (66):

(66)　a.　[s Jân　raft *va*　meri　dast　tekân　dâd]
　　　　　John left　and Mary　hand sign　gave
　　　　　'John left and Mary waved'

　　　b.　Jân [VP xandid *va*　dast　tekân　dâd]
　　　　　John　smiled and　hand sign　gave
　　　　　'John smiled and waved'

　　　c.　Jân [AP puldar *va*　mašhur] bud
　　　　　John　rich　and famous　was
　　　　　'John was rich and famous'

　　　d.　Jân [PP bâ　meri　*va*　bâ　fred] raft
　　　　　John　with Mary　and with　Fred left
　　　　　'John left with Mary and Fred'

　　　e.　[NP Jân　*va*　meri] raftand
　　　　　John　and Mary left
　　　　　'John and Mary left'

The same pattern is found outside Indo-European, for example in Finno-Ugric with Finnish *ja* and Hungarian *és*; in Caucasian with Georgian *da* (Vogt 1971:212); and in Tagalog with the co-ordinator *at* (Schachter and Otanes 1972:540).

It is equally possible however to find that the sentential co-ordinator is used for some, but not all phrasal levels, as in Fijian (see (67)) where the 'with' strategy is used at the NP level in the form of the preposition *kei*, thus giving the pattern S – VP – AP – PP – *NP:

(67)　a.　[s E　　a　　raici Mere ko Jone { ka / *kei } raici Raijieli ko Bili]

　　　　　DECLAR PAST see　Mere ART Jone { and / with } see Raijieli ART Bili

　　　　　'Jone saw Mere and Bili saw Raijieli'

　　　b.　Era　　　　[VP cici { ka / *kei } qito] na　gone

　　　　　DECLAR 3PL　　run { and / *with } play ART child

　　　　　'The children run and play'

c. Au a   raica rawa na waqa [$_{AP}$ levu $\begin{Bmatrix} ka \\ *kei \end{Bmatrix}$ totoka]

I   PAST see can ART ship   big $\begin{Bmatrix} and \\ *with \end{Bmatrix}$ beautiful

'I can see the big and beautiful ship'

d. Au a   lako [$_{PP}$ ki na sitoa $\begin{Bmatrix} ka \\ *kei \end{Bmatrix}$ ki na vale

                                           ni   yaloyalo]

I   PAST move   to ART shop $\begin{Bmatrix} and \\ *with \end{Bmatrix}$ to ART house

                                      of   image

'I went to the shop and to the theatre'

e. Au a   raica [$_{NP}$ na turàga $\begin{Bmatrix} *ka \\ kei \end{Bmatrix}$ na   marama]

I   PAST see   ART chief $\begin{Bmatrix} *and \\ with \end{Bmatrix}$ PAST lady

'I saw the chief and the lady'

2.1.3 *'With' strategy*

In this very common strategy it is either the case that the co-ordinating particle is identical to the preposition or postposition marking the comitative sense of 'with', or alternatively one of the conjuncts is inflected with a comitative case form. The source of this strategy is clearly the semantic proximity of many NP conjunctions like '[$_{NP}$ John *and* Mary] agreed' to a corresponding comitative 'John agreed *with* Mary', a proximity which has led some transformationalists (Lakoff and Peters 1969) to posit that the comitative has a deep-structure source in the conjunction. What is striking about this strategy, however, is that even in languages which do have the same surface morpheme for the conjunction and the comitative, it is commonly the case that devices exist for keeping the two constructions apart. What is more, the same morpheme may well be used for *all* cases of NP conjunction (not only those which are closely related to the comitative) and even for conjunction of other categories.

A good example of this is Fijian *kei* mentioned above, (67e). This sentence might well be translated as 'I saw the chief *with* the lady' as well as 'I saw the chief *and* the lady'. With subject NPs, however, the conjunction is clearly marked by verb agreement, as illustrated in (68):

(68)   *Erau*   lako mai e na siga Vakaraubuka
      DECLAR (3DU) move here on ART day Friday
      [$_{NP}$ na turaga *kei* na   watina]
         ART chief with ART wife
      'The chief and his wife are coming on Friday'

The conjunction can be marked as [+Separate] by means of verbal particles (e.g. *dui* = separately, *ruarua* = both; cf. example (55)) and furthermore, the whole conjoined NP may be topicalized:

(69)   [NP Na turaga *kei* na watina] rau lako mai e na siga
       ART chief   with ART wife   3DU move here on ART day
       Vakaraubuka
       Friday
       'The chief and his wife are coming here on Friday'

Verb agreement with the conjoined subject is also a feature of the Amerindian language Walapai referred to by Fillmore (1968:82). Here the comitative/instrumental is marked by case, as is the conjunction (Redden 1966:160–1):

(70)   a. ɲa-č ɲikwái-č-a   avon-a-*m*   taθ-k-wíl
         I-NOM clothes-PL-DEF soap-DEF-with wash-I-CONTINUOUS
         'I washed the clothes with soap'
      b. [NP Hátθáù-a-č   hmaɲ-*m*] hwák tiáitavm   yú-č-k-yu
         puppy-DEF-NOM boy-with two   very happy be-PL-3-PROG
         'The puppy and the boy are both very happy'
      c. [NP Wàlpáìkwáùk   háìkùkwáùk-m]   íče
         Walapai speech white man speech-with we speak
         'We speak Walapai and English'

As in Fijian, there is no verb agreement with object NPs, though contextual factors as in (70) may point to the conjunction rather than the comitative.

In Japanese, example (71), and Korean, example (72), the two constructions are kept apart by a different device, the position of the case markers for subject, theme and object. In the case of the conjunction, one such marker follows the entire construction (the individual members are not separately marked):

(71)   [NP John *to*   Mary] *ga*   kekkonsita
       John with Mary SUBJ married
       'John and Mary married'

(72)   [NP Čon *kwa* meari] nin   koŋwon-il kotko issottha
       John with Mary THEME park-OBJ   walk do(PAST)
       'John and Mary were walking in the park'

In the case of the comitative, however, the comitative NP is not a component part of the subject or theme, as shown for Japanese in (73) and Korean in (74) (Kuno 1973:116):

(73)   Mary ga   John to   kekkonsita
         Mary SUBJ John with married
         'Mary married John'

(74)   Meari nɨn   Čon kwa koŋwon-ɨl kotko issòttha
         Mary THEME John with park-OBJ   walk do(PAST)
         'Mary was walking with John in the park'

A further ingenious device is reported in Margi (Nigeria) by Hoffman (1963). In this language two morphemes are involved, depending on the total number of individuals involved in the conjunction, *àgá* if only two, and *kàkà* if more than two (Hoffman 1963:238, 250):

(75)   a. [NP Mád   *àgá* mwaləǹy]
            Madu with friend
            'Madu and his friend'

         b. [NP Madə *kàkà* mwálnyíyar]
            Madu with friends
            'Madu and his friends'

Both *àgá* and *kàkà* independently have the meaning of comitative 'with', with apparently no concomitant restriction on numbers. A string of the form NP *àgá* NP which involves more than two individuals must therefore be interpreted as the comitative rather than the conjunction. Furthermore, when the conjuncts are pronouns, the order of persons is absolute: 1st – 2nd – 3rd, so a discrepancy from this order also indicates the comitative, as in (76b) (Hoffman 1963:236):

(76)   a. Àmá'ír   y-àgá-ndà
            went away I-with-them
            'I went away with them'

         b. Àmá'ír   nd-àgá-yṳ̀
            went away they-with-me
            'They went away with me'

An interesting procedure which seems common amongst languages using the 'with' strategy is to indicate the plurality (or in general the number) of a conjoined NP by marking the first conjunct. In general this occurs only when the first conjunct is a pronoun, this pronoun then indicating the person and number of the whole NP, whilst further NPs following the co-ordinator are to be understood as included in that number. Thus we have in Fijian, (77) (Milner 1967:67) and in Margi, (78) (Hoffman 1963:238) (EXCL = Exclusive):

(77)   a. [NP *keirau*   *kei* na turaga]
            1DU(EXCL) with ART chief
            'the chief and I'

        b. [NP *keitou*   *kei* mosese]
            1 TRIAL(EXCL) with Mosese
            'Mosese, someone else, and me'

(78)   [NP *nà'y*   *àgá*-já]
            We(EXCL) with-him
            'he and I'

Occasionally however this procedure may be extended to full NPs in the first conjunct, when a plural version of the full NP exists with the independent meaning of 'X and others'. In Logbara (Uganda) for example, the phrase *ɔ̀dǐrǐ pǐ* means 'Odiri and his followers'. It may be combined with the 'with' strategy as in (79) (Crazzolara 1960:339):

(79)   Ɔ̀dǐrǐ pǐ etsá   Mìrìá *bɛ*   àma-rí àkúa
        Odiri   arrive Mírí͘a with our   village
        'Odiri and Miria arrived at our village'

It should also be noted that in such cases the conjuncts may be split by the verb, suggesting perhaps an intermediate stage between the straightforward comitative and straightforward conjunction. The same occurs in Fijian (Milner 1967:67):

(80)   *Keirau*   lako *kei* Samu
        1DU(EXCL) go   with Samu
        'Samu and I are going'

In Russian, which has a freer word order than either Logbara or Fijian, the conjuncts are optionally split:

(81)   a. [NP *My s*   toboj] idem
                we with you   go

        b.   *My* idem *s*   toboj
                we go   with you
                'You and I are going'

Although the 'with' strategy is generally restricted to NP conjunction, it is possible to find languages in which it has been extended to other categories. According to the information provided by Hoffman on Margi, for instance, the *àgá* comitative preposition/co-ordinating particle may also be used to conjoin adjectives, as in example (82) (Hoffman 1963:261):

(82)   dəl [$_{NP}$ dəgàl *àgá* dzəgàm kàkàmtə] nà
         river   large with deep   very   that
         'that very large and deep river'

It is not known however whether the same particle is permitted to conjoin prepositional phrases, as predicted by the category hierarchy, or any further categories. Other possible cases are Shuswap (British Columbia) *mƚ/mt-*, which as well as meaning 'together with' appears to conjoin at least NPS and VPS (Kuipers 1974:174); and Welsh *a/ac* (Jenkins 1959:138) which is the co-ordinating particle for the entire category hierarchy, including s, but which is etymologically identical to the instrumental preposition *â/ag*, both causing the spirant mutation (Pedersen 1908:514):

(83)   pe   llefarwn *â*   thafodau [$_{NP}$ dynion *ac*   angylion]
         though I speak with tongues   men   and angels
         'though I speak with the tongues of men and angels'

Comitative 'with' is however expressed in modern Welsh by the preposition *gyda(g)*, etymologically 'together with' and possessing the same form as its final element.

Under the heading of the 'with' strategy it is finally necessary to discuss those languages which permit at the NP level either the 'with' strategy or the 'and' strategy. In this case, the 'and' strategy is the general one, whereas the 'with' strategy is both syntactically and semantically restricted. A good example of this is Russian, where the *s* ('with') form can conjoin only two conjuncts, while the *i* ('and') form can conjoin any number, as illustrated in (84):

(84)   a. [$_{NP}$ Petja, Ivan *i*   Volodja] sotrudničajut
            Petja, Ivan and Volodja   collaborate(PL)
            'Petja, Ivan and Volodja collaborate'

         b. [$_{NP}$ Petja *s*   Ivanom] sotrudničajut
            Petja with Ivan   collaborate(PL)
            'Petja and Ivan collaborate'

         c. Petja sotrudničaet   *s*   Ivanom
            Petja collaborates(SG) with Ivan
            'Petja collaborates with Ivan'

d. *[Petja *s*   Ivanom *s*   Volodej] sotrudničajut
  Petja with Ivan   with Volodja collaborate(PL)
  'Petja and Ivan and Volodja collaborate'

In addition there are semantic restrictions in that the conjuncts with the
s form must be thought of either as acting together (as in (84b)), or
being located together (cf. Miller 1971):

(85)   a. [$_{NP}$ Volga $\begin{Bmatrix} i \\ s \end{Bmatrix}$ $\begin{Bmatrix} \text{Oka} \\ \text{Okoj} \end{Bmatrix}$] slivajutsja tam

    Volga $\begin{Bmatrix} \text{and} \\ \text{with} \end{Bmatrix}$ Oka   merge(PL) there

    'The Volga and the Oka merge there'

    b. [$_{NP}$ Volga $\begin{Bmatrix} i \\ s \end{Bmatrix}$ $\begin{Bmatrix} \text{Oka} \\ \text{Okoj} \end{Bmatrix}$] vidny   s   ètogo mesta

    Volga $\begin{Bmatrix} \text{and} \\ \text{with} \end{Bmatrix}$ Oka   visible(PL) from this   point

    'The Volga and the Oka are visible from this point'

    c. [$_{NP}$ Volga $\begin{Bmatrix} i \\ {}^*s \end{Bmatrix}$ $\begin{Bmatrix} \text{Oka} \\ \text{Okoj} \end{Bmatrix}$] byli   udivitel'no čistymi

    Volga $\begin{Bmatrix} \text{and} \\ {}^*\text{with} \end{Bmatrix}$ Oka   were(PL) surprisingly clean

    'The Volga and the Oka were surprisingly clean'

In (85a) the 'and' and 'with' forms are more or less equivalent. In (85b),
however, the 'with' form requires that the two rivers be located together
and visible in one glance, while the 'and' form permits them to be visible
in opposite directions. In (85c) we are interested simply in attributing
cleanness to two rivers, and not in their combined action or location,
hence the 'with' form is impossible.

Romanian, (86), behaves very similarly to Russian, except for the
existence of a third possibility combining the 'and' and 'with' forms:

(86)   a. [$_{NP}$ Ion *şi*   Bill] au   venit
      Ion and Bill have(PL) come

    b. [$_{NP}$ Ion *cu*   Bill] au   venit
      Ion with Bill   have(PL) come

    c. [$_{NP}$ Ion *şi*   *cu*   Bill] au   venit
      Ion and with Bill have(PL) come
      'John and Bill have come'

In this case, the combined form (86c) shares the same syntactic and
semantic restrictions as the 'with' form (86b).

2.1.4 *Pronoun strategy*

In this strategy, which appears to be restricted to NP conjunction, the conjuncts are simply linked by a plural pronoun which indicates the number and person of the conjoined NP. There is an obvious similarity between this strategy and the procedure already discussed (examples (77), (78)) by which under the 'with' strategy the first conjunct may itself be a pronoun indicating the number and person of the whole NP. The pronoun strategy itself however uses a pronoun as a link, which adds no further information, between two already fully specified conjuncts. An example of this is to be found in Tahitian (Tryon 1970:67):

(87)   'Ua reva ātu [$_{NP}$ Peu *rāua* 'o Terii]
        PERF leave away   Peu 3DU ART Terii
        'Peu and Terii left'

In Tahitian it is also possible to form what is in effect a zero-strategy conjunction with a pronominal first conjunct indicating the overall number and person of the conjoined NP (i.e. essentially like the Fijian and Margi examples, but without the 'with' co-ordinator) (Tryon 1970:67):

(88)   'Ua reva ātu [$_{NP}$ *māua*   'o Peu]
        PERF leave away   1DU(EXCL) ART Peu
        'Peu and I left'

Such forms as (88) existed also in Old Icelandic:

(89)   Annarr verðr   nú skilnaðr [$_{NP}$ *okkarr* Helga]   en
        another shall be now parting   1DU(GEN) Helgi(GEN) than
        ek aetlaða
        I expected
        'There shall be a different parting between Helgi and me than I
        expected'   (Brennu-Njáls Saga)

However a direct linking of fully specified conjuncts on the Tahitian model appears to have been impossible. A misleading parallel is the first complex phrase of the following example from Old Icelandic:

(90)   [$_{NP}$ *þeir* Kári *ok* Grímr *ok* Helgi] lǫgðu út mǫrgum
             they   Kari and Grim and Helgi lunged out many(DAT)
        spjótum   ok saerðu marga menn, en [$_{NP}$ *þeir* Flosi]
        spears(DAT) and wounded many men   and   they Flosi
        gátu ekki   at gǫrt
        got nothing accomplished

'Kari and Grim and Helgi lunged out with many spears and wounded many men, and Flosi and his men accomplished nothing'   (Brennu-Njáls Saga)

The first complex phrase appears to be a combination of the pronoun and the 'and' strategies. Note however that the pronoun does not intervene between the conjuncts but rather precedes them, as in the simpler forms with one specified NP: '[NP *þeir* Flosi]'. The two complex phrases in (90) are in fact exactly parallel in construction, with 'Flosi' in the second replaced by the conjunction '[NP Kári *ok* Grímr *ok* Helgi]' in the first. Since the pronoun indicates the overall number and person of the NP, in the case of one (singular) NP as the second conjunct, the meaning can only be 'NP and others'. When the second conjunct itself is plural, however, the set may be restricted to that number (as the context indicates in the example given), but it may well include others. The first complex phrase could have the meaning: 'Kari, Grim, Helgi and their men'.

A further example of the pure pronoun strategy is to be found in Kpelle, a West African Language (Welmers 1973:306):

(91)   [NP Surɔŋ `tà   nɛnî]    `tí   pà
           man   they woman   they came
        'A man and a woman came'

Kpelle also permits the simpler construction in which the pronoun is the first conjunct (Welmers 1973:306)

(92)   [NP `Tà   Sumo]   `tí   pà
           they Sumo   they came
        'He/she and Sumo came'

This suggests the principle that any language which permits the pure pronoun strategy will permit the simpler construction as in (88), (89) and (92), though not necessarily vice versa.

2.1.5 *'Dual' strategy*
A rare strategy available to the Samoyed languages Nenets (Tereščenko 1973:19) and Enets, side by side with the standard zero strategy, appears to allow two NPs to be conjoined by marking each with the ending of the dual number, as illustrated for Nenets in (93):

(93)   [NP ńakasxa'   papasxa']
           older brother(DU)   younger brother(DU)
        'the older brother and the younger brother'

Enets in addition permits the dual marker to be attached to the first NP alone, a variation on the theme of marking the first conjunct with the number of the whole co-ordination.

2.2 Presection

In a majority of languages it would appear that presection is simply handled by a combination of standard conjunction and negation strategies at any particular level, for example in English:

(94)   John is [AP *not* rich, *and* happy]

Examples such as (94) are often ambiguously interpretable as cases of rejection if the scope of negation is taken to include the second conjunct. It is also generally possible to form co-ordinations of more than two members with similar ambiguities:

(95)   a. John is [AP *not* rich, happy *and* wise]

         b. John is [AP *not* rich, *not* happy *and* wise]

In languages like English therefore, apart from the distinct behaviour of adversative forms (cf. section 1.2), there is little to justify a separate treatment of presection.

   In some other languages, however, a strategy distinct from the combination of conjunction and negation is available, even though it may arise historically from such a combination. Examples may be found in the classical languages with the forms *neque/nec* (Latin) and οὔτε (Greek). These particles are also used in postsection, and, repeated, in rejection. For presection, however, they combine with standard co-ordinators to form the pairs *neque/nec . . . et . . .*, *neque/nec . . . . . . que* in Latin and οὔτε . . . . . . τε in Greek. Such forms are unambiguously interpretable as presection as in the following example from Latin (Kühner and Stegmann 1955:48):

(96) eques Romanus [AP *nec*   infacetus *et*   satis   litteratus]
     knight Roman   and not dull   and moderately literate
     'a not dull and moderately literate Roman knight'   (Off.3.38)

The special form *nec* may be replaced by the standard negator *non*, or by a combination of *et non* with no difference in meaning.

2.3 Postsection

Like presection, postsection is in a majority of languages simply handled by a combination of standard conjunction and negation strategies. Justification for a separate treatment may again be found, however, in languages which possess a separate strategy. In the classical languages,

for example, the forms are the reverse of those found in presection: (*et
...*) *neque/nec* in Latin and (... τε) οὔτε ... in Greek, with the
exception that the initial co-ordinating particle is optional (Latin
examples in (97) from Kühner and Stegmann 1955:49/39):

(97)   a. qui [$_{VP}$ *et* rem agnoscit   *neque* hominem
           who   and affair recognizes and not men
           ignorat]
           is ignorant of
           'who recognizes the affair and is not ignorant of the man'
                                                        (Flacc. 46)

        b. aut [$_{VP}$ facere iniuriam *nec*   accipere], aut et   facere
           or   to do injustice and not to suffer or and to do
           et accipere
           and to suffer
           'either to do an injustice and not to suffer one, or both to do
           (an injustice) and to suffer one'
                                                        (Rep. 3.23)

The combined forms *neque* and *nec* have dissolved into separate
negation and conjunction in the majority of Romance languages, but
survive in the Italian form *nè* (Meyer-Lübke 1900:259):

(98)   [$_S$ Ha   voluto far   cosi, *nè*   io lo   condanno]
           he has wanted to do thus and not I him blame
           'He wanted to do so, and I don't blame him'

A similar particle may also be found in Estonian *ega*, in addition to the
standard co-ordinators for conjunction *ja* and *ning*, and the standard
negator *ei* (Päll, Totsel and Tukumtsev 1962:406):

(99)   Vane Hirm [$_{VP}$ magas enamasti hammikupoolel *ega*
           old   Hirm   slept mostly   mornings in   and not

        vajanud siis tõeliselt mingit valgust]
        needed then basically any   light
        'Old Hirm slept mostly in the mornings and basically did not
        need then any light'

Further justification for a separate treatment of postsection may be
sought in the existence in some languages of a special co-ordinating
particle co-occurring with a standard negator in the following conjunct.
An example of this may be found in Tagalog, which uses the co-
ordinator *nang* (or *na/-ng*) with a following negator *hindi* or *wala*, the
standard co-ordinator for conjunction being *at* (Schachter and Otanes
1972:544):

(100)   [_S Nakakapagbisikleta si   Manuel $\begin{Bmatrix} nang \\ na \end{Bmatrix}$ (*hin*)*di* humahawak
        ride bicycle   TOP Manuel   and   not   hold
        sa manibela]
        to handlebars
        'Manuel can   ride   a   bicycle   and   not   hold   on   to   the
        handlebars'

A similar particle appears to be present in Vietnamese *chứ*, side by side
with the zero strategy for standard conjunction (Thompson 1965:262). It
is not known to me however to what extent these two particles may be
used at phrasal levels.

2.4 *Disjunction*

A number of languages are cited by Döhmann (1974:41–2) as permitting
identical expression of disjunction and conjunction, whether by means
of simple juxtaposition (Sumerian, Ancient Egyptian, Chinese), or by
the use of an identical co-ordinator (Sanskrit, Tarahumara, Dakota,
Aymará).

In the case of simple juxtaposition, the existence of a separate and
distinct disjunction strategy does not appear to be precluded. Sumerian,
which is stated by Poebel (1923:154) not to distinguish between conjunction and disjunction, also possessed, according to S. Langdon
(1911:175) a repeated postposition for disjunction alone: ... *enna* ...
enna. Similarly in Ancient Egyptian, the particle *r-pw* could optionally
be suffixed to the final element of the disjunction (Gardiner 1973:68–9),
and Chinese possesses the disjunctive particle *hao*. Indeed, it is not clear
whether there are any languages at all which can express disjunction
solely by simple juxtaposition. Even the Samoyed languages, generally
sparse with co-ordinating conjunctions, do appear to have some devices.
In Nenets for example the form *nibt'a*, in origin the third person
singular conditional of a negative auxiliary verb, links at least NPS
(Tereščenko 1973:17)

(101)   [_{NP} pydă *nibt'a* pydăr]
            he   or   you
            'he or you'

Sel'kup, which is the most liberal of the Samoyed group with co-
ordinating conjunctions, has the repeated form *qaj* ... *qaj* ...
(Prokof'eva 1966:412), but no forms at all are cited by Tereščenko
(1966b, 1973) for Enets. It is interesting to note that a more limited use

of simple juxtaposition may be found in more familiar languages for the disjunction of numerals, for example German *drei-vier* and Russian *tri-četyre* (three or four).

Of the particles which are claimed to indicate either disjunction or conjunction, Tarahumara *hari* and Dakota *ka/k ʔa* are at least doubtful. The Tarahumara dictionary of Thord-Gray (1955) does not cite the particle quoted, but lists instead postposed *ave* and *napega* (among others) for conjunction, and postposed *chawe* or *chauke* for disjunction. In the Dakota text of Stark (1962), the form *ka/k ʔa* is unequivocally glossed as 'and', and a distinct particle *iš* is glossed as 'or'. Further information on Aymará *sá* is difficult to find.

Nevertheless, in certain environments, the distinction between 'and' and the sense of 'or', in which it is indifferent which of the elements is chosen, may be a minimal one. Compare *I like apples and pears* with *I like apples or pears*. It is not surprising, therefore, that some merging of *and* and *or* does exist. Sanskrit *uta*, at least from a historical point of view, is a good example of this. In origin, as indicated by cognate forms from Iranian (Old Persian *utā* > Middle Persian *uδ* > Modern Persian *o* (Oranskij 1963:74)) it indicates conjunction, though in later forms of Sanskrit its main function seems to be as an indicator of disjunction (MacDonell 1927:149). Korean . . . *ina* . . . *ina* may be glossed as '(either . . .) or . . .' or '(both . . .) and . . .' or 'and/or' (Martin and Lee 1969:309) with the sense that is is unimportant which is chosen. A further variation is provided by Georgian, which possesses unequivocal conjunction (*da*) and disjunction (*an*), but permits the latter to be reinforced by the former (*anda*) as disjunction (Vogt 1971:212–3).

On the whole, however, it is rare to find anything unusual in disjunction. The majority of languages appear to possess at least one unequivocal strategy and this is invariably permitted at sentential and at phrasal levels. Examples are English *or*, Estonian *või*, Russian *ili* and Japanese *ka*. Some languages possess two forms (Latin *aut*, *vel*; Georgian *an*, *tu*; Vietnamese *hay*, *hoặc*) where the first form in each case suggests that the alternatives are mutually exclusive and it is important which is chosen, while the second indicates indifference of choice (whether the alternatives are mutually exclusive or not).

2.5 *Rejection*

Strategies for rejection may consist simply in a combination of standard conjunction and standard negation, as in Arabic *la* . . . *wa la* . . . , permitted at sentential and all phrasal levels. Distinct strategies frequently consist of iterated particles, for example Turkish *ne* . . . *ne* . . . (see (102), from Lewis 1967:208); Russian *ni* . . . *ni* . . . ; Tagalog *ni* . . . *ni*

... (Schachter and Otanes 1972:543); Hungarian *se* ... *se* ... or *sem* ...
sem ...; Tamil ... *illai* ... *illai* (Beythan 1943:156); Albanian *as* ... *as*
... (see (103), from Rost 1887:164); Latin *neque* ... *neque* ... or *nec* ...
nec ....

(102) Bu sabah [NP *ne*   çay *ne* kahve] içtim
     this morning neither tea nor coffee I drank
     'This morning I drank neither tea nor coffee'

(103) S˙ kam [NP *as*   buk   *as* ui]
     not I have   neither bread nor water
     'I have neither bread nor water'

Note that further negation of the verb form may also be permitted or
required, as in (103).

Etymologically, such particles as those cited above are very often, and
not surprisingly, traceable to a combination of conjunction and negation. Examples of this are Latin *neque* (<*ne* + *que*, cf. section 2.2) and
Albanian *as* (<*a* + *sɛ*) (Pekmezi 1908:217).

Occasionally, the particle (for example Estonian *ega*, cf. example
(99)) is not iterated, but simply combined with standard negation as in
(104) below from Estonian (Päll, Totsel and Tukumstev 1962:407):

(104) Ta ei lainud enam kuhugi   kaugemale
     he not went more anywhere further
     [NP *ei* suvel   *ega*   talvel]
       not summer in and not winter in
     'He didn't go anywhere further any more, neither in summer
     nor in winter'

Because of the logical correspondence of $\bar{p}.\bar{q}$ and $\overline{p \lor q}$, however, the
strategy for rejection may be based not on a conjunction of negations
but on a negation of disjunction. An obvious example of this is English
not ... *either* ... *or*, but it also occurs in Sanskrit *na* (*vā*) ... *vā* ...
(Döhmann 1974:49).

2 Complementation

MICHAEL NOONAN

0 Introduction

In this chapter we are concerned with sentential complementation, hereafter referred to simply as 'complementation'. By complementation we mean the syntactic situation that arises when a notional sentence or predication is an argument of a predicate. For our purposes, a predication can be viewed as an argument of a predicate if it functions as the subject or object of that predicate. So, for example, the subject of (1), *Elliot*:

(1)   Elliot annoyed Floyd

can be replaced by various syntactic configurations that are notionally predications, i.e. consist of a predicate and a string of arguments:

(2)   a. *That Elliot entered the room* annoyed Floyd
        b. *Elliot's entering the room* annoyed Floyd
        c. *For Elliot to enter the room* would annoy Floyd

The italicized constituents in (2) are all sentential subjects of *annoy* and therefore subject complements of *annoy*. Similarly, *Nell*, the object of *remember* in (3):

(3)   Zeke remembered Nell

can be replaced by a predication that also functions as the object of *remember*, as we see in (4):

(4)   a. Zeke remembered *that Nell left*
        b. Zeke remembered *Nell's leaving*
        c. Zeke remembered *to leave*

The italicized portions of (4) are object complements of *remember*. As illustrated in (4c), complements may be truncated in the sense that the notional subject and certain other elements of a complete sentence may be absent. Predicates like *remember, see, think, cause,* etc. that take subject or object complements are referred to as 'complement-taking predicates' (CTPS).

Not all embedded sentences can be considered complements; relative clauses, purpose and manner clauses, locative and temporal clauses, etc. are not complements since they are not arguments of verbs. None of the italicized strings in (5) is a complement:[1]

(5)　a. Alf saw the man *that Pearl knows*

　　　b. Roscoe hit Floyd *to cause trouble*

　　　c. *On entering the room*, Irv saw Max standing by the window

　　　d. *When Zuma grows up*, she'll be a truck driver

　　　e. Nelson entered the room *carrying a briefcase*

Further, in this chapter we are not concerned with cases that fit the semantic definition of complementation given above, but where the main predicate is syntactically reduced to a non-verbal form, for example an adverb, as in:

(6)　a. Oddly, Zeke eats leeks (cf. It is odd *that Zeke eats leeks*)

　　　b. Strangely enough, Lucille knows Sanskrit

The organization of this chapter will be as follows: section 1 will discuss the morphology of complements, section 2 the syntax of complements, and section 3 the semantics of complementation. Section 4 will discuss complement systems. Section 5 will briefly discuss noun complementation.

1　The morphology of complements

1.1　*Complement types*
Even within a single language, complements can come in a variety of forms. English, for example, has four main forms for its complements, i.e. it has four main *complement types*. These complement types are illustrated in (7):

(7)　a. *That Cartier defeated Dugué* would be significant
　　　　(*that*-clause)

　　　b. *For Cartier to defeat Dugué* would be significant
　　　　(infinitive clause)

　　　c. *Cartier's defeating Dugué* is significant
　　　　(gerundal or verbal noun clause)

　　　d. Nelson saw *Cartier defeating Dugué*
　　　　(participial clause)

Other languages may have a greater or lesser number of complement types. For instances, Irish has only two complement types, illustrated in (8) (NZN = Nominalization):

(8)   a. Dúirt   sé *go   dtiocfadh   sé*
          said(3SG) he COMP would come he

          'He said that he would come'
          (*go*-clause)

    b. Is maith liom   *iad   a   fheiceáil*
          COP good with me them COMP see(NZN)
          'I like to see them'
          (verbal noun)

Some languages may have the same number of complement types as English, but may have different sorts of complements. For example, Lango, a Nilotic language, has four main complement types:

(9)   a. Àtín òpòyò   *ní   àcégò   dɔgólá*
          child remembered(3SG) COMP closed(1SG) door

          'The child remembered that I closed the door'
          (indicative)

    b. Àtín òpòyò   *òcègò   dɔgólá*
          child remembered(3SG) closed(3SG) door
          'The child remembered to close the door'
          (paratactic complement)

    c. Àtín òpòyò   *cèggò   dɔgólá*
          child remembered(3SG) to close(INF) door
          'The child remembered to close the door'
          (infinitive)

    d. Àtín òmítò   *ní   àcég   dɔgólá*
          child wanted(3SG) COMP close(1SG) door
          'The child wanted me to close the door'
          (subjunctive)

A complement type is identified basically by (1) the morphology of the predicate; (2) the sorts of syntactic relations it has with its arguments; and (3) the external syntactic relations of the complement construction as a whole.

1.2 Complementizers
Complement types often have associated with them a word, particle, clitic, or affix whose function it is to identify the entity as a complement.

Such forms are known as *complementizers*. Derivational affixes, such as English *-ing*, which are used to convert a form from one part of speech to another are not considered here to be complementizers. More than one complementizer may occur with a given complement type. Alternatively, some complement types may have no complementizer associated with them at all. In English, the particle *that* in (7a) is a complementizer associated with a complement type named after it, the *that*-clause. The particle *if* can also function as a complementizer with this same complement type, as in:

(10)   I don't know if Zeke knows Harry

Most infinitives have the complementizer *to*, but some have no complementizer. Neither the verbal noun nor participial complement types have complementizers in English. In Lango, there is only one complementizer, *ní*, and it is used with two distinct complement types, the indicative in (9a) and the subjunctive in (9d), which differ from each other inflectionally. The *ní* complementizer is the main morphological distinguisher between the indicative complement type and the paratactic complement, which are otherwise similar morphologically, though the syntactic properties of the two differ considerably (section 2.4). The Lango paratactic and infinitive complements lack complementizers altogether.

The use of a complementizer with a given complement type is sometimes optional or contextually determined. (11a) and (11b) are both possible:

(11)   a. Perry knows *that Hugh is vulnerable*

        b. Perry knows *Hugh is vulnerable*

When *that*-clauses are subjects, however, the use of *that* is obligatory:

(12)   a. *That Hugh is vulnerable* is remarkable

        b. *Hugh is vulnerable is remarkable

English *that* can be contrasted with the behavior of the complementizer *go* in Irish, which is obligatory in all contexts:

(13)   a. Tá a fhios   agam *go   léifidh   sí   an leabhar*
            COP its knowledge at me COMP read(FUT) she the book
            'I know that she'll read the book'

        b. *Tá a fhios agam *léifidh sí an leabhar*

The English complementizer *to* associated with infinitives is also dependent on context, but the principles governing its distribution are rather different from those governing the distribution of the *that*-complementizer. As indicated above, the use of *that* is optional with object complements, but obligatory with subject complements; the distribution is therefore syntactically determined. There are syntactically determined aspects of the distribution of the *to*-complementizer also – when infinitives are in other than object position the *to*-complementizer is obligatory. But in object position, the distribution of *to* is governed, rather arbitrarily, by the CTP. With complement-taking predicates like *force*, *want*, and *allow* the use of *to* is obligatory:

(14)   a. Evelle forced Jerry to change his plans
        b. *Evelle forced Jerry change his plans

(15)   a. Joe wants Pierre to retire
        b. *Joe wants Pierre retire

(16)   a. Henry allowed Dick to speak
        b. *Henry allowed Dick speak

The predicate *help* can occur with or without *to*:

(17)   a. Leonid helped Boris to see the error of his ways
        b. Leonid helped Boris see the error of his ways

To is ungrammatical with *make* and *let*:

(18)   a. *Bert made Jimmy to blush
        b. Bert made Jimmy blush

(19)   a. *The judge let Spiro to go
        b. The judge let Spiro go

In Yaqui, one complement type takes two complementizers: *ke*, a particle that precedes the clause, and *kai*, a clause-final clitic. With this complement type, one or both of the complementizers must be present. This is illustrated in (20) (data from Lindenfeld 1973; Carlos Seguín, personal communication):

(20)   a. Tuisi tuʔi _ke_   hu hamut bwika-_kai_
          very good COMP the woman sing-COMP
          'It's very good that the woman sings'
        b. Tuisi tuʔi _ke hu hamut bwika_
        c. Tuisi tuʔi _hu hamut bwika-kai_
        d. *Tuisi tuʔi _hu hamut bwika_

Complementizers typically derive historically from pronouns, conjunctions, adpositions or case markers, and, rarely, verbs, and so may resemble words currently used in these capacities.[2] The English complementizers *that*, *if* and *to* are derived from and thus resemble the pronoun *that*, the conjunction *if*, and the preposition *to* respectively. Similar examples can be cited from a great number of languages. In Kanuri, an East Saharan language, clitics otherwise functioning as accusative and dative case markers may be affixed onto finite verbs and function as complementizers (data from Lukas 1967):

(21)   Àvá-nzə́-yè   shí-*rò*   kúŋə́nà cìn
        father-his-NOM him-DAT money give(3SG)
        'His father gives him money'

(22)   *Sávà-nyì ìshìn-rò*   təmǎŋə́nà
        friend-my come-3SG(DAT) thought (1SG PERF)
        'I thought my friend would come'

(23)   Sávà-nyì íshìn
        friend-my come(3SG)
        'My friend is coming'

In Russian, an interrogative and relative pronoun *čto* functions also as a complementizer:

(24)   *Čtó* ty   čital?
        what you read
        'What were you reading?'

(25)   Ja ne znaju, *čtó* ty   čital
        I NEG know what you read
        'I don't know what you were reading'

(26)   Ja ne znaju, *čto* ty   čital
        I NEG know COMP you read
        'I didn't know that you were reading'

As a pronoun, *čto* is always stressed (24–5). As a complementizer, as in (26), it is not stressed. Maori illustrates the common tendency to use the adposition associated with direction toward and indirect objects as a complementizer for complements with determined time reference (cf. section 3.1.1; Clark 1973):

(27)   E   hoki ana au *ki* te kaainga
        PRES return PROG I to the village
        'I'm going back to the village'

(28)   ka   hoatu te   taurekareka *ki* te   rangatira
        AORIST given the slave   to the chief
        'The slave was given to the chief'

(29)   E   hiahia ana   raatou *<u>ki</u>*   *te   haere*
        PRES want   PROG they   COMP the go
        'They want to go'

English *to* has the same range of uses as Maori *ki*. In Uzbek, a particle *deb* 'saying' functions as a complementizer (Abduzuxur Abduazizov, personal communication; and Sjoberg 1963):

(30)   *Bu ɔdam bir ǰoǰa-ni   oǧirladi <u>deb</u> aytti   u*
        this man one chicken-OBJ stole   COMP said(3SG) he
        'He said that the man stole a certain chicken'

Sometimes the same complement type takes on different meanings with different complementizers. In Jacaltec, for instance, the sentence-like complement type can occur with several complementizers, either individually or in combination. One of these complementizers, *chubil*, implies that the information in the complement is accorded a high degree of credibility, while another, *tato*, is used with complements about which there is some reservation on the part of the speaker or even outright disbelief. These differences are illustrated by the following sentences (Craig 1977):

(31)   a. Xal naj *<u>tato</u> chuluj   naj presidente*
        said ART COMP will come ART president
        'He said that the president would come'

        b. Xal naj *<u>chubil</u> chuluj naj presidente*
        'He said that the president will come'

(31a) would be a report of an assertion whose credibility is open to doubt. (31b), on the other hand, presents the reported assertion as a fact, since either the 'he' in (31b) is reliable, or the speaker has good reason to believe that the statement is true. In Kabre, a Gur language, the subjunctive complement can occur with the complementizers *né* and *zì* (SJNCT = Subjunctive):

(32)   a. Màlàbá   àbàló *<u>né</u>* *ísé*
        pressed(1SG PERF) man   COMP run(3SG SJNCT)
        'I forced the man to run'

        b. Màlàbá   àbàló *<u>zì</u>* *ísé*
        pressed(1SG PERF) man   COMP run(3SG SJNCT)
        'I pressed the man to run'

With the *né* complementizer in (32a), there is an implication that the man ran, but in (32b) with *zì* there is no such implication.

1.3 *The morphology of complement types*
1.3.1 *Sentence-like complement types*
All languages have some sort of sentence-like complement type, one that without its complementizers has roughly the same syntactic form as a main clause. In a sentence-like (hereafter, s-like) complement type, the predicate has the same syntactic relation to its subject and its other arguments that it has in syntactic main clauses: it remains syntactically and morphologically a verb, and any case marking in subjects or objects will have the same form as in main clauses (but see sentences (43–6) from Wappo below). Further, if the verb in main clauses is inflected for subject or object agreement in some language, then the verb in any s-like complement type in that language will also be inflected for subject or object agreement. In English, the sentence:

(33)   Burt *is* a chicken farmer

is identical in form to the s-like complement in (34):

(34)   Max knows *that Burt is a chicken farmer*

The form taken by the complements in (35) and (36) is not s-like:

(35)   Max wants Burt *to be* a chicken farmer

(36)   Burt's *being* a chicken farmer worries Max

Neither of the above complements meet the criteria for s-like complement types; the notional subject of the complement does not bear in either case the same syntactic relation to its predicate that it does in main clauses. In (35), the complement subject has been raised to object position in the matrix clause (cf. section 2.2). In (36), the complement subject has an associative (or genitive) case relation to its predicate. In neither case is the predicate inflected for subject agreement as in (33) and (34) above.

That a complement type is s-like does not preclude the possibility that its syntax may differ in certain respects from that of main clauses. In German, for example, the word order in s-like complements differs from that in main clauses:

(37)   Er ist schlau
         he COP cunning
         'He is cunning'

(38)   Es ist wahr, dass er schlau   ist
        it COP true   COMP he cunning COP
        'It's true that he's cunning'

In (37) the adjective *schlau* follows the copular verb *ist*, but in complement in (38), the verb comes last. In Irish, many verbs have so-called 'dependent' forms which occur only in subordinate clauses and after a few verbal particles. For example, the main clauses

(39)   *Tá* sé ina   dhochtúir
        COP he in his doctor
        'He's a doctor'

(40)   *Chonaic* Seán an mhuc
        saw   John the pig
        'John saw the pig'

when embedded as complements become respectively:

(41)   Tá a fhios   agam *go bhfuil sé ina   dhochtúir*
        COP its knowledge at me COMP COP   he in his doctor
        'I know that he's a doctor'

(42)   Tá a fhios   agam *go bhfaca Seán an mhuc*
        COP its knowledge at me COMP saw   John the pig
        'I know that John saw the pig'

In Wappo, the subjects of main clauses are marked with a suffix *-i* (Li and Thompson 1976a):

(43)   Chic-i   c'ic'a ṭ'a-taʔ
        bear-SUBJ bird   kill-PAST
        'The bear killed the bird'

(44)   Ce k'ew-i   tuc'a-khiʔ
        that man-SUBJ big-PREDICATOR
        'That man is big'

When sentences like these are embedded as s-like complements, their internal syntax doesn't change except that the subject marker *-i* cannot occur with the subjects of these clauses (*ʔah* is the irregular subject form of the first person pronoun):

(45)   ʔah *chica c'ic'a ṭ'a-taʔ*   haṭiskhiʔ
        I   bear bird kill-PAST know
        'I know that the bear killed the bird'

(46)   ʔah *ce k'ew tuc'a-khiʔ* haṭiskhiʔ
        'I know that the man is big'

1.3.2 *Indicative versus subjunctive sentence-like complements*

In many languages there is more than one s-like complement-type. When such a distinction exists, the form that most closely resembles declarative main clauses is referred to as *indicative*. Non-indicative s-like complement types usually have a special non-indicative stem or conjugation; they may also differ from indicatives in occurring with modal particles or special complementizers.

Non-indicative s-like complement types can be referred to by the semantically neutral term *subjunctive*. For a particular language, a term with more semantic content such as optative, irrealis, potential, etc. might be more appropriate. Indicative and subjunctive verbal forms are said to differ in *mood*, and there are rarely more than two s-like mood distinctions available in complement systems, though a number of languages have more than two mood distinctions available for use outside the complement system (see chapter III:4).

Indicative–subjunctive distinctions in complementation are attested in a number of language families. Only languages that distinguish tense and/or aspect in their verbal morphology, however, will be likely to have an indicative–subjunctive distinction.

English distinguishes an indicative from a (rather moribund) subjunctive in complementation. The subjunctive differs from the indicative only in the morphology of the verb. The indicative and subjunctive use the same complementizer, *that*:

(47) a. King Melvin suggested *that Natasha <u>was</u> drawn and quartered*

     b. King Melvin suggested *that Natasha <u>be</u> drawn and quartered*

(48) a. I insisted *that Roscoe <u>lives</u> here*

     b. I insisted *that Roscoe <u>live</u> here*

The (a) sentences above contain indicatives, while the (b) sentences contain subjunctives. In Lori, usually considered a dialect of Persian, the subjunctive has a prefix and a special conjugation distinguishing it from the indicative. As with English, the complementizer is the same (data from Stan Murai):

(49) Zine   eteqad dar *ke   pia tile-ye   <u>dozid</u>*
      woman belief have COMP man chicken-OBJ stole(3SG INDIC)
      'The woman believes that the man stole the chicken'

(50) Zine   væ pia xas   *ke   tile-ye   <u>be-doze</u>*
      woman from man wanted COMP chicken-OBJ 3SG SJNCT-steal
      'The woman wanted the man to steal the chicken'

In Romanian, both the verb conjugation and the complementizer differ:

(51)   El spune că   *citeşte*   *o carte*
        he says   COMP read(3SG INDIC) a book
        'He says that he's reading a book'

(52)   El vrea   să   *citescă*   *o carte*
        he wants COMP read(3SG SJNCT) a book
        'He wants to read a book'

In Russian, the subjunctive is identical in form to the indicative past tense. The complementizer is the same for both moods, but the subjunctive is always accompanied by the modal particle *by*:

(53)   Ja verju, *čto   Boris pridët*
        I   believe COMP Boris will come(INDIC)
        'I believe that Boris will come'

(54)   Ja verju, *čto   Boris prišël*
        I   believe COMP Boris came(INDIC)
        'I believe that Boris came'

(55)   Ja ne verju, *čto   by   Boris prišël*
        I   NEG believe COMP SJNCT PCL Boris come(SJNCT)
        'I don't believe that Boris will come/came'

As the Russian case illustrates, subjunctives tend to have fewer inflectional possibilities than indicatives. The complement in (55) is neutral to a future or past interpretation, though the predicate is marked for perfective aspect. Past and future reference in Russian is clearly marked on indicatives, however, as (53) and (54) show. Many of the tense distinctions associated with subjunctives in the literature turn out on closer inspection to be aspectual distinctions. In Classical Greek, for example, the indicative present and aorist contrast along both a time and an aspect dimension. The present is imperfective and refers to time coextensive with the time of speaking; the aorist is perfective and refers to time prior to the act of speaking (Goodwin 1892, Smyth 1920):

(56)   Speúdousi   pròs tèn kómēn
        hasten(3PL PRES) to   the village
        'They are hastening to the village'

(57)   Éspeusan   pròs tèn kómēn
        hasten(3PL AORIST) to   the village
        'They hastened to the village'

In the subjunctive, the tense distinction is lost and only the aspectual distinction remains between present and aorist:

(58) Efobeîto   *mè speúdōsi*   *pròs tèn kómēn*
      afraid(3PL IMPERF) NEG hasten(3PL PRES SJNCT) to   the village
      'He was afraid that they should be hastening to the village'

(59) Efobeîto   *mè speúsōsi*   *pròs tèn*
      afraid(3SG IMPERF) NEG hasten(3PL AORIST SJNCT) to   the
      kómēn
      village
      'He was afraid that they should hasten to the village'

In Bemba, the indicative distinguishes twenty-four tense–aspect categories (Givón 1971, 1972). In the subjunctive, only a restricted number of present and future distinctions is possible (some examples are provided in section 3.1.1) all of which appear to be the products of tense copying. In fact, many tense distinctions exhibited by subjunctives are not independently meaningful, but are the result of tense-copying (cf. section 2.6).

The subjunctive may also neutralize aspectual distinctions. In Lango, the indicative has a three-way aspectual contrast, distinguishing a progressive, a habitual, and a perfective:

(60) Àkwànnò   búk
      read(3SG PROG) book
      'He's reading a book'

(61) Kwánó   'búk
      read(3SG HABIT) book
      'He reads a book (all the time)'

(62) Òkwànò   búk
      read(3SG PERF) book
      'He read a book (all the way through)'

In the subjunctive, these distinctions are neutralized:

(63) Dákó òdìò   icó *ní* 'kwál   'búk
      woman pressed(3SG) man COMP read(3SG SJNCT) book
      'The woman { to read a book (all the time)'
      pressed { to read a book (all the way through)' }
      the man

On the other hand, the subjunctive may have as many inflectional categories as the indicative, as for instance in Ossetic (Abaev 1964).

One inflectional distinction follows from the definition of subjunctive complement as s-like: if the indicative has subject–verb or object–verb agreement, the subjunctive will almost invariably code these categories as well. Inflectional categories of subjunctives will be mentioned again briefly in section 1.3.4.

Subjunctives often bear some regular relation to another part of the verbal paradigm. The Russian example mentioned above where the subjunctive is morphologically identical to the past tense is rather atypical, the more usual pattern being that where the subjunctive resembles the future tense form as in the following example from Pashto:

(64)   Zə bə dā kitáb *vúlvaləm*
        I   PCL this book read(ISG PERF FUT)
        'I will read this book'

(65)   Zə ğvárəm   če   dā kitáb *vúlvaləm*
        I   want(ISG) COMP this book read(ISG PERF SJNCT)
        'I want to read this book'

The future construction includes the particle *bə* but the verb forms are identical in the two cases. The subjunctive and imperative paradigms are frequently similar.

It seems that all languages with subjunctive complements can use subjunctives as main clauses (though the reverse may not be true – Irish has a somewhat rare subjunctive in main clauses that is not used in complementation). Main clause subjunctives tend to be used in modal, hortative, or imperative senses. Consider the contrast between indicative and subjunctive clauses in French:

(66)   Dieu vous *bénit*
        God you bless(INDIC)
        'God blesses you'

(67)   Dieu vous *bénisse*
        God you bless(SJNCT)
        'May God bless you'

Subjunctive main clauses may be accompanied by the subjunctive complementizer even though there is no overt complement-taking predicate accompanying the subjunctive, as in this example from Romanian:

(68)   *Să*   continuăm
        COMP continue(IPL SJNCT)
        'Let's continue'

1.3.3 *Paratactic complements and verb serialization in complementation*
Parataxis and verb serialization may be used in complementation. These
constructions have much in common syntactically:

1. Both consist of a subject NP followed by a series of verb
   phrases.
2. Each verb phrase contains a fully inflected verb.
3. No marker of coordination or subordination links the two
   verb phrases.
4. No special verb forms are used: if the first verb in the series
   is indicative, all the rest will be too.

There are a number of important differences between the constructions,
but only one, relating to the matter of one versus two assertions, has a
direct bearing on their use in complementation.[3] In this section, only
examples of parataxis will be given.

In the paradigm cases of parataxis, the matrix clause and the
paratactic complement each constitute clauses which could stand by
themselves as independent sentences with approximately the same
meaning. Below are some indicative–paratactic pairs from Lango:

(69) a. Dákó òkòbbì ìcó *ní* àtín òkwɔrɔ kál
      woman told(3SG DAT) man COMP child sifted(3SG) millet
      'The woman told the man that the child sifted millet'

   b. Dákó òkòbbì ìcó òkwɔrɔ kál
      woman told(3SG DAT) man sifted(3SG) millet
      'The woman said it to the man, he sifted millet'
      (The woman told the man to sift millet (and he did))

(70) a. Àtín òpòyò *ní* 'dákó òkwɔrɔ kál
      child remembered(3SG) COMP woman sifted(3SG) millet
      'The child remembered that the woman sifted millet'

   b. Àtín òpòyò òkwɔrɔ kál
      child remembered(3SG) sifted(3SG) millet
      'The child remembered it, he sifted millet'
      (The child remembered to sift the millet (and he did))

The (a) sentences above have indicative complements, the (b) sentences
paratactic complements. In the (a) sentences there is an obligatory
complementizer *ní*, and the complement includes its notional subject. In
the (b) sentences, the complement consists of a verb phrase without a
subject NP. The verb in these cases does not form a syntactic constituent
with its notional subject, even in (69b) when the verb occurs next to it

(*icó* 'man' in (69b) is the indirect object of *òkòbbì* 'she told it to'). The complementizer *ní* cannot occur with paratactic complements. In (69b), both *dákó òkòbbì ìcó* 'the woman said it to the man' and *òkwɔ̀rɔ̀ kál* 'he sifted the millet' can stand as independent clauses with approximately the same meaning as in the paratactic construction.

Paratactic complements are fairly common in sub-Saharan Africa, especially with CTPS whose complements are implied to be true, as is the case for many causative predicates, as in this example from Luo (Creider 1974):

(71)   əmîyɔ   ɔnyâŋgo *orì·ŋgo*
        gave(1SUBJ 3SG OBJ) Onyango ran(3SG)
        'I gave it to Onyango, he ran'
        (I made Onyango run)

and immediate perception predicates, as in the following Hausa example:

(72)   Nǎ   gán shì *yánà   aikì*
        1SG(PERF) see him be at(3SG) work
        'I saw him, he is working'
        (I saw him working)

Paratactic complements may occur in other environments as well, as in Diegueño (M. Langdon 1970):

(73)   ʔənʸa· puy ʔəxap-x-vu
        I   there go in-1SG-UNREALIZED SPECIFIC
        əwa·rp-x   uma·w
        want-3PL SUBJ 3SG OBJ UNREALIZED not(3PL)
        'I'll go in there, they won't want it'
        (They won't want me to go there)

The predicates in paratactic constructions can typically be inflected for any verbal category that indicative complements can be inflected for. Further, paratactic complements will typically agree with their CTPS in tense–aspect marking. See section 2.4 for discussion of this and other problems relating to parataxis in complementation.

1.3.4 *Infinitive complements*
The term 'infinitive' has been used for rather different sorts of syntactic entities. The word 'infinitive' itself, meaning 'not limited' (e.g. by person, number, tense), would suggest itself for use with complement types that do not express inflectional distinctions. Such a classification of complement types into inflected versus non-inflected categories, how-

ever, would not provide a particularly useful classification. In this chapter the term will be used somewhat differently referring instead to verb-like entities that do not bear syntactic relations to their notional subjects; i.e. their subjects do not take nominative case marking or condition verb agreement (where otherwise appropriate for subjects), nor are they marked in the associative (genitival) case. The notional subjects of infinitives are typically equi-deleted (section 2.1), raised (section 2.2), or made objects of adpositions, as in (74):

(74)   *For him to abandon Radical Syndicalism* would be terrible for
         the movement

But because infinitives are verb-like, the relations that they may establish with their objects (as in the phrase *abandon Radical Syndicalism* in (74)) are the same as those established by verbs in s-like complements.

Except for subject agreement (and mood), infinitives may be inflected for all verbal categories such as tense–aspect, voice, object agreement, etc. In most cases, however, infinitives like subjunctives are inflected for fewer of these categories than indicative complements in the same language. It seems possible to arrange verbal inflections (minus subject agreement and mood) along a scale like that in Table 2.1. It applies to all non-indicative complement types:

Table 2.1. *The relationship of verbal inflection to non-indicative complement types*

full range of tenses	past vs. non-past (morphologically may correspond to the perfect/non-perfect distinction in the indicative)	aspect	voice, transitivity, causative, desiderative, object agreement
1	2	3	4

Generally speaking, the further to the left an item is on this scale, the less likely it is to be coded on a non-indicative complement. The categories in set 4 are almost always coded on infinitive and subjunctive complements if they are coded on indicatives. (An exception is Hungarian, which has object agreement in verbs but lacks it in infinitives–data from Edith Moravcsik). When infinitive and subjunctive complement types differ in the number of inflectional categories they code, the s-like subjunctive will likely code more, but tense coding on subjunctives is more likely to be the product of tense copying (section 2.6).

Classical Greek provides an example of a language whose infinitives can code inflectional categories 1–4 in Table 2.1. Greek also illustrates another important point, namely that certain inflectional categories of infinitives may be manifested only in certain contexts. The Greek indicative in active voice is coded for the following tense–aspect categories: present, (past) imperfective, future, aorist (basically, a perfective past), (present) perfect, and pluperfect (past perfect). The infinitive can be coded for all of these save imperfective and pluperfect. When infinitive complements are used for reported speech, their tense distinctions parallel in use their indicative counterparts:

(75)   Fēsì   grápsai
       say(3SG) write(AORIST INF)
       'He says that he wrote'

(76)   Fēsì   gegrafénai
       say(3SG) write(PERF INF)
       'He says that he has written'

(77)   Fēsì   gráfein
       say(3SG) write(PRES INF)
       'He says that he's writing'

(78)   Fēsì   grápsein
       say(3SG) write(FUT INF)
       'He says that he'll write'

Apart from their use in reported speech constructions, however, the future and perfect infinitives are rather rare (Goodwin 1892), and the present and aorist infinitives simply code aspect in the manner described for subjunctives in section 1.3.2. In English, the infinitive construction can code a past/non-past distinction, as well as aspect and voice. The past/non-past distinction is illustrated below:

(79)   I believe Walt *to be a flat-earther*

(80)   I believe Walt *to have been a flat-earther*

The morphology used for the past in (80) (*have* followed by a past participle) codes secondary or relative pasts (perfect tenses) in indicative clauses. In Russian, infinitives cannot be coded for tense, although tense categories are coded on verbs. Russian infinitives are, however, coded for aspect and voice. An aspect distinction coded on infinitives in Russian is illustrated below:

(81)   Ja xoču *každyĭ den' igrat'*   *na rojale*
       I   want every day   play(IMPERF INF) on piano
       'I want to play the piano every day'

(82)   Ja xoču *sygrat'*   *vam*   *melodiju*
       I   want play(PERF INF) to you tune
       'I want to play you a tune'

In Lango, infinitives are not coded for tense or aspect, though aspect is an important category in indicative complements, but are coded for transitivity and orientation (which corresponds very roughly to voice – see Noonan and Bavin Woock 1978b):

(83)   Ámìttò   *nὲnnὸ*   *gwók*
       want(1SG) see(TRANS INF) dog
       'I want to see the dog'

(84)   Ámìttò   *nénô*
       want(1SG) see(INTRANS INF)
       'I want to see'

(85)   Ámìttò   *nên*
       want(1SG) see(SECONDARY ORIENTATION INF)
       'I want to be seen/be visible'

The morphology of the infinitive construction may betray its origins in another grammatical category. In Jacaltec, for example, the infinitive is marked with the irrealis suffix *-oj*, but differs from the ordinary irrealis future in not taking subject agreement affixes (Craig 1977). In many languages, the infinitive shows clear signs of being derived from a nominal construction. This appears to be the case for most Indo-European infinitives which derive historically from case-marked nominalizations (Buck 1933, Lehmann 1974, Jeffers 1975). For this reason, complementizers with infinitives frequently derive from adpositions or articles.

Infinitive complement types resemble paratactic complements in many respects. Both are verb phrases that lack overt subject NPS. They differ in that paratactic complements can be inflected for subject agreement whereas infinitives cannot, and paratactic complements are syntactically not subordinate clauses, whereas infinitives are and may, therefore, occur with a complementizer while paratactic complements may not. In languages that lack subject–verb agreement and do not have complementizers for infinitives a problem may arise in deciding whether or not a given complement is an infinitive or a paratactic complement. For example, in Sre (Manley 1972) verbs are not conjugated for subject agreement. Since a complementizer does not occur in the following example, the complements could be interpreted as either infinitives or paratactic complements.

(86)   Kɔn khay pal rəgəy təlɔŋ rɛ
        child his   must be able try   swim
        'His child has to be able to try to swim'

The complements in (86) would be interpreted as paratactic, however, only if each of the complements were capable of standing alone as an independent clause without substantial change of meaning for the whole. Since this is not possible in these cases, these complements are considered infinitives.

Infinitives are widely distributed across languages, though perhaps somewhat less commonly than nominalizations. They are frequently involved in clause-union phenomena (section 2.3).

1.3.5 Nominalized complements

Nominalized complements are predications with the internal structure of noun phrases. The predicate becomes nominalized, assuming the form of a verbal noun, and takes over the role of head noun of the noun phrase. The arguments may assume associative (genitival) relationships with the predicate. The nominalized predicate may occur with articles, case markers, adpositions, and in some cases may even be pluralized.

The relations that a nominalized predicate has with its arguments are the single most important feature distinguishing nominalizations from other sorts of complements. In a few cases, both notional subject and object may have an associative relation with the nominalized predicate. English provides an example of this sort:

(87)   *Algernon's shooting of the aardvark* drew international attention

The notional subject of the nominalized predicate *shooting* is coded in the associative case, while the notional object establishes its associative relation to the predicate via the preposition *of*. The more common situation, however, is that where only the subject bears an associative relation to the predicate and the object is coded with the usual object marker. Uzbek provides an example of this sort (NZR = Nominalizer):

(88)   Xɔtin bu ɔdam-niŋ ǰoǰa-ni   oǧirla-š-i-ni
        woman this man-GEN chicken-OBJ steal-NZR-3SG-OBJ
        istadi
        wanted(3SG)
        'The woman wanted the man to steal the chicken'

The notional subject of *oǧirla-* 'steal' is *ɔdam* 'man' which is marked in the genitive case with *-niŋ*. The suffix *-i-* 'his' coded on the nominalized predicate *oğirla-š-* reinforces the associative relationship. The notional direct object of *oğirla-*, *joǰa* 'chicken', takes the ordinary direct object marker. *Oğirla-š-* 'stealing' as the direct object of *istadi* 'wanted', is also marked with the direct object marker. In a few rare cases, the nominalized predicate may have only an associative relation with its notional object. This situation holds in Irish, where the notional subject is either equi-deleted or raised:

(89)   Is ionadh liom   *Seán* a   bhualadh Thomáis
        COP surprise with me John COMP hit(NZN) Thomas(GEN)
        'I'm surprised that John hit Thomas'

It is also possible for neither argument to bear an associative relation to the nominalized predicate. In English, this situation occurs most frequently when the complement is an object of a preposition (see Visser 1973 for more examples and discussion):

(90)   I disapprove of *children smoking pot*

Nominalized complements vary considerably as to the verbal categories they can retain, ranging from those that can express few verbal categories to those that retain all verbal categories. In Squamish, for instance, nominalized complements can retain all of the verbal inflections, clitics, and sentence particles found in main clauses. Compare (92) and (91) (Kuipers 1967):

(91)   Na č-n   wa   c'aq'-an-umi
        fact DECLAR-ISG PROG hit-TRANS-2SG OBJ
        'I was hitting you'

(92)   Č-n   łč-iws   *kʷi n-s-na*   *wa*
        DECLAR-ISG tired-body ART ISG POSS-NOM-fact PROG
        c'aq'-an-umi
        hit-TRANS-2SG OBJ
        'I'm tired of hitting you'

In Squamish, all nominals, including proper nouns, are always accompanied by articles. Nominalized complements conform to this principle, taking the article *kʷi*.

Nominalized complements can also occur with nominal categories such as case markers and number inflections. In Turkish, case inflections are placed on verbal nouns according to the general principles for placement of case categories in the language. Briefly, the absolute codes non-specific direct objects, which, in the case of nominalized predicates, signals non-specific or imperfective aspect. The accusative case codes specific direct objects, or perfective nominalizations. The dative case is used for goals:

(93)   *Çaliş-mak*   istiyor
        work-NZR(ABS) want(3SG)
        'He wants to work'

(94)   *Ekmek al-mağ-i*   unuttu
        bread take-NZR-ACC forgot(3SG)
        'He forgot to get bread'

(95)   *Yürü-meğ-e*   başladik
        walk-NZR-DAT began(1PL)
        'We began to walk'

Plural affixes are found on nominalized predicates in Ossetic (Abaev 1964), marking imperfective aspect:

(96)   *Xæts-yn-tæ* sistoï   *kuyrttat-imæ*
        fight-NZR-PL started(3PL) Kurtatin-with
        'They started to fight with the Kurtatins'

The form of a nominalization is more likely to be idiosyncratic relative to the verbal paradigm than is the verb-like infinitive, which will likely have a regular relation to the verbal paradigm.

Some of the points in this section are treated in greater detail in chapter III:7.

1.3.6 *Participial complements*

Participles are adjectival or adverbial forms of verbs. The role of participles in complementation is usually limited even in languages that make extensive use of participles. The reason for this is that, in their role as adjectives, participles are not the heads of constructions, but rather modify some noun which functions as the head; i.e. in complementation, participles function as attributive, not predicate, adjectives.

Since complements are, by definition, predications functioning as arguments of predicates and predicates are the heads of predications, complements will normally be rendered as constructions having their predicates as heads, whether surfacing as verbs or nouns. Because of their syntactic properties, participles will normally be used in complementation only when the special semantic properties of participles can be exploited (see section 3.1.5).

The only place in complement systems where participles are regularly found is in complements to immediate perception predicates (section 3.2.12). Here the object of the immediate perception predicate is head and the participle a qualifying clause.[4] Examples of such constructions can be found in Classical Greek:

(97)   a. Eîde   autòn   *paúonta*
            saw(3SG) him(ACC) stop(PART PRES MASC SG ACC)
            'He saw him stopping'

        b. Eîde   autòn   *paúsanta*
            saw(3SG) him(ACC) stop(PART AORIST MASC SG ACC)
            'He saw him stop'

(98)   a. Eîde   autèn   *paúousan*
            saw(3SG) her(ACC) stop(PART PRES FEM SG ACC)
            'He saw her stopping'

        b. Eîde   autèn   *paúsāsan*
            saw(3SG) her(ACC) stop(PART AORIST FEM SG ACC)
            'He saw her stop'

The pronouns *autòn* and *autèn* function as heads of their respective constructions, the participles agreeing with them in gender, number and case. The participles are also inflected for present and aorist tenses, and again these distinctions here are used only to reflect aspectual contrasts (cf. section 1.3.2). Participles, in their role as complements to immediate perception predicates, do not have tense, but may encode aspectual distinctions. Participles may also code voice distinctions. Notice that the so-called present and past participles in English, when used as complements to immediate perception predicates, encode active and passive voice respectively:

(99)   We saw the army defeating the enemy

(100)   We saw the army defeated by the enemy

Both participles above have both complement and relative interpretations.

There are some instances of participles being used as complements of CTPs other than immediate perception predicates. In Classical Greek, participles could also function as complements to predicates in reported discourse, as we see below:

(101)   Éggellen autoùs   paúontas
         report(3SG) them(ACC) stop(PART PRES MASC PL ACC)
         'He was reporting that they were stopping'

(102)   Éggellen autoùs   paúsantas
         report(3SG) them(ACC) stop(PART AORIST MASC PL ACC)
         'He was reporting that they stopped'

In cases like this, participles can code tense. In a few cases, participles are also found as complements to modal predicates, as in the Latin gerundive (Greenough 1903) and the Hindu-Urdu gerundive (Bailey 1956). As a non-indicative complement type, participial complements follow the scale in Table 2.1 (section 1.3.4) in the verbal categories they encode.

Adverbial participles, which may head adverbial clauses (chapter II:4) may also be used as complements. They differ from adjectival participles in their inability to agree with any head noun. In Catalan adjectival participles agree with their head noun in number (Yates 1975):

(103)   a. la classe *dirigent*
           'the ruling class'

        b. les classes *dirigents*
           'the ruling classes'

The adverbial participle is used in Catalan as a complement to immediate perception predicates and is invariant:

(104)   a. Vaig   veure   la dona *passant* per   la duana
           go(1SG) see(INF) the woman go(PART) through ART customs
           'I saw the woman go through customs'

        b. Vaig   veure   les dones *passant* per   la duana
           go(1SG) see(INF) the women go(PART) through ART customs
           'I saw the women go through customs'

1.3.7 *Summary*
In the last few sections, characteristic features of the various complement types have been discussed and illustrated. Some of the more important features are summarized in Table 2.2.

2.0 The syntax of complementation

We have defined complementation as the grammatical state where a predication functions as an argument of a predicate. In contrasting this (universal) semantic characterization with the surface characteristics of sentences containing complements, a process terminology is useful, especially where cross-linguistic comparisons are made. In the sections that follow, we will use process terminology to describe *equi-deletion*, *raising*, and other semantic phenomena.

Table 2.2. *Summary of complement types*

complement type	part of speech of predicate	syntactic relation of subject to predicate	range of inflectional categories	other characteristics
indicative	verb	same as main clause	same as main clause	s-like form (nearly) identical to declarative main clause
subjunctive	verb	same as main clause	typically reduced	s-like form that differs from declarative main clause – when main clause, often used in hortative or imperative senses
paratactic	verb	predicate may agree with subject but doesn't form constituent with it	same as indicative	interpreted as separate assertion; syntactically not a subordinate clause; can't take complementizer
infinitive	verb	predicate can't form constituent with subject	reduced; can't take subject–verb agreement	relations with object same as indicative
nominalization	noun	associative relation between subject and predicate	reduced; may take nominal categories such as case and number	may have internal structure of NP; frequent gradation between nominalizations and infinitives
participle	adjective or adverb	subject is head, rest of predication is modifier	reduced; may take adjectival inflections when agreeing with subject	syntactically may conform to principles governing adjectives

2.1 *Equi-deletion*

As discussed above, certain complement types may be truncated or reduced in the sense that certain components normally found in main clauses may be absent from them. Consider the following sentences:

(105)   Zeke wants *Norma to plant the corn*

(106)   Zeke wants *to plant the corn*

In (105), Zeke is the main clause (or matrix) subject, Norma the complement subject. In (106), Zeke is both matrix and complement subject, but notice that Zeke in (106) is not mentioned twice, corresponding to its two semantic roles. That is, we don't have a sentence like

(107)   *Zeke$_i$ wants Zeke$_i$/him$_i$ to plant the corn

in place of (106). The second mention of *Zeke* has been deleted to produce (106) by a process known as equi-deletion. Equi-deletion (equi) deletes subjects of complements when they are coreferential with (i.e. refer to the same individual or thing as) some argument in the matrix. In (106) the complement subject has been equi-deleted under identity with the matrix subject.

It is possible to have equi-deletion under identity with matrix arguments other than subject. In Irish, for example, objects of prepositions regularly condition equi:

(108)   Ba   mhaith liom   theacht
         would be good   with me come(NZN)
         'I want to come'

The notional subject of *teacht* 'come' is deleted under identity with the pronominal portion of *liom* 'with me'. When the notional subject of the complement is not coreferential with a matrix argument, it is overt, like *í* in:

(109)   Ba   mhaith liom   í   a   theacht
         would be good   with me her COMP come(NZN)
         'I want her to come'

In English, direct objects can condition equi in the case of three-place predicates like *force*:

(110)   The woman forced the man to winnow the millet

In (110), the subject of the infinitive is deleted under identity with the direct object of *force, man*.

The application of equi always results in a non-s-like complement type.

Languages can differ in the conditions under which equi can occur. English, as sentences (106) and (110) illustrate, allows equi under identity with either matrix subject or direct object. Lango, for example, allows equi only under identity with subjects, never with direct objects:

(111)   Dákó   àmìttò   ní   'lócà ryét   kàl
         woman want(3SG) COMP man winnow(3SG SJNCT) millet
         'The woman wants the man to winnow the millet'

(112) Dákó àmìttò *ryὲttò* *kàl*
woman want(3SG) winnow(INF) millet
'The woman wants to winnow the millet'

(113) Dákó òdìò lócà *ní* *'ryὲt* *kàl*
woman pressed(3SG) man COMP winnow(3SG SJNCT) millet
'The woman pressed the man to winnow the millet'

In (111), there is no coreference between matrix arguments and complement subject, so equi doesn't apply and the complement remains s-like
(subjunctive). In (112), the notional matrix and complement subjects
are coreferential, so the complement subject has been equi-deleted,
resulting in a non-s-like complement (infinitive). In (113), a condition of
coreference exists between matrix object and complement subject, but
whereas the English example, (110), exhibits an infinitive (evidence that
equi has applied), the Lango example retains a sentence-like (subjunctive) complement. In (113), *lócà* 'man' is not repeated as a noun in the
complement clause under the usual conditions governing coreference in
discourse. The complement predicate, however, is conjugated for a
third person singular subject.

Some languages make very restricted use of equi. In Albanian, for
example, neither identity with matrix object or subject normally conditions equi (data from Ferit Rustemi):

(114) Gruaja deshi *njeriu* *ta* *vjedhë* *pulën*
woman wanted(3SG) man(NOM) COMP steal(3SG SJNCT) chicken
'The woman wanted the man to steal the chicken'

(115) Njeriu deshi *ta* *vjedhë* *pulën*
man wanted(3SG) COMP steal(3SG SJNCT) chicken
'The man wanted to steal the chicken'

(116) Gruaja e detyroi njeriun *ta* *vjedhë* *pulën*
woman PRO forced man(ACC) COMP steal(3SG SJNCT) chicken
'The woman forced the man to steal the chicken'

In (114) *njeriu* 'man', the subject of the complement predicate *vjedhë*
'steal', is not coreferential with any argument in the matrix. In (115), the
complement subject is ellipted anaphorically and is represented by the
third singular inflection of *vjedhë*. The complement subject, however,
cannot be said to be equi-deleted in (115) because (i) the complement is
still s-like (sentences do not require overt subject NPs in Albanian), and
(ii) example (115) could mean either 'the man wanted to steal the
chicken' or 'the man wanted *him* to steal the chicken', where 'man' and
'him' are not coreferential. The deletion of the second mention of *njeriu*

with either gloss follows the usual discourse conditions on anaphoric ellipsis and is not the product of a sentence-internal process like equi. In (116), the complement is s-like, and equi has not (and could not have) applied even though a relation of coreference exists between matrix object and complement subject.

Equi-deletion is a common process, especially when conditioned by coreference of complement subject to matrix agent or experiencer (typically encoded as subjects, but note the Irish example, (108) above). Deletion under identity with other arguments is rarer. Where equi-deletion exists, it is usually obligatory.

Equi must be distinguished from other kinds of deletion, as indicated in the discussion above. In many languages, subject arguments (and all other arguments, for that matter) need not be overtly mentioned when their reference is clear from the discourse context. In the following sentence from Malay, for example,

(117)   Saya mĕningat *bahwa sĕdang mĕnchuri ayam*
        I   remember COMP   MIDDLE steal   chicken
        'I remember that he was stealing the chicken'

the subject of the complement is not overt, nor is there any agreement affix in the predicate to reference it. This sentence would only be felicitious if it were clear from discourse context who the subject was. The deletion in this case has nothing to do with equi and the complement can be thought of as an independent sentence:

(118)   Sĕdang mĕnchuri ayam
        MIDDLE steal   chicken·
        'He was stealing the chicken'

(118) is a perfectly good sentence under the same conditions as (117). The conditions governing deletion in these cases are essentially the same as those governing pronominalization of arguments in English. Further, subjects may not be overt when they have a general or non-specific reference, as in:

(119)   *Eating guavas* is fun

A non-s-like complement type occurs in English in these cases, but equi has not applied since conditions for coreference have not been met, i.e. there is no matrix argument which the subject can be identical to.

2.2 Raised arguments

In addition to outright deletion via equi, there is another method whereby arguments may be removed from their predications resulting in a non-s-like complement type. This method involves the placement of an argument notionally part of the complement proposition (typically the subject) in a slot having a grammatical relation (e.g. subject or direct object) to the CTP. This movement of an argument from a lower to a higher sentence is called *raising*. Sentence (121) differs from sentence (120) in that raising has applied to (121), moving the complement subject into the matrix as direct object:

(120)   Irv believes Harriet is a secret agent

(121)   Irv believes *Harriet* to be a secret agent[5]

Harriet has a different grammatical status in (120) and (121). This is attested by the fact that when *Harriet* in (120) is pronominalized, the subject form *she* results, whereas when *Harriet* in (121) is pronominalized, the object form *her* appears:

(120')   Irv believes she is a secret agent

(121')   Irv believes *her* to be a secret agent

This is consistent with the view that Harriet is the subject of the complement verb *is* in (120) and has been raised to become the object of the matrix verb *believe* in (121). The sort of raising illustrated in (121), is called subject to object (Subj–Obj) raising.

We have conclusive evidence for raising when the putatively raised form is *semantically* an argument of the complement clause but *syntactically* a part of the matrix clause. For instance, *believe* is a two-place predicate; it takes as subject an experiencer argument and as object the thing believed. It's possible, however, to raise the subject of the object complement of *believe*, as in (121). But notice that the truth value doesn't change. What Irv believes is not *Harriet* (in fact he could distrust Harriet completely), but rather *that Harriet is a secret agent*. In other words, even though *Harriet* in (121) is the direct object of *believe*, and thus syntactically part of the matrix clause, semantically *Harriet* remains part of the complement, which is what Irv believes, just as in (120).

Now contrast the behavior of complements of *believe* with those of *force* in the following repeated examples:

(121)   Irv believes Harriet to be a secret agent

(110)   The woman forced the man to winnow the millet

These two sentences look superficially similar, but only in (121) do we conclude that raising has taken place; *force* is a three-place predicate, taking as argument an agent, a patient, and an argument which codes the action that results from the agent's manipulation of the patient. *Man* in (110) is already an argument of *force* and therefore is not raised to the matrix from the complement. In (110), the subject of the complement clause is deleted by equi.

Case marking can provide clues about raising. Where pairs of sentences exist such as (120') and (121'), the object case marking on *her* provides definitive proof of raising. (Note that the opposite sort of movement, 'lowering' of arguments, does not occur.) Even pairs of sentences from different languages can help establish a raising analysis. In comparing the Albanian sentence (114) with its English counterpart,

(114)   Gruaja deshi   *njeriu   ta   vjedhë*   *pulën*
         woman wanted(3SG) man(NOM) COMP steal(3SG SJNCT) chicken
         'The woman wanted the man to steal the chicken'

(114')   The woman wanted *the man* to steal the chicken

We note first the identity of meaning. Since the predicate–argument relation is a meaning relation, if *deshi* and *wanted* mean the same thing, they must have the same sort of arguments. Assuming they do mean the same thing, the sentences are comparable. The noun *njeriu* 'man' in (114) is coded in the nominative case. Albanian distinguishes a nominative (*njeriu*) from an accusative (*njeriun*), so the presence of the nominative in (114) is an indication that no raising has occurred. In (114'), *man* is not marked for case, but if *man* is replaced by a pronoun we get *him*, which is marked in the object (= accusative) case. Words bearing the same semantic relation in Albanian and English, *man* and *njeriu* respectively, have different grammatical relations, and because of the object case marking on *him*, we can conclude that raising has taken place in English (but not Albanian). Needless to say, such comparisons must be used with great care. They provide hints rather than definitive proof. The ultimate proof comes from a comparison of the semantic analysis with the syntactic one in the manner described above.

When raising takes place, the complement appears in a non-s-like form, like the English infinitive, if such a form exists in the language. But notice that the existence of such forms *per se* is not proof for raising, as is the case in (110).

All the examples discussed so far involve Subj–Obj raising, but other sorts of raising exist as well. Complement subjects can also be raised to matrix subject position (Subj–Subj), as we see in comparing (122) with (123):

(122)   It seems that Boris dislikes vodka

(123)   *Boris* seems to dislike vodka

In (123), *Boris* has been raised from complement subject position to matrix subject position. There are also cases of raising from object position to subject (Obj–Subj) or object (Obj–Obj) position. Obj–Subj raising is illustrated below:

(124)   It's tough for Norm to beat Herb

(125)   *Herb* is tough for Norm to beat

Herb in (125) has undergone Obj–Subj raising. Obj–Obj raising does not occur in English, but is found in Irish:

(126)   D'éirigh   leis   *iad*   a   thabhairt   leis
        rose(3SG) with him them COMP bring(NZN) with him
        'He managed to bring them with him'

Iad 'them' has been raised from object position in the complement to object position in the matrix. The complement subject has been equi-deleted under identity with the pronominal form in *leis* 'with him' in the matrix. We know *iad* has been raised for a number of reasons, the most obvious of which is its position within the sentence. Irish is a VSO language, so objects ordinarily follow predicates:

(126') Thug   sé leis   iad
        brought he with him them
        'He brought them with him'

Yet in (126), *iad* precedes the predicate *thabhairt*, occupying the usual position for objects of the matrix verb *d'éirigh* 'rose'.
   Raising may be optional (without apparent effect on the truth value), as in the English sentences above, or obligatory. In Irish, one argument from a nominalized complement is raised to object in the matrix. The subject will be raised unless it is equi-deleted, in which case the object is obligatorily raised:

(127)   Is   ionadh liom   é   a   fheiceáil Sheáin   anseo
        COP surprise with me him COMP see(NZN) John(GEN) here
        'I'm surprised that he saw John here'

(128)   Is   ionadh liom   *Seán* a   fheiceáil anseo
        COP surprise with me John COMP see(NZN) here
        'I'm surprised to see John here'

In (127), the subject is raised into the matrix. It is then coded by the object form *é* 'him', rather than the subject form *sé* 'he'. In (128), the subject has been equi-deleted and the object *Seán* has been raised. In English there are a few CTPS for which Subj–Obj raising is obligatory. When the subject of the complement of *want* is not equi-deleted, it must be raised into matrix object position:

(129)   *I want that the man steal the chicken

(130)   I want *the man* to steal the chicken

In (129), no raising has occurred and the sentence is ungrammatical. Many languages, however, would translate (130) with a form resembling (129), e.g. Lango:

(131)   Ámìttò   ní   'lócà kwál   gwènò
         want(1SG) COMP man steal(3SG SJNCT) chicken
         'I want the man to steal the chicken'

where *lócà* 'man' remains the subject of *kwál* 'steal' since Lango does not allow Subj–Obj raising. English, on the other hand, does not allow Obj–Obj raising, which, as illustrated above, is possible in Irish.

Cross-linguistically, raising is not nearly as common as equi. Many languages do not employ any sort of raising at all (excluding from consideration here instances of clause union discussed in section 2.3). Perhaps the most common sort of raising is Obj–Subj, although this occurs only with evaluative CTPS such as *good*, *bad* and *hard*. The exact number of these evaluative CTPS that can trigger Obj–Subj raising will vary from language to language. English allows a rather open set of evaluative predicates to trigger Obj–Subj raising, whereas Lango allows Obj–Subj raising only with *ber* 'good':

(132)   *Twòl* bèr   àcámà
         snake good for eating
         'Snake is good to eat'

(133)   *Twòl ràc   àcámà
         'Snake is bad to eat'

(134)   *Twòl tèk   àcámà
         'Snake is hard to eat'

When arguments are raised, they assume the grammatical role (e.g. subject or object) that would ordinarily be held by the complement to which they notionally belong. In (135)

(135)   Floyd wants *Zeke* to drive

the raised argument *Zeke* is the direct object of *wants* and has been raised from an object complement of *wants*. Similarly, in

(136)   *Roscoe* seems to be a moonshiner

Roscoe has been raised from the subject complement of *seems*, which in turn has been extraposed to sentence-final position.[6]

2.3 *Incorporation of reduced complements into the matrix*
Any complement type that has fewer syntactic and inflectional possibilities than an indicative main clause, can be referred to as a *reduced* complement. s-like indicative complements are, by definition, non-reduced. The reduced complements considered so far retain some characteristics of independent clauses. For instance, the predicate in the complement may continue to govern a set of grammatical relations independent of those governed by the embedding verb. In the sentence

(137)   Nell made Dudley test the wort

Dudley is the direct object of *made*, while the infinite complement *test the wort* functions as the factitive object[7] of *made*; *wort* is the direct object of *test*. (137) illustrates two levels of grammatical relations governed by the matrix and complement predicates respectively, displayed as Figure 2.1.

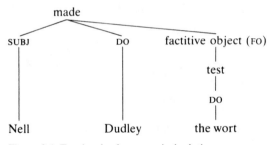

Figure 2.1 Two levels of grammatical relations

The notional subject of *test* has been equi-deleted under identity with the direct object *Dudley*. (137) and Figure 2.1 illustrate a variety of clause reduction where the complement predicate can maintain grammatical relations of its own, independent of the grammatical relations determined by the matrix verb. We will call this sort of clause reduction *simple clause reduction* (SCR). There is another variety of clause reduction which we will call *clause union* (CU) where the matrix and complement predicates share one set of grammatical relations. A few CTPs in French offer a contrast between SCR and CU. One such is *laisser*

(French data from Mathias 1978 and Beaubien, Sabourin and St-Amour 1976):

(138)   a. Roger laissera   Marie marcher
           Roger let(3SG FUT) Marie walk(INF)
           'Roger will let Marie walk'

        b. Roger laissera   Marie manger les pommes
           Roger let(3SG FUT) Marie eat(INF) the apples
           'Roger will let Marie eat the apples'

(139)   a. Roger laissera   marcher Marie
           Roger let(3SG FUT) walk(INF) Marie
           'Roger will let Marie walk'

        b. Roger laissera   manger les pommes à Marie
           Roger let(3SG FUT) eat(INF) the apples   to Marie
           'Roger will let Marie eat the apples'

The sentences in (138) illustrate SCR, while those in (139) illustrate CU. Contrast (138b) with (139b): in (138b), both *laissera* and *manger* have direct objects, *Marie* and *les pommes*, respectively. In (139b) the matrix and complement clauses have been merged to the degree that only one set of grammatical relations is shared between them. The grammatical relations in (138b) and (139b) can be displayed graphically in Figure 2.2.

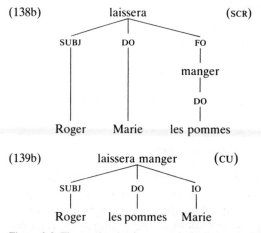

Figure 2.2 The two levels of grammatical relations in (138b) and (139b)

In (139b) the predicates of the matrix and complement predications have been merged and one set of grammatical relations is shared between them. *Marie*, the DO of *laissera* in (138b) becomes the indirect object of the merged predicate *laissera manger* as indicated by the indirect object marker *à*, while *les pommes* becomes the DO of the merged predicate. A full set of grammatical relations would include SUBJ, DO, IO, FO, and oblique object OO.[8] In a set of grammatical relations, there can be only one SUBJ, DO, IO, and FO, though there may be more than one OO.[9] In CU, the arguments of two notional predications must be made to conform to one set of grammatical relations. In the typical case, the SUBJ of the CTP will retain its grammatical role, as will the DO, IO, etc. of the complement predication. The DO of the CTP must take on the highest-ranking grammatical relation not filled by another argument in the merged predication. In (139b), this argument takes on the role of IO since the DO slot is already filled. If the IO slot is already filled, as in (140),

(140) Roger laissera   Marie donner   les livres *à Jean*
       Roger let(3SG FUT) Marie give(INF) the books to John
       'Roger will let Marie give the books to John'

CU will result in the DO of the CTP *laissera* becoming an OO as in (141):

(141) Roger laissera   donner   les livres à Jean *par Marie*
       Roger let(3SG FUT) give(INF) the books to John by Marie
       'Roger will let Marie give the books to John'

In sum, the hierarchy for determining the grammatical role of the notional DO of the CTP in CU is as follows:[10]

(142)   DO
         IO
         OO (often, though not invariably, expressed as a passive agent)

A more radical form of CU is *lexical union* (LU). LU results in the merged predicates forming a single lexical unit; the CTP typically is represented as an affix on the (notional) complement predicate. As an example of LU, consider the following sentences from Georgian:

(143)   a. Is movida
           he came
           'He came'

        b. Me mas movatanine
           I   him come(CAUSE)
           'I made him come'

(143b) represents an instance of LU where the predicates meaning 'come' and 'cause' have been merged into a single lexical unit. The distribution of grammatical roles in LU follows the same general principles as for other forms of CU.[11]

Many languages make rather extensive use of CU. Lahu is a case in point, where a very high percentage of cases of complementation will involve CU or, more rarely, LU. Below is a complex sentence from Lahu involving multiple CU and an instance of LU (Matisoff 1973):

(144)   ɔe   yâmî   thà? ɔyâpā thà? mɛ́ni thà? ɔ   cā
         mother daughter OBJ son   OBJ cat   OBJ rice eat(CAUSE)
         cɨ   tu   te   ve
         CAUSE UNREALIZED CAUSE COMP
         'The mother had her daughter make her son feed the cat rice'

All of the arguments save the highest subject ɔe 'mother' and the lowest object ɔ 'rice' are accompanied by the marker thà? in apparent violation of the principles summarized above. Thà? however, is not really a DO marker, but rather accompanies human non-subjects and focused constituents. The grammatical role of non-subjects is normally not marked on nouns, but is, rather, inferred from the sort of real-world object the argument represents and the sort of verbs present in the verbal complex.

2.4 Parataxis and serialization

Along with their syntactic similarities (section 1.3.3), paratactic and serial constructions have similar semantic ranges. Both, for instance, can be found in causative and immediate perception constructions. The two constructions differ in a number of respects, which can only be summarized here:[12] verbs in serial constructions have obligatory agreement in tense–aspect,[13] whereas paratactic constructions do not. For instance in Gã, the following tense–aspect distinctions are available:

(145)   a. Mìbà   (past)
            come(ISG PAST)
            'I came'

         b. Míbà   (perfect)
            come(ISG PERF)
            'I have come'

         c. Míbàà   (habitual)
            come(ISG HABIT)
            'I come'

In serial constructions, person and tense–aspect distinctions like those illustrated above will be found on each verb in the series:

(146)   a. Mìnyɛ́   mìbà   (past)
            be able(1SG PAST) come(1SG PAST)
            'I was able to come'

        b. Mínyɛ̄   míbà   (perfect)
            be able(1SG PERF) come(1SG PERF)
            'I have been able to come'

        c. Mínyɛ́ɔ   míbàà   (habitual)
            be able(1SG HABIT) come(1SG HABIT)
            'I'm able to come'

Further, each clause may be independently negated in parataxis whereas with serials only one negative is allowable and has the entire
construction within its scope. In parataxis, each verb may have a
different subject, as in this Lango example:

(147)   Ìcó òdìá   àcégò   dɔ́gólá
        man pressed(3SG SUBJ 1SG OBJ) closed(1SG SUBJ) door
        'The man pressed me, I closed the door'
        (The man forced me to close the door)

With serials, there is only one grammatical subject, whatever the
semantic subject of the following verbs may be, as in the following Akan
example (Schachter 1974: 258):

(148)   Mede   aburow migu   msum
        take(1SG) corn   flow(3SG) in water
        'I caused the corn to flow into the water' or
        'I poured the corn into the water'

Clearly, *aburow* 'corn' is the semantic subject of 'flow', yet the verb
takes first person concord.
    The syntactic differences noted above correlate with a crucial seman-
tic difference, namely that paratactic constructions contain two assertions, i.e., each clause is separately asserted, whereas serial constructions contain just one, encompassing the entire construction. In this
way, serial constructions resemble more ordinary sentences with subordinate clauses. Independent aspect marking and negation would seem
a necessary consequence of a clause that constitutes a separate assertion, as would a lack of obligatory subject agreement. The two-assertion
aspect of parataxis will be discussed in section 3.1.4.
    One criterial characteristic of both serial and paratactic constructions
is that only the first verb in the series can have an overt subject NP, i.e.
serial and paratactic constructions consist of a subject NP and its verb
phrase, followed by one or more verb phrases. The notional subject of

each verb following the first is represented only by subject–verb agreement, and is coreferential with either the subject or object of the preceding verb or the first verb in the series. But unlike the infinitive which is also subjectless, the verb in the paratactic complement is fully inflected for person and tense–aspect if these are inflectional categories in the language. Paratactic and infinitive complement types contrast in Lango:

(149)   Án àpóyò   àcégò   dɔ́gólá   (paratactic)
        I   remembered(1SG) closed(1SG) door
        'I remembered it; I closed the door'
        (I remembered to close the door)

(150)   Án ápòyò   cèggò   dɔ́gólá   (infinitive)
        I   remembered(1SG) close(INF) door
        'I remembered to close the door'

In (149), the second predicate àcégò is fully inflected for person and tense–aspect. In (150), the second predicate cèggò 'to close' is an infinitive, inflected neither for person nor tense–aspect.
In the sentence

(151)   Dákó òdìò   ìcó òkwàlò   gwènò
        woman pressed(3SG) man stole(3SG) chicken
        'The women pressed the man; he stole the chicken'
        (The woman forced the man to steal the chicken)

the noun ìcó 'man is notionally the object of òdìò 'pressed' and the subject of òkwàlò 'stole', but from a syntactic point of view, it functions only as the object of òdìò. This is crucial for the claim that serial and paratactic complements never have overt subject NPs. There are two simple demonstrations of the syntactic status of ìcó in (151). First, when ìcó is pronominalized, the verb òdìò is inflected for third person singular object, as in:

(152)   Dákó òdìέ   òkwàlò   gwènò
        woman pressed(3SG SUBJ 3SG OBJ) stole(3SG SUBJ) chicken
        'The woman forced him to steal the chicken'

Note that the object suffix -έ differs from the subject pronoun έn 'he, she'. Pronominalized direct objects in Lango appear as object affixes replacing the final -ò, but pronominalized subjects can appear only as inflections in the verb or can appear as a subject pronoun accompanied by the subject agreement inflection. If ìcó in (151) is pronominalized by either of the techniques available for subjects, the result is ungrammatical:

(153) *Dákó òdìò   òkwàlò   gwènò
       woman pressed(3SG) stole(3SG) chicken
       'The woman forced him to steal the chicken'

(154) *Dákó òdìò   έn òkwàlò   gwènò
       woman pressed(3SG) he stole(3SG) chicken
       'The woman forced him to steal the chicken'

((153) is grammatical with the reading 'The woman forced it to steal the chicken'.) Second, the tonal contour of *òkwàlò* 'stole' in (151) supports the interpretation of *icó* as the syntactic object of *òdìò but not the syntactic subject of *òkwàlò*. In the third person singular perfective, the inflection of the verb varies depending on whether or not the verb is accompanied by an overt subject pronoun. In a word like *òkwàlò* the tone will be high (´) on the second syllable if the verb is accompanied by an overt pronominal subject, but low (`) if the verb is not accompanied by an overt pronominal subject. This is not a matter of tone sandhi, but is a grammatically conditioned feature. These patterns are illustrated below:

(155) έn òkwálò   gwènò
       he stole(3SG) chicken
       'He stole the chicken'

(156) òkwàlò   gwènò
       stole(3SG) chicken
       'He stole the chicken'

In (155) the tone pattern on the verb is *òkwálò* with a high tone on the second syllable because of the overt pronominal subject *έn*. while in (156) the tone pattern is *òkwàlò*. with a low tone. because of the lack of an overt pronominal subject. This tone alternation is found in subordinate clauses too. as illustrated below:

(157) Dákó òtàmò   ní 'έn òkwálò   gwènò
       woman believed(3SG) COMP he stole(3SG) chicken
       'The woman believed that he stole the chicken'

(158) Dákó òtàmò   ní òkwàlò   gwènò
       woman believed(3SG) COMP stole(3SG) chicken
       'The woman believed that he stole the chicken'

In the paratactic construction, repeated here below,

(159) *Dákó òdìé   òkwàlò   gwènò
      woman pressed(3SG SUBJ 3SG OBJ) stole(3SG SUBJ) chicken
      'The woman forced him to steal the chicken'

the tonal pattern of *òkwàlò* is clearly the same as in (156) and (158) where the verb lacks an overt nominal subject. So, despite the presence of its notional subject immediately before it, *òkwàlò* behaves tonally as though it had no overt nominal subject, so the pronoun -*έ* is indeed the syntactic object of *dì* 'press'.

From the standpoint of complementation, many aspects of the syntax and semantics of paratactic constructions resemble those of adjacent and logically connected sentences in discourse, rather than the main predicate–subordinate relationship that otherwise obtains in complementation. For instance, (149) could well be rendered in English as

(160)   I remembered it; I closed the door

and (151) as:

(161)   The woman pressed the man; he stole the chicken.

and perhaps do more justice to the semantic and grammatical relations involved in those sentences than the somewhat more idiomatic translations given above. It should be noted, however, that from a phonological point of view, (149) and (151) are single sentences. They have an intonational contour like that of single sentences, and rules of external sandhi that do not operate across sentence boundaries operate within paratactic constructions (Noonan and Bavin 1981).

Another manifestation of the difference between paratactic complements and other sorts of complements in Lango has to do with the possibility for utilizing 'switch-reference' morphology. In ordinary subordinate clauses, both indicative and subjunctive, a verb inflected for third person must have a prefix indicating whether the subject of the subordinate clause is the same or different from the subject of the CTP. In the third person singular perfective, the prefix indicating same subject (ss, non-switch reference) is *è*-, and the unmarked prefix indicating a third person singular subject (which can be interpreted as switch reference) is *ò*-. These are illustrated below:

(162) Dákó òpòyò   ní   ècégò
      woman remembered(3SG SUBJ) COMP closed(3SG SS)
      dɔ́gólá
      door   (non-switch reference)
      'The woman remembered that she closed the door'

(163) Dákó   òpòyò   ní   òcègò
       woman remembered(3SG SUBJ) COMP closed(3SG SUBJ)
       dɔ́gólá
       door   (switch reference)
       'The woman remembered that he/she closed the door'

In (162), the subject of *ècégò* must be interpreted as *dákó* 'woman',
while in (163), the subject of *òcègò* must be interpreted as being
someone other than the woman. This opposition is available only in
subordinate clauses. Since the switch reference prefix *ò-* is phonologically identical to the ordinary main clause third person singular perfective prefix *ò-*, (164) is a possible sentence,

(164) Òcègò   dɔ́gólá
       closed(3SG SUBJ) door
       'He closed the door'

whereas (165) is not:

(165) *Ècégò   dɔ́gólá
       closed(3SG SUBJ) door
       'He closed the door'

The prefix *è-* indicating non-switch reference is possible only in subordinate clauses, and is not found in adjacent sentences in discourse. So
the English

(166) The woman hit the man. She ran away

where the subject in both clauses is the same, as in (162), cannot be
rendered by

(167) *Dákó òjwàtò   ìcó . Èŋwécò
        woman hit(3SG SUBJ) man   ran away(3SG SS)
        'The woman hit the man. She ran away'

where the second verb *èŋwécò* has the non-switch reference prefix *è-*,
but can be rendered by

(168) Dákó òjwàtò ìcó. Òŋwɛ̀cò

where the second verb has the *ò-* prefix. (168) can also mean:

(169) The woman hit the man. He ran away

Paratactic constructions resemble in this respect constructions like (168) more than other complement constructions like (162) and (163), since switch reference morphology is not available in parataxis. The sentence

(170)   *Dákɔ́ òpòyò   ècégò   dɔ́gólá
         woman remembered(3SG SUBJ) closed(3SG SS) door
         'The woman remembered to close the door'

is ungrammatical because of the è- non-switch reference prefix on ècégò, even though the subjects of òpòyò and ècégò must be interpreted as being coreferential. The meaning of (170) would have to be rendered by

(171)   Dákɔ́ òpòyò   òcègò   dɔ́gólá
         woman remembered(3SG SUBJ) closed(3SG SUBJ) door
         'The woman remembered to close the door'

where the form òcègò, which in true subordinate clauses indicates switch reference, is used in this case where the subjects must be interpreted as coreferential.

2.5 Distribution of complements within sentences

As we have seen, complements function as subjects or objects. They are usually positioned in sentences just like other subjects or objects, but in many languages there are strong preferences, or even outright constraints, on the distribution of complements that result in different distributional patterns for complements than for other grammatical structures filling the same grammatical roles. For instance, the nominalized complement in English can occur in subject position in both declarative and interrogative sentences:

(172)   a. Floyd's leaving town is significant
         b. Is Floyd's leaving town significant?

The s-like complement type in English, however, may occur in subject position in declarative sentences, but not in interrogative sentences that are formed by placing an auxiliary element in sentence-initial position:

(173)   a. That Floyd left town is significant
         b. *Is that Floyd left town significant?

Restrictions on the distribution of complement types are, in fact, quite widespread in English:[14]

(174)   a. I believe John's having left to have upset you
         b. *I believe that John left to have upset you

(175)   a.   *For John to be executed* would be regarded by many people as outrageous

   b.   *Many people would regard *for John to be executed* as outrageous

Constraints on the distribution of complement types normally take the form of restrictions against the placement in sentence-initial, or, more commonly, in sentence-medial position of complements whose heads are verbs. Languages may deal with such restrictions by making use of ordinary word-order possibilities or by employing special constructions which, typically, remove s-like complements to the end of a sentence. The process of moving a complement to the end of a sentence is called 'extraposition'. This process is syntactically distinct from ones such as passive involving arguments other than complements. Complements moved to the end of the sentence are referred to as 'extraposed'.

The example (173b) violates the constraint in English against having complements with verbal heads in medial position; however, this sentence can be rendered grammatical by extraposition, as in (176):

(176)   Is it significant that Floyd left town?

Notice that in (176), the complement has been removed to sentence-final position and its original place in subject position taken over by the pronoun *it*. Replacement of the extraposed complement by a proform is not found in all languages.

In a few cases, extraposition seems to be obligatory, even though the non-extraposed sentence would not violate the ordinary constraints on the placement of complements. In such cases, extraposition is governed by the CTP. In English, the predicates *seem* and *appear* have obligatory extraposition of their subjects:

(177)   a.   *That Floyd is drunk seems to me

   b.   It seems to me that Floyd is drunk

   c.   *That Floyd is drunk appears to me

   d.   It appears to me that Floyd is drunk

Extraposition normally has the effect not only of removing the complement from its grammatical position, but also of depriving it of its grammatical role. In the sentence

(178)   It's significant that Floyd is drunk

the extraposed clause no longer functions as the subject. Evidence for this includes the fact that *it* can be raised like a subject (as in (179a)) and equi-deleted like a subject (as in (179b)):

(179)   a. I want *it* to be known that Zeke is a Libertarian

       b. It is known to be impossible for Zelda to have written *War and Peace*
        (cf. It is known that *it* is impossible for Zelda to have written *War and Peace.*)

In Irish, extraposition from subject position is often associated with an impersonal CTP, i.e a form used when there is no overt subject:

(180)   Feictear   dom *go*   *bhfuil slaghdán air*
       seem(IMPERS) to me COMP COP   cold   on him
       'It seems to me that he has a cold'

The verb *feic-* 'see, seem' is inflected in the impersonal present. The s-like complement *go bhfuil slaghdán air* has been extraposed from the normal subject position immediately following the verb to sentence-final position. Extraposition in (180) is obligatory since Irish requires all s-like complements to occur in sentence-final position.

So far we have only considered extraposition from subject, but extraposition from object is also found and is reasonably common especially in the sov languages of the Middle East, for example Persian, Armenian, and Uzbek. Eastern Armenian, an sov language, has a constraint like that of Irish (vso), requiring s-like complements to occur in sentence-final position. The ordinary sov word order of Eastern Armenian is illustrated in (181) (data from Galust Mardirussian and Bill Vespassian):

(181)   Mard-ə hav-ə   gojatshav
       man-the chicken-the stole
       'The man stole the chicken'

s-like object complements, however, do not occur preverbally as objects normally would, but rather are extraposed to sentence-final position:

(182)   Kənik-ə   imanuma *vor* *mard-ə hav-ə*   *gojatshav*
       woman-the knows   COMP man-the chicken-the stole
       'The woman knows that the man stole the chicken'

In Persian (sov), s-like complements, both indicative and subjunctive, must be extraposed, but reduced complements may only be extraposed when, as nominalizations, they are objects of prepositions (data primarily from Zohreh Imanjomeh):

(183) a. Æli goft   *ke   Babæk bimar æst*
           Ali said(3SG) COMP Babak sick is
           'Ali said that Babak is sick'

       b. *Æli *ke Babæk bimar æst* goft
           (Extraposition is obligatory with s-like complements.)

(184) a. Mæn šoruʔ   *be avaz xand-æn* kærdæm
           I beginning to song recite-NZR did(1SG)
           'I began to sing'

       b. Mæn šoruʔ kærdæm *be avaz xand-æn*
           (Extraposition possible with nominal complements.)

(185) a. Mæn *adæd-æn-e*   Babæk-ra færman dadæm
           I   come-NZR-ASSOC Babak-OBJ order gave(2SG)
           'I ordered Babak to come'

       b. *Mæn færman dadæm *adæd-æn-e Babæk-ra*

       c. *Mæn Babæk-ra færman dadæm *adæd-æn(-e)*
           (Extraposition not possible with nominalized complements
           unless they are objects of prepositions.)

In Uzbek, also sov, extraposition is only possible with s-like complements. The language distinguishes extraposed complements with the
optional complementizer *ki* from non-extraposed complements with *deb*
'saying'. These latter complements are used in reported discourse (data
from Abduzukhur Abduazizov):

(186) a. Men bu ɔdam-niŋ joja-ni   oğirla-gan-i-ni
           I this man-GEN chicken-OBJ steal-NZR-3SG POSS-OBJ
           bilaman
           know(1SG)
           'I know that this man stole the chicken'
           (Nominalized complement, extraposition not possible.)

       b. Men bilamen   ki   bu ɔdam joja-ni   oğirladi
           I   know(1SG) COMP this man chicken-OBJ stole(3SG)
           'I know that this man stole the chicken'
           (Extraposition obligatory with this sort of s-like
           complement.)

       c. Xɔtin bu ɔdam joja-ni   oğirladi deb dedi
           woman this man chicken-OBJ stole(3SG) saying said
           'The woman said that this man stole the chicken'
           (Extraposition not possible with this sort of s-like
           complement.)

In sov languages, extraposition is usually related to the possibility for postposing other sorts of sentence elements, typically oblique arguments. Extraposition need not, however, be accompanied by such a possibility. Uzbek seldom postposes oblique arguments but extraposes s-like complements frequently. Extraposition of subject complements in Irish has no parallel in any other rule of postposition.

Another topic that must be mentioned here is the parenthetical use of predicates, such as *believe*, *think*, *suppose*, and *regret*. In their non-parenthetical use, these verbs express positive propositional attitudes to the proposition embodied in their complement (see sections 3.1.2 and 3.2.2). Such a use is illustrated below:

(187)   Floyd believed that radical syndicalism is the best form of government

In stating (187), one would most likely be making an assertion about Floyd's former belief, not radical syndicalism. It is possible, however, to use *believe* parenthetically in such a way that the assertion is invested in the complement, especially with a first person singular subject and verb in the present tense. When used parenthetically, the position of the CTP is freer than usual: the CTP and its subject may be placed initially or after any major sentence constituent:

(188)   I believe radical syndicalism is the best form of government

(189)   Radical syndicalism is, I believe, the best form of government

(190)   Radical syndicalism is the best form of government, I believe

In one possible interpretation of (188) and the most likely interpretation of (189) and (190), *believe* is used parenthetically; the main assertion constitutes a claim about radical syndicalism not the belief of the subject of the matrix predicate *believe*. The function of the parenthetical verb in these sentences is 'to modify or weaken the claim to truth that would be implied by a simple assertion'.[15]

The syntactic effect of the parenthetical use of the CTP is to make the complement the main clause. Notice that the complementizer *that*, normally optional with *believe*, cannot be used when the CTP is used parenthetically:

(191)   *That radical syndicalism is, I believe, the best form of government

(192)   *That radical syndicalism is the best form of government, I believe

This is true also of languages where the use of the complementizer is ordinarily obligatory. Indicative complements in Lango are always accompanied by the complementizer *ní* except when the CTP is used parenthetically, in which case *ní* is not used. Only affirmative predicates can be used parenthetically, so with a negative predicate the complementizer cannot be ommited:

Negative predicates: parenthetical use not allowed

(193) Pé àtámó   ní   Òkélò dàktál
       NEG believe(1SG) COMP Okello doctor
       'I don't believe that Okello is a doctor'

(194) *Pé àtámò Òkélò dàktál
       'I don't believe that Okello is a doctor'

Parenthetical uses of affirmative predicates

(195) Àtámò   Òkélò dàktál
       believe(1SG) Okello doctor
       'I believe Okello is a doctor'

(196) Òkélò, àtámó, dàktál
       'Okello, I believe, is a doctor'

(197) *ní Òkélò, àtámó, dàktál

So far as I am aware, all languages can use predicates like *believe* parenthetically, but not all languages allow for the movement of the CTP and its subject into the complement clause. Irish, for instance, does not seem to allow either the deletion of the complementizer or the movement of the parenthetical into the complement clause:

(198) Is eagal liom   go   bhfuil an bás   aige[16]
       COP fear with me COMP COP   the death at him
       'I'm afraid that he'll die'

(199) *Is eagal liom $\begin{Bmatrix} \text{fuil} \\ \text{tá} \end{Bmatrix}$ an bás aige

(200) *Tá an bás, is eagal liom, aige

It is possible to place the parenthetical at the end, but this seems to result in two independent clauses since

(201) Is eagal liom

can stand by itself as a sentence meaning 'I'm afraid it's so'.

2.6 *Sequence of tense/mood restrictions*

Many languages that employ tense or mood morphology restrict in various ways the tense or mood categories allowable in complements. Sequence of tense or mood restrictions may take any one of the following forms:

(i) Tense categories may be copied onto the complement from the CTP. In English, for example, reported speech (indirect discourse) may be marked with the primary tense of the CTP, the original tense appearing as secondary tense where possible.[17] A primary tense is one which makes reference to only one point in time, which is always relative to the time of the utterance. Secondary tenses make reference to a primary tense *and* one additional point in time. One common secondary tense is the secondary past, or perfect, formed in English with the auxiliary *have*. In *Zeke had come by the time Zelda cashed her check*, the verb complex *had come* references two points in time: the past time when Zeke came, and the past time, following Zeke's arrival, when Zelda cashed her check (see Figure 2.3).

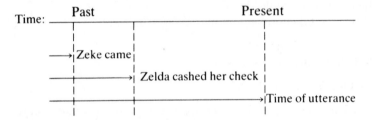

Figure 2.3 Time reference

The verb simplex in *Zelda cashed her check* refers only to one point in time as it contains no secondary tenses. The (b) sentences below evidence tense-copying.

(202)　a. Floyd said 'I *came*'　　　　past
　　　　b. Floyd said that he *had come*　　past + sec. past

(203)　a. Floyd said 'I'm coming'　　　present
　　　　b. Floyd said that he was coming　past

(204)　a. Floyd said 'I'll come'　　　　future
　　　　b. Floyd said that he would come　past + sec. future

Tense copying represents an attempt to mold the complement to the subjective viewpoint of the speaker and is frequently associated with other changes in the complement (cf. section 3.2.1). English and other languages use the distinction between primary and secondary time reference for various semantic purposes. Instead of (204b) we can say

(205)   Floyd said that he'll come

which lacks tense copying. The future in the complement represents a primary tense distinction, i.e. relative to the time of the utterance. The future reference in the complement in (204b) is relative to the time reference of the CTP and is therefore secondary. The most likely interpretation of (205) is that Floyd is still expected, whereas with (204b), Floyd has either already arrived or isn't coming.

Tense copying is not universal in reported speech. In Russian, for instance, reported speech is expressed in the tense in which the statement was originally made, regardless of the tense of the CTP:

(206)   Boris skazal, čto   prisël
          Boris said   COMP came(MASC SG)
          'Boris said that he came'

(207)   Boris skazal, čto   prixodit
          Boris said   COMP come(3SG)
          'Boris said that he's coming'

(208)   Boris skazal, čto   pridët
          Boris said   COMP come(3SG FUT)
          'Boris said that he will come'

These Russian sentences have no counterparts like the English (202b), (203b) and (204b).

(ii) Tense possibilities may be restricted on the complement because of the semantics of the CTP. For instance complements to the verb *promise*, when s-like, must employ future morphology:

(209)   I promise that I'll come

(210)   *I promise that I came

(210) is grammatical in those dialects where *promise* = 'swear'. The reason for this, of course, is that the thing promised necessarily follows the act of promising in time. We include here also complements in paratactic and serial constructions which must have the same time reference as the CTP. Paratactic and serial complements typically occur in semantic environments with determined time reference (section 3.1.1).

(iii) Choice of mood may be governed by the tense in the matrix. In such cases, the usual semantic role assigned to mood distinctions appears to be neutralized. An example of mood distinctions governed by tense is found in Classical Greek. In indirect discourse, the indicative follows matrix verbs in non-past tenses, while the optative follows past tenses. Classical Greek does not employ tense copying (Goodwin 1892):

(211)   Légei   hóti gráfei
         say(3SG PRES) COMP write(3SG PRES INDIC)
         'He says that he is writing'

(212)   Eîpen   hóti gráfoi
         say(3SG PAST) COMP write(3SG PRES OPTATIVE)
         'He says that he was writing'

2.7 Negative raising

Negative raising is the name applied to the situation where a negative marker appears to be removed from the complement clause with which it is logically associated and raised to the ordinary position for negatives within the matrix clause.[18] It occurs in the great majority of the world's languages. In the following examples, the (b) sentences have a raised negative:[19]

(213)   a. I think that Floyd didn't hit Roscoe

         b. I don't think that Floyd hit Roscoe

(214)   a. Zeke believes that Martians don't live in caves

         b. Zeke doesn't believe that Martians live in caves

(215)   a. Hugh wants Mary Ann not to win

         b. Hugh doesn't want Mary Ann to win

Negative raising occurs with only a restricted set of CTPS; for other CTPS, the presence of the negative in the complement results in a different meaning:

(216)   I regret that Floyd didn't hit Roscoe

(217)   I don't regret that Floyd hit Roscoe

Generally speaking, only propositional attitude predicates (such as *believe* or *deny*), desiderative predicates (*want*), and modal predicates (*can* or *be able*) allow for negative raising without change of truth value.

3.0 The semantics of complementation

Complementation is basically a matter of matching a particular complement type to a particular complement-taking predicate. The basis for this matching is the semantic relation between predicate and complement that is inherent in the meaning of the CTP, defining the relation of the predicate to the action or state described in the embedded predication, and the discourse function of the complement itself. Additional factors in this matching are the semantic possibilities inherent in the morphology and syntax of the complement type. The complement type, composed as it is of certain kinds of grammatical material – a nominalization, a sentence-like complement type, etc. – and connected to the matrix hypotactically or paratactically, either contributes or fails to contribute certain sorts of information to the construction as a whole and so is intrinsically better suited for certain kinds of CTPs and to certain discourse functions. In this way, different complement types can be used with the same CTP, exploiting their inherent meaning potential. The choice of complementizer may also affect the meaning potential of a complement.

3.1 *The semantics of complement types*
There are several factors that can affect the semantic potential of a complement type:

(i) inherent modality, such as mood distinctions

(ii) degree of reduction

(iii) choice of complementizer

(iv) method of syntactic relation to the matrix clause: sub-ordination versus parataxis

(v) grammatical status of the notional predicate: verb, noun (in nominalized complements), adjective (in participial complements)

These factors will be taken up in order below.

3.1.1 *Mood distinctions*
The term *mood* will be used in this chapter to refer to a grammatical category, while *modality* will refer to a semantic category. The two are related in that mood categories can usually be viewed as grammatical-izations of modalities.

As mentioned in section 1.3.2 the term *indicative* in complementation refers to the mood which most closely resembles that of simple declarative sentences. *Subjunctive* is the neutral term used to describe any opposing mood distinction in complementation; other terms such as optative, potential and consequential, carry with them more specific mood designations.

The essence of the subjunctive in complementation is the coding of complements that are in some way *dependent*. A complement is dependent if some aspect of its meaning or interpretation follows from information given in the CTP. Not all dependent complements, however, are coded as subjunctives in any given language with an indicative-subjunctive distinction. Three sorts of dependency are important here:

> (i) time reference dependency
>
> (ii) truth-value (epistemic) dependency
>
> (iii) discourse dependency

A complement has dependent or determined time reference (DTR) if its time reference is a necessary consequence of the meaning of the CTP. A complement is truth-value dependent if the complement construction containing it involves an explicit qualification of commitment to the truth of the proposition embodied in the complement. A complement is discourse dependent if it is part of the background or common ground of the participants in a discourse.[20]

The most basic of these dependencies is time-reference dependency, and the property of DTR is almost always included in the modalities represented by the subjunctive. A complement having DTR typically refers to a future world-state relative to the time reference of the CTP. For example, in the sentence:

(218)   José ordered João to interrogate Smith

João's interrogation of Smith must be thought of as following José's order. That is, the complement has a future time reference relative to the time reference of the CTP *order*, even if both events, the order and the interrogation, took place in the past relative to now. José could not, for example, order João to do something in the past relative to the act of ordering, thus ruling out a sentence like (219):

(219)   *José is ordering João to interrogate Smith yesterday

CTPs that represent commands, requests, intention, desires, and expressions of necessity, ability, or obligation are among those whose complements have DTR.

Complements to many CTPs have independent time reference (ITR). The time reference of the complement in (220) is in no way logically bound by the time reference of the CTP:

(220)   I know that $\begin{cases} \text{Zeke ate the leek} \\ \text{Zeke is eating the leek} \\ \text{Zeke will eat the leek} \end{cases}$

CTPs that have complements with ITR include those that assert, report, comment on as background, or make truth-value judgements about their complements.

Lori is a language that utilizes its indicative/subjunctive opposition to express the ITR/DTR distinction. In Lori, both indicative and subjunctive complements use the complementizer *ke*, but the two moods differ in inflection. The indicative is conjugated for tense, but the subjunctive is not since it is only used for complements with DTR. The indicative/subjunctive distinction is illustrated below:

Indicative

(221)   Zine   fekr   i-kone   ke   pia tile-ye
         woman thought PROG-do(3SG) COMP man chicken-OBJ
         dozi
         stole(3SG INDIC)
         'The woman thinks that the man stole the chicken'

(222)   Zine   go ke pia tile-ye   dozi
         woman said COMP man chicken-OBJ stole(3SG INDIC)
         'The woman said that the man stole the chicken'

(223)   Zine   naraxæte ke   pia tile-ye   dozi
         woman regrets   COMP man chicken-OBJ stole(3SG INDIC)
         'The woman regrets that the man stole the chicken'

(224)   Zine   va šak e ke pia tile-ye   dozi
         woman from doubt is COMP man chicken-OBJ stole(3SG INDIC)
         'The woman doubts that the man stole the chicken'

Subjunctive

(225)   Zine   pia-ye vadašt   ke   tile-ye   bedoze
         woman man-OBJ forced(3SG) COMP chicken-OBJ steal(3SG SJNCT)
         'The woman forced the man to steal the chicken'

(226)   Zine   va pia xas   ke   tile-ye   bedoze
         woman from man wanted COMP chicken-OBJ steal(3SG SJNCT)
         'The woman wanted the man to steal the chicken'

(227)   Pia kušeš   kerd ke tile-ye   bedoze
         man attempt did COMP chicken-OBJ steal(3SG SJNCT)
         'The man tried to steal the chicken'

(228)   Pia xoš-eš   i-a   ke   tile-ye
         man pleasantness-his PROG-come COMP chicken-OBJ
         le bedoze
         PL steal(3SG SJNCT)
         'The man likes to steal chickens'

(229)   Pia   i-tares   ke   tile-ye   bedoze
        man PROG-be able COMP chicken-OBJ steal(3SG SJNCT)
        'The man is able to steal the chicken'

As we see in the last three examples, complements with DTR don't have
to represent future events, but may simply represent potential events or
states. The range of DTR complements includes those whose time
reference is the same as the CTP, such as complements to phasal (or
aspectual) predicates like *begin*, those that are timeless in the sense that
they represent general conditions or states, such as certain complements
of *like*, and those that have no time reference because they represent
non-events (as distinct from those that are simply potential) such as
certain complements of *try*. What all these have in common, of course,
is that their time reference is determined by the meaning and use of the
CTP so that only one time reference, the one determined by the CTP, is
possible for these complements.

Indicative/subjunctive oppositions like the one illustrated above
for Lori are fairly common. Bulgarian, like Lori, has its
indicative/subjunctive opposition built on ITR/DTR. The indicative and
subjunctive have distinct complementizers (*če* and *da* respectively) and
differ in inflectional possibilities; the indicative is inflected for tense
while the subjunctive is invariable and uses the same person–number
inflections as the indicative present (data from Ilya Talyev):

Indicative

(230)   Misli,   če   vie ste umoren
        think(3SG) COMP you COP tired
        'He thinks that you're tired'

(231)   Dobre, če   te   sreštnax
        good   COMP you met(1SG)
        'It's good that I met you'

(232)   Čux,   če   toj mu   dal   parite
        heard(1SG) COMP he to him gave(3SG) money
        'I heard that he gave him the money'

Subjunctive

(233)   Mislja   da   ida
        think(1SG) COMP go(1SG SJNCT)
        'I intend to go'

(234) Iskam   da   kupja
       want(1SG) COMP buy(1SG SJNCT)
       'I want to buy'

(235) Moga   da   vidja
       be able(1SG) COMP see(1SG SJNCT)
       'I can see'

(236) Veče započnaxa da   minavat
       already began(3PL) COMP pass by(3PL SJNCT)
       'They've already begun to pass by'

Truth-value dependent complements are those whose CTP expresses a kind of propositional attitude toward the truth of the complement, for example CTPS such as *think, believe, doubt, deny* and *be possible* (cf. section 3.2.2). Complements to such predicates have ITR. It is fairly rare to find a syntactic contrast between complements of propositional attitude CTPS and others that, for example, denote assertions with verbs like *say* or reports of such assertions. Vestiges of such systems are found in Central Asia, however. There one can find a contrast between truth-value dependent complements associated with an ordinary complementizer, and assertions or reports of assertions associated with an adverbial participial form of, for example, *say* or *do*. Such a distinction was illustrated for Uzbek in section 2.5, where the verb 'know' expresses a propositional attitude and takes an extraposed complement with the complementizer *ki*. The verb 'say', on the other hand, expresses no propositional attitude, takes a non-extraposed complement, and is preceded by *deb* 'saying'.

A much more common situation is for languages to distinguish between positive propositional attitudes and negative or dubitative propositional attitudes and group the former with assertions and reports of assertions as the indicative, and the latter with DTR complements as the subjunctive. It is common to find a class of indicative complements that includes not only those of positive propositional attitude verbs such as *believe*, but complements to commentative or factive predicates such as *regret*. These complements typically represent propositions taken as background to a discourse, and are normally presupposed to be true (Kiparsky and Kiparsky 1970, Kempson 1975, Wilson 1975; cf. section 3.2.4). Hypotheticals line up with negative or dubitative propositional attitudes as subjunctive, though they may be associated with a special hypothetical or conditional mood in some languages (cf. chapter III:4). Contrafactives like *pretend* pose special problems (cf. section 3.2.3). We can distinguish in this way complements that have *realis* modality versus those that have *irrealis* modality. Realis modality is associated with complements whose propositions are asserted as a fact or commented on as a factual or actual event or state. Irrealis modality carries with it no such implication; what one can infer about a complement with irrealis modality comes directly from the CTP. Table 2.3 displays the distribution of realis and irrealis modality relative to some complement roles.

Table 2.3. *Realis and irrealis modality in complement roles*

	Complement role
REALIS	assertion report of assertion positive propositional attitude background (factive)
IRREALIS	negative propositional attitude hypothetical proposition DTR (commands, requests, intentions, desires, etc)

Russian is an example of a language for which a realis/irrealis distinction underlies the indicative/subjunctive opposition:

Indicative

(237) Ja govorju, čto   Boris pridët
       I say   COMP Boris will come
       'I say that Boris will come'

(238) Ja dumaju, čto   Boris pridët
       I think   COMP Boris will come
       'I think that Boris will come'

(239) On govoril, čto   Boris pridët
       he said   COMP Boris will come
       'He said that Boris will come'

(240) Ja ljublju, čto   Boris pridët
       I like   COMP Boris will come
       'I like it that Boris will come'

Subjunctive

(241) Ja somnebajus', čtoby Boris prišël
       I doubt   COMP Boris come(SJNCT)
       'I doubt that Boris will come/came'

(242) Ja ne verju, čtoby Boris prišël
       I NEG believe COMP Boris come(SJNCT)
       'I don't believe that Boris will come/came'

(243) Ja xoču, čtoby Boris prišël
       I want COMP Boris come(SJNCT)
       'I want Boris to come'

(244) Ja bojus', čtoby Boris ne prišël
       I fear   COMP Boris NEG come(SJNCT)
       'I'm afraid that Boris will come'

(245) Ja prikazal, čtoby Boris prišël
       I ordered COMP Boris come(SJNCT)
       'I ordered Boris to come'

(246) Nužno, čtoby Boris prišël
       necessary COMP Boris come(SJNCT)
       'It's necessary for Boris to come'

Languages that utilize indicative/subjunctive opposition for realis/ irrealis distinction, like Russian and Persian, frequently do not have tense distinctions available for their subjunctives even though tense distinctions are coded in the indicative. While tense distinctions would be useless (*qua* tense distinctions) in the DTR range of the subjunctive, there is no logical reason why they could not be used with subjunctive complements to propositional attitude predicates as they are in English:

(247)
I don't believe that { Floyd skipped town / Floyd is skipping town / Floyd will skip town }

Yet neither Persian nor Russian (as glosses to some of the above sentences indicate) have tense distinctions in the subjunctive.

One sort of limited exception to this is found in Bemba (Givón 1971, 1972). Bemba has a basic realis/irrealis distinction in its mood categories, but divides the irrealis modality between two subjunctives. The first, called by Givón the 'subjunctive of uncertainty', encodes negative propositional attitudes. The second, the 'subjunctive of coercion', is associated with DTR contexts. Indicatives in Bemba have a large number of tense–aspect distinctions, including a number of futures representing different degrees of futurity. The subjunctive of uncertainty, like the Russian and Persian subjunctives discussed above, has no tense distinctions available, utilizing only a simple aspect distinction. The subjunctive of coercion, however, does have tense distinctions, contrasting a non-future with the various futures available in Bemba:

(248)   A-à-ebele   John ukuti a-y-e
         he-PAST-tell John COMP he-leave-SJNCT
         'He told John to leave'

(249)   A-léé-eba John ukuti a-y-e
         'He is telling John to leave'

(250)   A-kà-eba John ukuti a-kà-y-e
         'He will tell John to leave (tomorrow)'

(251)   A-ká-eba John ukuti a-ká-y-e
         'He will tell John to leave (after tomorrow)'

Tense marking in these is simply a matter of tense copying (section 2.6) since the marking is dependent on that of the CTP.

A complement is discourse dependent if the proposition it contains constitutes part of the common ground or background to a discourse. Discourse-dependent complements include complements to commentative (factive) predicates and complements to those negative propositional attitude predicates that constitute denials, such as *deny* or *not believe*.[21]

There are a few complement systems, Spanish among them, that group together discourse-dependent complements with DTR complements and complements of negative propositional attitude predicates to form a non-assertive modality which is coded in the subjunctive (Hooper 1975, Terrell and Hooper 1974, Klein 1977, Guitart 1978). The indicative encodes assertions, reports of assertions, and complements of predicates with positive propositional attitudes; such complements can be called *assertive* (NB not all complements in this class are assertions in the technical sense of this term).

In Spanish, the distribution of indicative and subjunctive complements parallels the Russian case exemplified above except that discourse-dependent complements are coded in the subjunctive. Thus, sentence (252)

(252)   Lamento   que   Juan salga   esta noche
         regret(1SG) COMP John leave(3SG SJNCT) this night
         'I regret that John will leave tonight'

employing the subjunctive is grammatical, whereas

(253)   *Lamento   que   Juan sale   esta noche
         regret(1SG) COMP John leave(3SG INDIC) this night

employing the indicative is not. The same sentence in Russian is grammatical only with the indicative:

(254) Sožaleju, čto Ivan uedet   segodnja
       regret(1SG) COMP Ivan leave(3SG PERF FUT INDIC) today
       večerom
       evening
       'I regret that Ivan will leave tonight'

Complements of commentative predicates like *regret* are discourse dependent because in saying sentences like (252), one must assume (if one is being sincere) that the hearer already knows the information in the complement. This information is the common ground or background to the discourse and the function of the sentence is to comment on this information (cf. 3.2.4). (252) would have an indicative complement in Persian and Russian.

The tense distinctions available in the Spanish subjunctive are used mostly in tense copying, but can, as when used with complements to commentative predicates, be used to represent real, independent tense distinctions. The greater the range of the subjunctive, in particular when it has the ability to code non-assertive ITR complements, the more likely it is to be able to express independent tense.

The three semantic distinctions underlying the indicative/subjunctive oppositions described above can be displayed as in Table 2.4.

Table 2.4. *The three semantic distinctions underlying indicative–subjunctive oppositions*

			Complement role
ASSERTIVE	REALIS		assertion
			report of assertion
			positive propositional attitude
		INDEPENDENT TIME REFERENCE	background (factive)
NON-ASSERTIVE	IRREALIS		negative propositional attitude
			hypothetical
		DETERMINED TIME REFERENCE	commands, requests, intentions, desires, etc.

I do not intend to imply that the hierarchy of complement roles given in Table 2.4 is always observed in indicative/subjunctive oppositions, though in most cases it is. In Modern Literary German, for instance, the

subjunctive is used for reports of assertions, but is only used sporadically and somewhat idiosyncratically elsewhere in the hierarchy. For
example, complements to *wollen* 'wish' are in the indicative when the
main verb is in the present tense, but in the subjunctive when the main
verb is past (Lockwood 1968):

(255)   Wir wollen,   dass er es tut
        we wish(PRES) COMP he it do(PRES INDIC)
        'We wish that he'd do it'

(256)   Wir wollten,   dass er es täte
        we wish(PAST) COMP he it do(PAST SJNCT)
        'We wish that he did it'

Cases like this illustrate the conventionalized use of mood present in
mood government (section 2.6). Such cases represent a considerable
reduction or even loss of the original modal character of the subjunctive
and the subsequent grammaticization of the use of the subjunctive in a
portion of its former range.[22]

The meaning differences between indicative and subjunctive complement types can be exploited with a given CTP allowing for the expression
of a variety of implication relationships. For instance, in Bemba (Givón
1971, 1972) the realis/irrealis modality opposition expressed by the
indicative/subjunctive distinction may be used with the same coercive
verb to indicate a difference in implication:

(257)   John a-à-koonkomeshya Robert a-à-boombele
        John 3SG-PAST-order   Robert 3SG-PAST-work(INDIC)
        'John ordered Robert (long ago) and Robert worked (long
        ago)'

(258)   John a-à-koonkomeshya Robert a-bomb-e
        John 3SG-PAST-order   Robert 3SG-work-SJNCT
        'John ordered Robert to work (and Robert may or may not
        have worked)'

The complement in (257) can be inferred to be a factual event. The
subjunctive in (258), however, carries no implication that the event it
encodes is a real or actual event.

3.1.2 *Degree of reduction*
There is a general principle in complementation that information tends
neither to be repeated nor lost. Exceptions to this are easy enough to
find, but the principle holds true in the great majority of cases. For this
reason, reduced complements, which are likely to lack tense distinctions

(see section 1), are typically associated with predicates whose complements have DTR. Infinitives, for example, are frequently restricted to DTR contexts since their use elsewhere would result in information loss. Indicative complements are normally excluded from DTR contexts since they are typically coded for tense, and therefore the expression of tense in such cases is redundant.

In English, infinitives, with a couple of exceptions to be discussed below, are associated with DTR contexts, while indicatives are associated with ITR contexts. Infinitives occur as complements to predicates expressing commands, requests, intentions, desires, etc. They do not normally occur as complements to predicates that are assertive, commentative, or express propositional attitude, all of which take indicative complements in English. The exceptions to this are instructive in that they show how various factors may override the general principles governing the distribution of complement types in a language. *Believe*, a propositional attitude predicate, can take either infinitive or indicative complements:

(259)   I believe Zeke to be an idiot

(260)   I believe that Zeke is an idiot

Sentences like these can be used, straightforwardly enough, to make a statement about propositional attitude. But such sentences can also be used to assert the proposition embodied in the complement; that is, the function of the statement is not simply to express a propositional attitude, but rather to present the proposition embodied in the complement as an assertion. The function of *believe* and similar verbs especially in sentences like (259) is simply to soften the force of the assertion, guiding the hearer to a proper appreciation of the complement proposition in its context, rather than being in itself part of what is asserted (see Urmson 1963). The use of *believe* here is in many respects like the parenthetical use of this predicate described in section 2.5. The time reference of *believe* in such cases represents the time reference of the asserted proposition. When (259) is used to assert the complement proposition, there is, then, only one significant time reference, that of the asserted proposition. So an infinitive can be used without loss of information.[23]

Like *believe*, *promise* can also take an infinitive or indicative complement:

(261)   I promise to go at nine

(262)   I promise that I'll go at nine

Notice, however, that infinitives are only possible with *promise* if the subject of *promise* and the complement predicate are coreferential, so that *I promise that John will go* is not the same as *I promise John to go*; in the latter *John* is a dative argument, not a raised subject. The reason for this has to do with the 'controllability factor' associated with infinitives (see below). Unlike *believe*, whose complements have ITR, complements to *promise* have DTR: the thing promised must follow the act of promising. We would predict, then, that *promise* would take infinitive complements only, which as (262) illustrates, is clearly not the case. The reason for the acceptability of (262) probably derives from the fact that it (and (261)) is semantically related to one meaning of (263):

(263)   I'll go at nine

(263) can be used as an assertion, but it is far more likely to be used in performing the illocutionary act of promising, in which case it means about the same thing as (262). In (262) and its parenthetical equivalent (264)

(264)   I'll go at nine, I promise

the nature of the speech act is made explicit, unlike (263), but the illocutionary force of the statement is the same as (263). (262), then, can be looked at as a 'syntactic blend' (G. Lakoff 1974) of the semantically equivalent statements (261) and (263), consisting of a statement like (263), with the illocutionary force of a promise, and the CTP *promise* as in (261), making the nature of the speech act explicit.

Because reduced complement types like infinitives tend to be used in DTR contexts, they are not discourse dependent. Their time reference is either fixed, in which case there is a necessary sequencing of matrix and complement states or events, or the time reference is simply irrelevant, in which case the CTP amounts to a comment or judgement on any potential occurrence of the complement event or state. The latter case can be illustrated by sentences like:

(265)   I like to eat snails

(266)   It's odd for camels to drink vodka

One consequence of fixed time reference is the implication (where semantic–pragmatic factors permit) that the matrix event or state is in some way responsible for, or at least affects, the complement state or event. This was called the 'controllability factor' by Riddle (1975b). This controllability factor does not, of course, hold in ITR contexts, and thus the distinction between the ITR of s-like complements and the DTR of reduced complements can be exploited with given CTPs to create meaning contrasts:

(267) a. I remembered that I closed the door

    b. I remembered to close the door

(268) a. Zeke decided that he was a bootlegger

    b. Zeke decided to be a bootlegger

(269) a. Nell told Enrico that he was a good singer

    b. Nell told Enrico to be a good singer

The complements in the (a) sentences above refer to states of affairs that exist independently of the action or state described in the matrix, whereas in the (b) sentences, there is a clear dependence between the matrix and complement proposition.

A further consequence of the controllability factor is that, if the CTP can be interpreted as an action, then the complement can be interpreted as an action even though the complement in isolation refers to a state. For instance

(270) Floyd is a nice boy

(271) Floyd is an acrobat

describe two states attributed to Floyd. When the above propositions are made infinitival complements, as in

(272) Floyd tried to be a nice boy

(273) Floyd tried to be an acrobat

they are interpreted actively, describing actions not states. Again, the difference between these reduced complement types and non-reduced complement types can be exploited for semantic effect:

(274) a. Floyd remembered that he was a nice boy

    b. Floyd remembered to be a nice boy

(275) a. Max convinced Floyd that he was a nice boy

    b. Max convinced Floyd to be a nice boy

(276) a. Floyd pretended that he was a nice boy

    b. Floyd pretended to be a nice boy

The (a) sentences have the state interpretation, while the (b) sentences express some notion of activity.

3.1.3 *Complementizers*

When a form functions as a complementizer and something else, its meaning outside the complement system will likely be related to its use in complementation. The complementizer, then, may not be simply a neutral marker of a complement type but may bring with it a meaning that can affect the semantics and therefore the distribution of the complement type it is associated with. A straightforward example of this is the English particle *if*, which functions as a sentence connective in

(277)   I'll leave if Zeke comes

and as a complementizer in

(278)   I doubt if Zeke knows

The constructions in (277) and (278) are clearly different; as one illustration of this difference, (279) but not (280) is a possible sentence:

(279)   If Zeke comes, I'll leave

(280)   *If Zeke knows, I doubt

As a sentence connective, *if* sets up a relation between antecedent and consequent states or events; the consequent does not hold unless the condition stated in the antecedent holds. As a complementizer, *if* is mostly used with complements where the usual positive implications associated with a given CTP are not meant to hold. For instance, complements of *nice* normally are given a factive interpretation, i.e. presupposed to be true:

(281)   It was nice that Zeke came

(282)   It wasn't nice that Zeke came

It is reasonable to infer from both (281) and (282) that Zeke in fact came. When the matrix is stated conditionally, the complement is not meant to have a factive interpretation and *if* is chosen as the complementizer:

(283)   It would be nice if Zeke came

Similarly, complements of *know* as in

(284)   Alf knows that Zeke came

are assigned a factive interpretation. This interpretation can be cancelled with *if* as complementizer:

(285)   Alf knows if Zeke came (but I don't)

It doesn't follow from (285) that Zeke came. But the predicate *doubt*, which expresses a negative propositional attitude amounting to a denial of the proposition embodied in its complement, as in

(286)   I doubt that Zeke came

can also take complements with *if*, as in:

(287)   I doubt if Zeke came

The effect of *if* as a complementizer is to cancel positive implications, and it has no effect on negative ones, so (286) and (287) are roughly synonymous.

In conditional constructions like (277) and (279), the *if*-clause represents a non-actual or irreal state or event. The irrealis modality of the consequent is identified by *will/would* or some other indicator of futurity. In complementation, *if* is likewise associated with non-actual or irreal modality; none of the complements in (283), (285), or (287) can be taken as a real or actual event. Irrealis modality seems to underlie both uses of *if*, the meanings being clearly related.

Bolinger (1972) has claimed the *that*-complementizer and the *that*-demonstrative in English are similarly related in that the distribution of the *that*-complementizer is affected by its ultimately demonstrative function.

In many languages adpositions function as complementizers (cf. section 1.2). Their meaning outside complementation may relate directly to their use in complementation. As one example, the Irish preposition *gan* translates English 'without' in its use with nominal and phrasal adjuncts:

(288)   D'imigh sé gan   leabhar
         left   he without book
         'He left without a book'

(289)   D'imigh sé gan   mé a   fheiceáil
         left   he without me COMP see(NZN)
         'He left without seeing me'

In complementation, *gan* is used to negate noun complements:

(290)   D'iarr mé air   gan imeacht
         asked I   on him NEG leave(NZN)
         'I asked him not to leave'

Semantically, *gan* is negative in all its uses. Even in (288), *gan* could be roughly translated as 'not with'. The negative aspect of *gan* predominates in (289) and (290).

3.1.4 *Manner of syntactic relation to the matrix*

Notional complements may be rendered (1) as subordinate clauses or (2) as verb phrases in paratactic constructions, in which case they are syntactically on a par with the clause containing the CTP (see section 2.4). This syntactic difference can be exploited to create semantic contrasts between paratactic and subordinate complement types.

In Lango, the subjunctive and the paratactic complement types can both be used with a large number of CTPS. One example of this contrast is given below:

(291)   Dákó   òdìò   ìcó   òkwàlò   gwènò
        woman pressed(3SG) man   stole(3SG) chicken

                                              (paratactic)
        'The woman forced the man to steal the chicken'

(292)   Dákó   òdìò   ìcó   nì   'kwál   gwènò
        woman pressed(3SG) man   COMP steal(3SG SJNCT) chicken

                                              (subjunctive)
        'The woman pressed the man to steal the chicken'

With (291), we can legitimately infer that the man in fact stole the chicken, while with (292), we can make no such inference: we only know that the woman put pressure on the man to do what she wanted him to do. Paratactic complements have interpretations as 'realized' states or events; subjunctive complements have an 'unrealized' interpretation. This semantic difference follows from the syntax. Since the Lango paratactic complement behaves syntactically like a juxtaposed independent sentence, saying (291) amounts to making two assertions:

(293)   Dákó   òdìò   ìcó   òkwàlò   gwènò
        woman pressed(3SG) man   stole(3SG) chicken
        'The woman pressed the man. He stole the chicken'

Since each of the component predications represents an independent assertion, it follows that the complement would be interpreted as a fact. (292), however, represents a single assertion; the interpretation of the complement is mediated through the semantics of the CTP, which in this case does not allow an implicative interpretation. The semantic difference, then, between parataxis and hypotaxis (subordination) in complementation involves the number of assertions the construction contains; each clause in the paratactic construction is a separate assertion, whereas in hypotaxis·there is a single assertion involving both CTP and complement.

Paratactic complements typically occur in DTR environments, especially in causative and immediate perception contexts. The reason for this is that the nature of these situations, a cause and an effect, an action and its perception, lend themselves particularly well to coding as two separate though logically connected events. The complement in these cases can be interpreted as a separate assertion, taking its place in the progression of the discourse without the mediation of the CTP. Hypotaxis in complementation is a device for qualifying the interpretation of a predication with the CTP acting as a sort of semantic filter.

Hypotaxis is the complementation device *par excellence* because the complement is, logically, an argument of the predicate and hypotaxis is a direct syntactic reflection of this semantic situation. The syntax parallels the semantics. Parataxis will likely be used in complementation only where the interpretation of the complement mediated through the CTP will be essentially the same as if it were coded as a separate assertion.

Serial constructions are in many respects intermediate between hypotaxis and parataxis. As in hypotaxis, notional complements in serial constructions form a single assertion with their CTPs. But like parataxis, the component verb phrases seem to be syntactically on a par.[24] The fact that a serialized construction typically represents one assertion and a paratactic construction two, affects their use in complementation. Both are usual in causative, immediate perception, and phasal contexts. Serial constructions alone are used in abilative and desiderative contexts because these are incompatible with the two-assertion aspect of parataxis. Parenthetical senses of predicates like *believe* are quite compatible with parataxis, but not serialization.

3.1.5 *Grammatical status of the complement predicate*
The part of speech (verb, noun, or adjective) of the complement predicate can be correlated with the use of the complement type that contains it, though how closely a complement type conforms to the 'ideal' distribution suggested by the grammatical status of its predicate depends on a number of factors, chief among which is the number and the kind of oppositions (distinct complement types) in the complement system. What follows are some generalizations about 'ideal' distributions. (We can define an 'ideal' distribution as a list of the uses that some grammatical entity is by nature best suited for and for which it is invariably used if it exists in the system at all.) Since complement predicates are coded as verbs in the great majority of cases (e.g. in s-like, paratactic, and infinitive complements) coding predicates as verbs can be viewed as the unmarked case, and indeed there are languages which allow this as the only possibility for coding predicates. We will therefore concentrate our attention here on the marked cases,

i.e. complement predicates as nouns or adjectives, noting that these forms always coexist in complement systems with predicates coded as verbs.

Nominalizations can be divided into two types: nominalized propositions and activity or state nominalizations. Nominalized propositions are referring expressions, i.e. they are used by speakers to refer to information given previously in a discourse or taken as background to a discourse. Nominalized propositions, then, are background information, discourse dependents and, of course, do not in themselves constitute assertions. Activity or state nominalizations are used to refer to kinds of activities or states, not to specific events or states constituting backgrounded information. Examples of each sort of nominalization are given below:

(294) *Nominalized propositions*

    a. *Zeke's hitting Roscoe* annoyed Floyd

    b. We regret *Floyd's flunking Flemish*

    c. *Floyd's flunking Flemish* is unlikely

    d. *Leo's drinking the metheglin straight down* caused him to pass out

    e. *Eating Beefos* made Mort sick

(295) *Activity or state nominalizations*

    a. Nell enjoys *shooting rabbits*

    b. *Eating grapes* is fun

    c. Henry is proud of *being tall*

    d. *Drinking mead* causes gout

    e. Arnold disapproves of *children drinking water*

Nominalizations of either sort result in a sort of objectification of the predicate, investing it with the status of a name. Nominalized propositions needn't be presupposed, as (294c) shows (activity or state nominalizations can't be presupposed since they're non-referential), but even when non-factive, they still represent backgrounded information. This is the essential characteristic of nominalized predications, though they may take on broader functions in the context of particular grammars.

As discussed in section 1.3.6, adjectivalized predications, or participles, because of the peculiarities of their syntax *vis-à-vis* other complement types, play a rather restricted role in complementation, being limited, normally, to use with immediate perception predicates, where, however, they are of reasonably frequent occurrence. The use of participles with immediate perception predicates follows from the use of participles generally.

As nominalization involves objectivalization of predicates, adjectivalization involves converting predicates into modifiers or qualifiers, specifying either attributes of nominals or attendant circumstances of events. An example of this latter use of participles is

(296)   Leaving the room, Gurt saw Burt

where the participial phrase *leaving the room* sets forth the circumstances under which the action of our primary concern, *Gurt saw Burt*, takes place. The two events are taken to be simultaneous and share a notional argument, *Gurt*.

These characteristic features of participles, the ability to express simultaneity with another event and the sharing of arguments with the main event, makes the participle quite suitable for use with immediate perception predicates: the event coded by the CTP and that coded by the complement must necessarily be simultaneous, and, furthermore, participants involved in the matrix and complement events can be said to be shared. For instance, if we say

(297)   Gurt saw Burt leaving the room

it follows for all practical purposes that

(298)   Gurt saw Burt[25]

Burt, then, is a shared participant in the two events coded in (297), and the events themselves must be viewed as simultaneous.

The characteristics of the participle that make it compatible with immediate perception predicates make it unsuitable for use with most CTPS. To give just one example, in the sentence

(299)   *I believe Brinck breaking his leg
          (cf. I believe that Brinck broke his leg)

the matrix and complement events do not necessarily occur simultaneously. Sentence (300), where the events do occur simultaneously, is possible.

(300)   I believe that Brinck is breaking his leg

but so is (301) possible:

(301)   a. I believe that Brinck broke his leg
        b. I believe that Brinck will break his leg

With immediate perception predicates, the two events are necessarily, not accidentally, simultaneous. Further, it does not follow from (299) (or its grammatical counterpart) that

(302)   I believe Brinck

3.2 *The classes of complement-taking predicates*
In the last section, characteristic semantic features of complement types were discussed. In this section, we will complete the discussion of the semantics of complementation by discussing semantic classes of CTPs. It should be made clear here that the classes of CTPs discussed below are meant to reflect the uses of CTPs in complementation rather than the full semantic properties of any given verb or set of verbs in any language. For instance, the English verb *tell* as a CTP has two main uses, one as an utterance predicate

(303)   Floyd told Zeke that Roscoe buried the mash

and another as a manipulative predicate:

(304)   Floyd told Zeke to bury the mash

It is certainly the case that there is a unified meaning of *tell* under which both uses are subsumed, but in this section we will consider each of the uses of *tell* and other verbs separately since they are what determine the choice of complement type.

References to notions like 'subject' in this, as in other sections, are meant to apply only in those languages where subjects and other grammatical relations can meaningfully be said to exist (cf. Schachter 1976 and Noonan 1977). 'Basic subjects' refer to subjects of active sentences.

3.2.1 *Utterance predicates*
Utterance predicates are used in sentences describing a simple transfer of information initiated by an agentive subject. The complement represents the transferred information, and the CTP describes the manner of transfer, the illocutionary force of the original statement, and can also give an evaluation of the speaker's (as opposed to the agent subject's) view of the veracity of the proposition encoded in the complement. The basic subject of the CTP is the entity to whom the original statement is attributed, i.e. the agent. The addressee may be expressed as a DO or IO in the matrix, but it is less likely to be overtly expressed than the agent. English verbs that can be used as utterance predicates include *say, tell, report, promise, ask*[26] etc., as we see in the following sentences:

(305)   Zeke said that Norm left

(306)   Herm told Rita that Norm left

(307)   The UPI reported that Norm left

(308)   Norm promised that he would leave

(309)   Nell asked if Norm left

The information given in the complement of utterance predicates can be presented in either of two ways: as a direct quotation (direct discourse) or as an indirect quotation (indirect discourse). The function of the direct quotation is to give the actual words of the speaker, while indirect quotations are adapted in varying degrees to the viewpoint of the speaker (the one who utters sentences like (305–9)). This adaptation involves the reorientation of the various deictic or shifter categories (Jakobson 1957), for example pronouns, locative markers, and tense markers (section 2.6). For instance, if the original statement was

(310)   I'll go there tomorrow

a direct quote would simply take the form:

(311)   He said, 'I'll go there tomorrow'

An indirect quote, on the other hand, might take the form

(312)   He said that he would come here today

where each of the shifter categories is appropriately modified to the viewpoint of the reporter.

Not all languages employ indirect quotes, or if they are used, they may be used only infrequently. Mayfield (1972) reports that Agta has no true indirect quotes. Shackle (1972) reports that true indirect speech is rare in Punjabi, and Bailey (1924) claims that indirect speech is hardly used at all in Shina.

With the exception of *promise* (discussed in sections 2.6 and 3.1.2) and similar predicates, complements to utterance predicates have ITR. This favors the use of ş-like complement types since they are the most likely to allow tense to be statable independently of the matrix. Further, by definition, direct discourse automatically results in s-like complements. Therefore, since all languages have ways of presenting direct quotes, all languages use s-like complements with utterance predicates, though other complement types can occur with predicates in this class for indirect discourse. There are, in fact, languages that use true s-like complements only with utterance predicates, for example Sherpa (T. G. Givón, personal communication).

Almost all languages distinguish direct from indirect discourse by means of intonation: there is typically a pause before and/or after the direct quote, while indirect discourse is treated like any other complement from the standpoint of intonation. In addition, some languages, for instance Bemba, use different complementizers for indicating direct versus indirect discourse (Givón 1972):

(313)   John a-à-ebele   *uku-ti* n-kà-isa
        John 3SG-PAST-say INF-say ISG-FUT-come
        'John said that I will come'

(314)   John a-à-ebele   *a-à-ti*   n-kà-isa
        John 3SG-PAST-say 3SG-PAST-say ISG-FUT-come
        'John said "I will come"'

The infinitive form of the defective verb *ti* 'say' is used as a complementizer with indirect quotes, while its simple past counterpart is used with direct quotes. In English, the complementizer *that* is optional with indirect quotes, but obligatorily absent with direct quotes:

(315)   a. *MacArthur said that 'I shall return'
        b. MacArthur said 'I shall return'

(316)   a. MacArthur said that he would return'
        b. MacArthur said he would return

With indirect quotes, subjunctive and other reduced complement types can also occur, though they are far less common in this context than indicative complements. When such complement types do occur with indirect quotes, their inflectional possibilities can be utilized to indicate tense distinctions. For instance, Latin is said to have three infinitives: a present, a perfect and a future (Greenough 1903). The future infinitive is only used in indirect discourse. The present and perfect infinitives, like the Greek present and aorist infinitives discussed in section 1.3.4, ordinarily represent imperfect and perfective aspect respectively. In indirect discourse, the tense markers on these infinitives assume a true time reference function:

(317)   Dīcunt   eum *iuvāre*   eam
        say(3PL PRES) him help(PRES INF) her
        'They say that he's helping her'

(318)   Dīcunt   eum *iūvisse*   eam
        say(3PL PRES) him help(PERF INF) her
        'They say that he helped her'

(319)   Dīcunt   eum *iūtūrum*   *esse*   eam
        say(3PL PRES) him help(FUT PART) be(PRES INF) her
        'They say that he'll help her'

Darden (1973) reports a similar phenomenon in literary Lithuanian. In such cases, then, the ITR context of complements to utterance verbs enables the time reference potential of this complement type to be realized.

Because the ITR context provided by indirect quotes so heavily favors indicative complements, the use of other complement types may be idiosyncratic. The German use of the subjunctive discussed in section 3.1.1 is an example of this sort; the use of the subjunctive there depends on the tense of the CTP. In English, the utterance predicate *report* can take infinitive complements in indirect discourse as well as the more expected indicative (as in (307) above):

(320)   The UPI reported Norm to have left

The idiomatic nature of this usage is revealed when we examine semantically similar predicates which do not take infinitive complements under the same conditions, for example, *say, announce*:

(321)   *John said Norm to have left

(322)   *John announced Norm to have left

For many speakers, however, the use of the infinitive with *report* is not wholly idiosyncratic, but rather reflects a meaning contrast. (320) differs from (307) in presenting the information given in the complement as less reliable, possibly contrary-to-fact whereas the information given in the complement in (307) is, from the speaker's point of view, more likely to be factual (Postal 1974). The use of the infinitive for indirect discourse in English has often been attributed to Latin influence, for example by Visser (1973).

While the use of such devices in English is peripheral at best, many languages possess regular devices for indicating the reliability of information given as indirect quotes. One such device was illustrated in section 1.2 for Jacaltec, where the complementizer marked an indirect quote as representing reliable or unreliable information.

3.2.2 *Propositional attitude predicates*
Propositional attitude predicates express an attitude regarding the truth of the proposition expressed as their complement. The propositional attitude may be positive as in the verbs *believe, think, suppose, assume*, etc., or negative as in *not believe, doubt, deny*, etc. Animate subjects of

such predicates are experiencers, as opposed to the agentive basic subjects of utterance predicates. Experiencers, however, needn't be overtly expressed. In sentences like

(323)   It's certain that Hugh will be defeated

(324)   It's possible that Perry will lose   .

the holder of the propositional attitude must be the speaker and therefore the experiencer is contextually redundant in such sentences.[27] Many languages do not have predicates such as *be certain*, using instead predicates like *believe* where the experiencer, the holder of the propositional attitude, is always overtly expressed. Further, some languages have only one true propositional attitude predicate, expressing a stronger or weaker commitment to the truth of the complement proposition via verb inflections, sentence particles or adverbs, complementizers, complement types, etc., and negative propositional attitude via negation.

Predicates expressing positive propositional attitude are the most likely predicates to be used parenthetically (section 2.5).

With first person subjects, English is likely to express degrees of certainty or commitment to a proposition by means of different CTPS (e.g. *be certain* versus *be possible*, *believe* versus *doubt*), negation, or by means of adverbials, for instance:

(325)   I sort of believe that the Mets will win (but I'm not certain)

When the subject is not first person, the speaker can still express varying degrees of commitment to the complement predication. In ordinary usage

(326)   Olaf thinks the Mets will win

suggests a negative propositional attitude on the part of the speaker. This negative attitude can be expressed overtly (not left to inference) as in:

(327)   Olaf stupidly believes that the Mets will win

(328)   Olaf stupidly guesses that the Mets will win

The tendency across languages is for the CTP to express the subject's propositional attitude, while adverbials, choice of complementizer and complement type normally express the speaker's propositional attitude.

In Jacaltec, the complementizers *chubil* and *tato* perform the function of indicating speaker propositional attitude with propositional attitude predicates, just as they do with utterance predicates (section 1.2; Craig

1977). Givón and Kimenyi (1974) report a similar situation in Kinyarwanda where the choice of *ko* and *ngo* as complementizers reflects a
neutral versus negative propositional attitude on the part of the speaker:

(329)   Yatekereže   ko   amazi yari   mare-mare
        think(3SG PAST) COMP water be(3SG) deep
        'He thought that the water was deep'

(330)   Yatekereže ngo amazi yari mare-mare
        'He (misguidedly) thought that the water was deep'

Speaker propositional attitude can also be indicated by choice of
complement type. Indicative versus subjunctive complements can be
used, as described in section 3.1.1, to indicate positive versus negative
propositional attitude.

Complements to negative propositional attitude predicates like *doubt*
not infrequently appear in the form of questions. This phenomenon
occurs in Irish:

(331)   An dtiocfadh   sé?
        Q   come(FUT) he
        'Will he come?'

(332)   Tá amhras orm   an dtiocfadh   sé
        COP doubt   on me Q   come(FUT) he
        'I doubt if he'll come'

English uses special complementizers, *if* and *whether*, under these
conditions. See section 3.1.3 for discussion of the use of *if* in such
sentences in English. The use of the interrogative form in Irish has a
similar explanation, namely that the question morphology indicates
uncertainty on the part of the speaker. Complements to utterance
predicates like *ask* that report questions exhibit this feature as well.

3.2.3 *Pretence predicates*

Pretence predicates are a semantically complex class whose subjects
may be either experiencers (*imagine*, some senses of *pretend*, *make
believe*) or agents (*fool (into thinking)*, *trick (into thinking)*, some senses
of *pretend*, *make believe*). These predicates have as a characteristic that
the world described by the proposition embodied in the complement is
not the real world. The status of the complement proposition in the real
world is not given, though there is a very general implication that the
proposition is false (Kempson 1975). The complements to these predicates have ITR.

The interesting aspect of these complements from the standpoint of complementation is the form of their complements in systems contrasting indicative and subjunctive complement types. Complements to pretence predicates are normally interpreted as hypothetical non-events, and hence would seem to be classified as irrealis or non-assertive (cf. section 3.1.1). One would expect, then, that in languages that used a realis irrealis or assertive/non-assertive contrast to underlie their indicative subjunctive distinction, complements to pretence predicates would be coded as subjunctives. This, however, is not the case: these complements are coded as indicatives. Russian, as illustrated in section 3.1.1, uses a realis irrealis distinction for its indicatives and subjunctives. Complements to *pritvorjatsja* 'pretend' are indicative; the subjunctive is unacceptable (data from Boris Palant):

(333)   Ja pritvorjalsja, čto   Ivan prišël
         I pretended   COMP Ivan came(INDIC)
         'I pretended that Ivan came'

(334)   *Ja pritvorjalsja, čtoby Ivan prišël
         I pretended   COMP Ivan come(SJNCT)
         'I pretended that Ivan came'

Similarly in Spanish, which uses an assertive/non-assertive distinction, only indicatives are possible with these predicates (data from Andres Gallardo):

(335)   Aparentaron   que vino
         pretended(3PL) COMP came(3SG INDIC)
         'They pretended that he came'

(336)   *Aparentaron   que viniera
         pretended(3PL) COMP come(3SG SJNCT)
         'They pretended that he came'

The reason for the indicative in these cases seems to derive from the fact that the pretence predicate establishes an alternative reality and the complement constitutes an assertion within that alternative reality. As an assertion, it is coded in the indicative. This serves to emphasize the fact that it is the function of the complement and its relation with its CTP that determine complement type, not entailment relations, as is often implied in the literature (e.g. Karttunen 1971b, Kiparsky and Kiparsky 1970).

3.2.4 *Commentative predicates (factives)*
The term 'commentative' has been chosen here over the more traditional term 'factive' because commentative is a more general term and more clearly characterizes the range of uses of these predicates.[28] Commenta-

tive predicates resemble propositional attitude predicates in that, when an overt human subject appears, the subject is an experiencer since the predicate gives information about mental attitudes. They differ from propositional attitude predicates in that they provide a comment on the complement proposition which takes the form of an emotional reaction or evaluation (*regret, be sorry, be sad*) or a judgement (*be odd, be significant, be important*). Both emotional evaluations and judgements are normally made on events or states that people take to be real (Rosenberg 1975). As a result, complements to commentative predicates have been said to be presupposed.[29] Further, sentences with commentative CTPs typically take the form of a comment expressed by the CTP on the complement proposition as topic (old, background information) so complements to commentative CTPs are discourse dependents (section 3.1.1).

Discourse-dependent complements have ITR (their time reference doesn't logically depend on the CTP), and therefore are normally in the form of indicative complements. Their discourse dependency would also make them compatible with nominalizations (section 3.1.5). English allows both s-like and nominalized complement types with these complements:

(337)   Nelson regrets that Perry got the nod

(338)   Nelson regrets Perry's getting the nod

Languages that employ an assertive/non-assertive distinction for their indicative/subjunctive opposition will use a subjunctive complement type for these complements.

Commentative predicates also occur with infinitive complements in English (Kiparsky and Kiparsky 1970, Spears 1973). The consequences of juxtaposing a commentative predicate and a DTR infinitive in English would seem to be predictable, namely the CTP would provide a comment on any potential occurrence of the proposition embodied in the complement consistent with the time reference of the CTP. The controllability factor (section 3.1.2) is not involved in the interpretation of infinitive complements of commentatives, since the complement does not refer to a specific event with a fixed time reference relative to the CTP.

When the 'any potential occurrence' interpretation of infinitives in these cases coincides with a pragmatic interpretation of the complement proposition as punctual (representing a single event), then the interpretation of s-like complements and infinitives may be virtually identical:

(339)   It was odd that Floyd came

(340)   It was odd for Floyd to come

In other cases, however, the two may differ considerably in meaning:

(341)   It's odd that turtles don't outrun rabbits

(342)   It's odd for turtles not to outrun rabbits

(341) amounts to a comment on the proposition

(343)   Turtles don't outrun rabbits

whereas (342) implies that turtles usually do outrun rabbits. (341) comments on the complement as representing a fact; non-reduced complements are interpreted as having independent existence and so can accommodate a factive interpretation. (342) comments on the complement as a potential occurrence. Judging a fact as odd is quite distinct from judging a potential occurrence as odd, hence the meaning difference.

In languages where adjectives are syntactically distinguished from verbs, there is a strong preference for coding commentative predicates as adjectives. Many languages have only adjectives filling this class of predicates, i.e. forms like *be sorry* in place of *regret*, etc.

3.2.5 *Predicates of knowledge and acquisition of knowledge*
This class of predicates has been called 'semifactive' (Karttunen 1971a, Terrell and Hooper 1974) and 'epistemic-qualifying' (Guitart 1978). These predicates take experiencer subjects and describe the state or the manner of acquisition of knowledge. Knowledge and acquisition of knowledge (KAK) predicates include *know, discover, realize, find out*, and *forget*, as well as perception predicates such as *see* and *hear* when used in a sense other than that of immediate perception (section 3.2.12) i.e. as in (344) but not (345):

(344)   I saw that Floyd left   (KAK sense)

(345)   I saw Floyd leave   (Immediate perception sense)

Dream is also a KAK predicate where the source of knowledge is not the real world (in most cultural contexts).

Excluding *dream* from further consideration here, complements to KAK predicates are presupposed to be true, since it only makes sense to assert knowledge or acquisition of knowledge about something one takes as a fact. Complements to KAK predicates, however, differ from complements to commentative predicates in that they do not necessarily constitute backgrounded material, but instead may be new in the discourse context, being part of what is asserted. One can assert both the manner of acquisition of knowledge as well as the content of the knowledge as new information, so that;

(346)   I discovered that Sally left Herman

can present the complement as new information (and could therefore be used appropriately where the content of the complement was not known), whereas;

(347)   I regret that Sally left Herman

cannot felicitously be used to present this information as new.

Since complements to KAK predicates have ITR, and are typically part of what is asserted (are not discourse dependent), they are normally encoded as indicative complements. When KAK predicates are negated or questioned, however, they may be used to express negative propositional attitude toward the complement proposition, in which case the usual syntactic consequences of negative propositional attitude follow in the context of a given language. In Spanish, such complements are put in the subjunctive (Guitart 1978), the usual procedure in Spanish for negative propositional attitude.

The predicate *know* has some unique properties. Unlike the other predicates of this class, *know* makes no assertion about manner of acquisition, only the fact of knowledge. As a result, its complements typically represent backgrounded material like commentatives. In addition to the fact of knowledge, however, *know* also asserts a positive propositional attitude toward its complement like *believe*, and unlike the commentative *regret*, which asserts an emotional reaction and comments on the complement as background. The form of complements with *know* cross-linguistically are like those of *believe* and unlike those of *regret* where the two differ. Evidently, expression of propositional attitude is a stronger determiner of complement type than backgrounding.

3.2.6 *Predicates of fearing*

Predicates of fearing, such as *be afraid*, *fear*, *worry* and *be anxious* have enough peculiarities cross-linguistically to merit dealing with them as a class. They are characterized semantically by having experiencer subjects and expressing an attitude of fear or concern that the complement proposition will be or has been realized. The complement has ITR.

One peculiarity of complements to predicates of fearing is that languages differ in the assignment of negation to such complements. In English, (348), Irish, (349), and Jacaltec ((350) data from Craig 1977), for example, the complement is expressed as a positive statement if it is interpreted affirmatively:

(348) He's afraid *that Floyd came*

(349) Is eagal léi   *go   dtiocfaidh sé*
       COP fear with her COMP come(FUT) he
       'She's afraid that he'll come'

(350) Chin   xiw   *tato chach ayc'ayoj swi'*   *te' ñah*
       COP(1SG) afraid COMP you   fall down top(3SG POSS) the house
       'I'm afraid that you'll fall from the roof'

In Latin, however, it is expressed as a negative if interpreted affirmatively, and as a positive if interpreted negatively (data from Greenough 1903):

(351) Vereor *ne   accidat*
       fear(1SG) NEG happen(3SG)
       'I fear that it may happen'

(352) Vereor *ut   accidat*
       fear(1SG) COMP happen(3SG)
       'I fear that it may not happen'

In Russian, a complement that is interpreted affirmatively is put in the negative (and in the subjunctive) if the complement represents simple possibility, but in the positive (and the indicative) if the complement is interpreted as something almost certain to occur:

(353) Ja bojus', *kak by   on ne prišël*
       I   fear(1SG) COMP SJNCT he NEG come(SJNCT)
       'I'm afraid that he may come'

(354) Ja bojus', *čto   on pridët*
       I   fear(1SG) COMP he come(FUT INDIC)
       'I'm afraid that he'll come'

As in the Russian case above, many languages possess devices to indicate the degree of certainty for the realization of the complement proposition. Russian changes the negation of the complement, uses its indicative/subjunctive distinction, and changes the complementizer (which is independent of the mood category switch since both *čto* and *kak* can occur with indicatives and subjunctives). When the indicative/subjunctive distinction is based on a realis/irrealis or assertive/non-assertive opposition, a language may use the indicative for more certain complements of fearing, and the subjunctive for less certain ones.

Predicates of fearing commonly occur with non-s-like complement types such as infinitives, especially when an equi-relation exists between notional subjects. In such cases, a meaning contrast between non-reduced and reduced complement types can be exploited:

(355) *Non-reduced complements*

    a. I was afraid that I fell asleep

    b. I was afraid that I would fall asleep

    c. I was afraid that I left

    d. I was afraid that I would leave

(356) *Reduced complements*

    a. I was afraid to fall asleep

    b. I was afraid to leave

(356) differs from (355) in the 'control factor' discussed in section 3.1.2 which is associated with complement types with DTR such as the English infinitive. In (356), the subject is presented as a potential controller of the complement event, whereas in (355) the subject is expressed as a simple experiencer of emotion.

In English, Irish, and a number of other languages, predicates of fearing are frequently used as parentheticals:

(357) John, I'm afraid, is a Democrat

3.2.7 *Desiderative predicates*
Desiderative predicates, such as *want*, *wish*, *desire* and *hope* are characterized by having experiencer subjects expressing a desire that the complement proposition be realized. In this respect, they can be looked on as being the opposite of predicates of fearing, expressing a positive as opposed to a negative feeling about the ultimate realization of the complement proposition.

Desiderative predicates divide up semantically into three usage classes. The first, the *hope*-class, has complements with ITR, as we see in the following examples:

(358) I hope that John came

(359) I hope that John will come

Hope-class predicates are the true counterparts of predicates of fearing since both types express an emotional attitude toward a proposition whose status is, for whatever reason, unknown, but which could turn out to be true. The *wish*-class predicates also have ITR complements,

(360)   I wish that John came/had come

(361)   I wish that John would come

but differ from those of the *hope*-class in that they are normally given a contrafactive interpretation, so that while the status of *John came* in (358) is simply unknown, the complement in (360) is implied to be false. This difference between *wish*- and *hope*-class predicates holds even when the complements have future reference; the complement in (362) is implied to be at least likely to be realized, whereas the complement in (363) is implied to be only a remote possibility:

(362)   I hope that Smith will resign

(363)   I wish that Smith would resign

If the complement proposition is incapable of realization, for whatever reason, it cannot be a complement of a *hope*-class predicate but can be a complement of a *wish*-class predicate:

(364)   *I hope that I was/were twenty again

(365)   I wish that I were twenty again

The contrafactive interpretation of *wish*-class predicates has its counterpart in the morphology of the verb complex. Notice that (363) uses the modal *would* while (362) has *will*; *will* expresses definite possibility, *would* has a less definite, hypothetical interpretation. In (365) the complement appears in the past subjunctive, a residual category in English used in hypothetical or contrafactive contexts. *Would* is the past subjunctive of *will*.

The third and last class is the *want*-class. Complements to *want*-class predicates have DTR, and express a desire that some state or event may be realized in the future. The complement in

(366)   I want John to come

can only have future reference. *Want*-class predicates resemble *wish*-class predicates in that their complements may refer to an unrealizable state of affairs.

(367)   He wants to be twenty again; he's a bit crazy

All languages share the three-way classification between the *hope*-, *wish*- and *want*-classes, but they do not all make the same formal distinctions. Most common is a distinction between the *wish*-class and either or both of the other two. Other languages may not make the same lexical distinctions that English does for the CTP verbs themselves, but they may have contrasting choices for complement types, or they may have reliability, irrealis or conditional markers on the CTP, on the complement predicate, or both.

The complement types used by these classes of predicates follow from their meaning. *Hope*-class predicates are usually associated with non-reduced complements. In Russian, for example, *hope*-class predicates take indicative complements:

(368) Ja nadejus', čto   Ivan prišël
       I hope(1SG) COMP Ivan came(INDIC)
       'I hope that Ivan came'

Spanish also uses an indicative with these predicates. *Hope*-class predicates differ from other desideratives also in their inability to allow negative raising (Horn 1978). Verbs used as *hope*-class predicates can often double as *want*-class predicates as in

(369) I hope to go

especially when an equi-relation exists between notional subjects. The complement type, then, is the same as for the DTR complements of *want*-class predicates, namely reduced complements, typically subjunctives or infinitives. These forms will be used if they are available in the system (see section 4). A frequently encountered situation for *want*-class predicates is the use of infinitives when an equi-relation exists between subjects, and subjunctives when no equi-relation exists. Lango provides an illustration of this:

(370) Dákó àmìttò   jwàttò lócà
       woman want(3SG) hit(INF) man
       'The woman wants to hit the man'

(371) Dákó àmìttò   ní   àtín 'jwát   lócà
       woman want(3SG) COMP child hit(3SG SJNCT) man
       'The woman wants the child to hit the man'

As the glosses to the above sentences show, English uses infinitives for both types of sentences, raising the complement subject to object position (section 2.2) when no equi-relation exists. This sort of situation is somewhat rare. A rather more common situation is exemplified by

Albanian, where even with an equi-relation the subjunctive is used (data from Ferit Rustemi):

(372)   Gruaja   deshi   njeriu   ta   *vjedhë*
        woman(NOM) wanted(3SG) man(NOM) COMP steal(3SG SJNCT)
        pulën
        chicken(ACC)
        'The woman wanted the man to steal the chicken'

(373)   Gruaja   deshi   ta   *vjedhë*   pulën
        woman(NOM) wanted(3SG) COMP steal(3SG SJNCT) chicken(ACC)
        'The woman wanted to steal the chicken'

Desiderative predicates are good candidates for lexical union (section 2.3) and examples can be found from many language families. Below is an example from Sanskrit (Gonda 1966):

(374)   Pibati
        drink(3SG)
        'He's drinking'

(375)   Pipāsati
        drink want(3SG)
        'He wants to drink'

In many languages, the subjunctive in a main clause has the force of a desiderative CTP plus complement, as in Catalan (data from Yates 1975):

(376)   Que tinguin   bon viatge
        COMP have(2PL SJNCT) good journey
        'Have a good trip' (I hope you have a good trip)

Some languages may use a mood other than the subjunctive to express desire in a main clause. The Greek optative is an example of this sort:

(377)   fúgoi
        flee(3SG OPTATIVE)
        'May he flee' (I want him to flee)

Cases like this can be difficult to distinguish from imperatives.

There are a number of cases of forms doing double duty. In Irish, for example, *maith* 'good' can be used both as a commentative and a desiderative predicate:

(378)   *Commentative*
        Is maith dhó   í   a   theacht
        be good to him her COMP come(NZN)
        'It's good for him that she came'

(379)   *Desiderative*
      Ba   mhaith liom   í   a   theacht
      be(COND) good   with me her COMP come(NZN)
      'I want her to come'

The syntactic difference between (378) and (379) involves the use of the
conditional mood (chapter III:4) on the supporting copula in the matrix,
and a change in preposition: *do* 'to' with the benefactee in the
commentative, *le* 'with' with the experiencer in the desiderative. In
Hebrew, the word *xošev* does double duty as a propositional attitude
predicate and as a desiderative: with indicative complements it means 'I
think' and with infinitive complements it means 'I plan' (data from Ora
Leivant):

(380)   Ani xošev še-ha-iš   ganav et ha-kesef
      I   think COMP-ART-man stole OBJ ART-money
      'I think that the man stole the money'

(381)   Ani xošev lignov   et ha-kesef
      I   plan steal(INF) OBJ ART-money
      'I plan to steal the money'

The control factor (section 3.1.2) associated with the DTR infinitive
accounts for the meaning shifts. The predicate meaning 'want' frequently does double duty as a modal predicate expressing 'need' or 'necessity'. Because of the DTR future orientation of *want*-class predicates, they
frequently come to be used as markers of future (as in many of the
Balkan languages).

3.2.8 *Manipulative predicates*

Manipulatives include the closely related causative and permissive
predicates, both involving an element of causation. We are concerned in
this section with 'efficient' not 'final' cause (Longacre 1976), since final
cause is normally expressed via adjuncts (e.g. purpose clauses, 'John
went *in order to please Harriet*'). Manipulative predicates express a
relation between an agent or a situation which functions as a cause, an
affectee, and a resulting situation. The affectee must be a participant in
the resulting situation. When the cause is a situation, the sentence may
be rendered not by a complement structure, but rather by a structure
like the English *because*-construction:

(382)   Floyd hit Roscoe because Zeke forced him

The meaning of (382) can also be rendered via complementation:

(383)   Zeke's forcing Floyd made him hit Roscoe

(384)   Zeke forced Floyd to hit Roscoe

Manipulative CTPs typically encode situations where the agent attempts to manipulate the affectee into performing some action or assuming some state.

Manipulative predicates may be simple (*cause*) or, when lexical structures in a language permit, they may in addition encode information about the manner of causation (*force*, *make*, *persuade*, *tell*, *threaten*, *let*, *cajole*), sometimes including an illocutionary act (*command*, *order*, *request*, *ask*, and other predicates that are primarily utterance predicates).

The nature of the causative relationship requires a specific temporal order of cause and effect, so complements to manipulative predicates have DTR and are reduced. Since there is an obligatory coreference between the affectee (the DO of the manipulative predicate) and the subject of the complement, the complement subject may be non-overt, resulting in an infinitive. This happens in English and in Spanish (Spanish data from Pat Seaver):

(385)   Max persuaded Nellie to run for mayor

(386)   Juan le   dejó   armar-la
        John him let(3SG) assemble(INF)-it
        'John let him assemble it'

In some languages, equi-deletion requires identity between subjects, so that a sentence-like reduced complement type (e.g. subjunctive) is used instead, as in Lango:

(387)   Dákó   òdìò   lócà nî   'tét   kwèrí
        woman pressed(3SG) man COMP forge(3SG SJNCT) hoe
        'The woman pressed the man to forge the hoe'

The causative relation itself is neutral as to whether the complement proposition is necessarily realized or non-realized. Many languages have devices to indicate such relationships. English, generally speaking, indicates the difference between realized versus non-realized interpretations of complement propositions lexically in the matrix CTP. For example, complements to *force* are interpreted as realized, whereas complements to *persuade* and especially *press* are not:

(388)   I forced Hugh to resign
        (implies Hugh resigned)

(389)   I persuaded Hugh to resign
        (implies that Hugh was convinced that he should resign, but carried no implication about his actual resignation)[30]

(390)   I pressed Hugh to resign
         (quite neutral as to whether or not Hugh resigned)

Other languages may mark this difference by choice of complement type. In the Lango sentence, (387), above, the complement is neutral as to whether it is realized or not. When the subjunctive of (387) is replaced by the paratactic complement of (391), the complement receives a realized interpretation:

(391)   Dákó   òdìò   lócà òtètò   kwèrí
         woman pressed(3SG) man forged(SG INDIC) hoe
         'The woman pressed the man; he forged the hoe'
         (The woman forced the man to forge a hoe)

Causatives, even more than desideratives, are good candidates for lexical union. Below is an example from Amharic (data from Mariam Assefa Morrisey):

(392)   Yɨmət'al
         come(FUT 3SG MASC SUBJ)
         'He'll come'

(393)   Yamət'əwal
         come(CAUSE FUT 3SG MASC OBJ 3SG MASC SUBJ)
         'He'll bring it' (He'll cause it to come)

3.2.9 Modal predicates

Broadly defined, modal predicates would include any predicate expressing modality which is epistemic (concerned with degree of certainty of knowledge) or deontic (concerned with moral obligation or permission). We have included predicates meeting the epistemic part of this definition in the category of propositional attitude predicates. Here we will restrict the term to just those predicates expressing moral obligation and moral necessity, and group these with predicates of ability which resemble them closely in syntactic properties. Modal predicates then, in English will include forms such as *can, be able, ought, should, may,* and *be obliged.* We note that most of these forms have epistemic interpretation as well, a frequently encountered situation across languages.

Modal predicates all have complements with DTR.[31] Complements to modals refer to either future events or states (relative to the time reference of the CTP):

(394)   Leon has to be in Fresno by three

or potential events or states-of-affairs:

(395)   Vladimir can eat a whole pizza

As a result, modals take reduced complements such as subjunctives and infinitives. Modal predicates may give the appearance of being one-place predicates

(396)   It's necessary for Leon to be in Fresno by three

or two-place predicates with an equi-deleted complement subject:

(397)   Leon must be in Fresno by three

Their use with subjunctives in many languages, as in the Albanian (see (398)) and Lori (see (399)) examples below, seems to argue for a two-place analysis, while purely semantic considerations favor the one-place analysis with subject raising:[32]

(398)   Njeriu mundeshte   te   vjedhë   pulën
         man   was able(3SG) COMP steal(3SG SJNCT) chicken
         'The man was able to steal a chicken'

(399)   Pia i-tæres   ke   tile-ye   bedoze
         man PROG-was able(3SG) COMP chicken(OBJ) steal(3SG SJNCT)
         'The man was able to steal a chicken'

Modal predicates are excellent candidates for clause or lexical union (section 2.3); English and other Germanic languages provide examples of clause union with these predicates. In English, a number of modal predicates such as *can, must, should, may,* etc. function as a special syntactic class of verbal auxiliaries with a set of unique syntactic properties (see Palmer 1968, Allen 1966). The Turkish 'necessitative' provides an example of lexical union with this class; *-meli* 'ought' can be suffixed to any verbal root to form a necessitative verbal stem (Lewis 1967):

(400)   Geldim
         'I came'

(401)   Geleceğim
         'I'll come'

(402)   Gelmeliyim
         'I ought to come'

In many languages, subjunctives used as main clauses may be given a modal interpretation, as well as the semantically related imperative sense.

3.2.10 *Achievement predicates*

Achievement predicates were discussed by Karttunen (1971a) under the name of 'implicative' predicates. Achievement predicates can be divided into positive and negative achievement classes. Positive achievement predicates such as *manage, chance, dare, remember to, happen to* and *get to* refer to the manner or realization of achievement. Negative achievement predicates, such as *try, forget to, fail* and *avoid* refer to the manner or reason for the lack of achievement in the complement predication. In both the positive and negative cases the complement has DTR since the time reference of the achievement (or lack of achievement) of the event will have the same time reference as the event (or its non-occurrence). Complements to achievement predicates, then, will take the form of reduced complements.

Complements to achievement predicates (especially negative achievement predicates) frequently represent names of activities or backgrounded propositions and so are compatible with nominalized propositions when these are available (cf. section 3.1.5):

(403)   Zeke tried eating spinach

(404)   Nelson avoids taking baths

3.2.11 *Phasal predicates (aspectuals)*

These predicates have been termed 'aspectuals' by Newmeyer (1969) and others. The useful term 'phasal' is derived from Longacre (1976). Phasal predicates refer to the phase of an act or state: its inception, continuation, or termination, and are represented in English by forms such as *begin, start, continue, keep on, finish, stop*, and *cease*. Complements to phasal predicates have DTR since the time reference of the above-mentioned phase of an event must be the same as that of the event itself. For this reason, phasal predicates are associated with reduced complements.

Phasal notions can be indicated by a variety of techniques aside from phasal predicates in complementation. Many languages have verb affixes or particles for indicating these notions. In some languages, continuation can be indicated by repeating the verb, as we see in this example from Tairora (Vincent 1973):

(405)   Otu   bi otu   bi otu   bi-ro
         go down go go down go go down go-3SG
         'He continued going down'

3.2.12 *Immediate perception predicates*

Immediate perception predicates include forms such as *see, hear, watch*, and *feel* where the predicate names the sensory mode by which the subject directly perceives the event coded in the complement. Also included in this class are predicates like *imagine*, where the event and its perception are entirely mental. Complements to immediate perception predicates have DTR since the immediate perception of an event must have the same time reference as the event itself. Complements to immediate perception predicates will therefore be reduced, though some exceptional cases are noted below.

As mentioned in sections 1.3.6 and 3.1.5, particles are frequently used in forming complements to immediate perception predicates. In these constructions, the subject of the complement proposition is treated as the DO of the CTP and the participle takes this DO as its head. A related construction is found in Lori ((406), data from Stan Murai), French ((407), data from June Mathias), Spanish ((408), data from Pat Seaver), and a few other languages where the complement takes the form of a relative clause with the DO as its head:

(406) Zine   pia-ye   di   ke   tile-ye   i-dozi
       woman man-OBJ saw COMP chicken-OBJ PROG-steal(3SG)
       'The woman saw the man stealing the chicken'

(407) Marie voit Roger qui   mange les pommes
       Marie sees Roger RPRO eat   the apples
       'Mary sees Roger eating the apples'

(408) Oigo   a Juan que toca   la guitarra
       hear(1SG) to John COMP play(3SG) the guitar
       'I hear John playing the guitar'

Both Spanish and French more commonly use infinitives as complements to these predicates.[33]

It is important to note, as Kirsner and Thompson (1976) point out, that semantically it is the entire event, not the argument coded as the matrix direct object, that is perceived. For example, in the sentence

(409)   I smelled Hank spreading the fertilizer

it is not Hank that is smelled. Similar arguments would apply for other instances of raising, for example with *want* in English.

A few languages use ordinary indicative complements with immediate perception predicates, creating a construction that may be identical to the KAK predicate use of perception predicates. Eastern Armenian appears to provide an example of this (data from Galust Mardirussian):

(410)   Kənik-ə   tesav   vor   mard-ə   hav-ə   gojats^hav
      woman-ART saw(3SG) COMP man-ART chicken-ART stole(3SG)
      'The woman saw the man steal the chicken'
      (The woman saw that the man stole the chicken)

Such cases may be difficult to distinguish from relative clause complements where the relative clause has been moved to postverbal position. Some languages differentiate immediate perception versus KAK uses of perception predicates by choice of complementizer. In Malay, for example, the complementizer *bahwa* is normally optional; it is optional with KAK uses of perception predicates but cannot be used with immediate perception senses. *Ingok* 'watch', which has no KAK counterpart, illustrates this (data from Eng-kwong Cheang):

(411)   Saya měn-ingok   (*bahwa) orang itu sědang
      I   TRANS-watch   (COMP)   man   the PROG
      měn-churi   ayam
      TRANS-steal chicken
      'I watched the man stealing the chicken'

Aside from the participles and relative clauses noted above, other sorts of complements otherwise not found in the complement system may be used with immediate predicates. Russian, for example, uses a special complementizer *kak* with the indicative complement type for complements to these predicates. In complementation, *kak* is otherwise used only with the subjunctive for predicates of fearing:

(412)   Ja videl kak   Boris čitaet knigu
      I   saw COMP Boris read book
      'I saw Boris reading a book'

The complement does not undergo tense copying. The KAK use of the above CTP would result in a sentence differing from (412) only in the substitution for *kak* of *čto*, the ordinary indicative complementizer.

Languages can distinguish between agentive (deliberate) and non-agentive (non-deliberate) perception. This is very frequently done in the case of visual perception, for example *watch* versus *see*. Only the non-deliberate forms have counterparts in KAK predicates.

3.2.13 *Negative predicates*
While in the great majority of the world's languages, negation is accomplished via a negative participle, or, more rarely, a negative conjugation or negative verbal stem, a few languages express negation as a CTP which takes the negated proposition as its complement (cf.

chapter 1:4).From a semantic point of view, this state of affairs is quite reasonable since negation can be expressed in logic as a one-place predicate. The rarity of overt negative predicates is more a reflection of the convenience of a negative particle versus a complement construction than of any semantic considerations.

An example of a negative predicate is provided by Fijian (Churchward 1941):

(413)   Ena lako ko koya
        FUT go   ART he
        'He will go'

(414)   Ena sega ni   lako ko koya
        FUT NEG COMP go   ART he
        'He won't go'

Another example is provided by Shuswap (Kuipers 1974):

(415)   X̣əqpnwéw'n
        understand(1SG)
        'I understand'

(416)   Tá? k s-x̣əpqnwéw'n
        NEG ART NZN-understand(1SG)
        'I don't understand'

Complements to negative predicates have DTR since the time reference of a preposition must be the same as its negation.

3.2.14 Conjunctive predicates

A few languages use verbs to translate English conjunctions like *and* and *and then*. Semantically, such conjunctions can be viewed as two-place predicates. Whether the complement to such predicates would have ITR or DTR would depend on the meaning of the predicate.

In Lango, there is a conjunctive predicate *té* meaning 'and then'. This predicate only appears in the habitual aspect and is conjugated for person, agreeing with the subject of the second conjoined clause. The second clause appears in the form of an infinitive, while the first clauses precedes *té* and is not marked as subordinate in any way:

(417)   Àcámò rìŋó àté   màttò   pì
        ate(1SG) meat and then(1SG) drink(INF) water
        'I ate meat and then I drank water'

(418)   Á'bínó   pìttò   kɔ́tí té   dɔ̀ŋɔ̀
        come(1SG) plant(INF) seeds and then(3SG) grow(INF)
        'I'll plant the seeds and then they'll grow'

(419) Òtèdò   rìŋó òté   càmmò
cook(3SG) meat and then(1PL) eat(INF)
'He cooked the meat and then we ate it'

This construction occurs frequently in Lango discourse.

4 Complement systems

With the exception of negative and conjunctive CTPS, all languages have about the same set of uses of CTPS and their complements. All languages do not, however, have the same number or kinds of complement types. In this section, we will examine the ways in which complement types are distributed among the various CTPS.

As mentioned in section 1, languages differ as to the number and kind of complement types available to them. English, for example, has an indicative, a rather moribund subjunctive, an infinitive, a nominalization, and a participle. Lango has an indicative, a subjunctive, a paratactic complement, and an infinitive. Lori has an indicative, a subjunctive, and a nominalization. Romanian has an indicative, a subjunctive, a little-used infinitive, and a participle. Irish has an indicative and a nominalization. As discussed in section 3, each of the complement types mentioned above has a special affinity for certain uses, but since the entire system must be accommodated, the range of any given complement type may be extended beyond its 'ideal' range. In general, the fewer the oppositions available within a complement system, the more likely a given complement type will be extended beyond its ideal range.

We will discuss briefly some representative complement systems. Compare, for example, the description of the Lango system presented below and that given in Noonan (to appear). Where the ranges of two complement types overlap, it is understood that either complement type could occur in that context.

All languages have an s-like indicative complement type, and all languages have some sort of reduced complement type in opposition to the indicative. Complement systems with two members tend to make their primary break at the ITR/DTR distinction, the morphology of the reduced complement type determining to a large degree any other semantic distinctions that may be present in the system. In Albanian, the indicative codes all ITR contexts, the subjunctive, DTR contexts. In Irish, however, the nominalized complement type is not only used in all DTR cases, but is also used in any context where the complement is backgrounded; the nominalized complement type is exploited both as the reduced complement type and as a nominal.

The Albanian subjunctive simply fills the role of reduced complement type; in a two-member system, a subjunctive is seldom used for more than this. This is true also for infinitives in two-member systems. The Albanian situation is typical of many Balkan languages, such as Macedonian, Bulgarian, and Modern Greek. The Irish situation described above is typical of the Celtic languages. A variation on this sort of two-member system is illustrated by Lahu, which contrasts an indicative complement type used in ITR contexts with an infinitive complement type used only in DTR contexts. Malay contrasts an indicative with an infinitive complement type which is distinguished from the indicative in that it cannot form a syntactic constituent with its notional subject and cannot occur with auxiliaries and particles. This complement type has DTR only, occurs only when its notional subject is equi-deleted under identity with the matrix subject or DO. This sort of system is often encountered in languages that do not inflect verbs for tense, aspect, and mood. Another sort of two-member system is found in Squamish and other American Indian languages, where the indicative complement is almost restricted to complements of utterance predicates; the nominalized complement type, which can express full tense–aspect and mood distinctions, is used elsewhere.

Three-member systems typically include indicative, subjunctive, and infinitive or nominalized complement types. In systems like this, the subjunctive frequently codes irrealis modality (section 3.1.1). In Russian, for example, the indicative is used in realis contexts with ITR and for complements to immediate perception predicates. The subjunctive codes irrealis contexts. The infinitive is used in DTR contexts where the complement subject has been equi-deleted under identity with matrix subject or direct object (see Brecht 1974). The subjunctive is used in all other DTR contexts. Persian has a similar system except that it replaces the infinitive with a nominal complement. The Persian nominalized complement has a greater range than the Russian infinitive, since it is used in all the contexts the infinitive is, as well as being used to code backgrounded complements. Lori and Eastern Armenian use their three-member opposition somewhat differently. The indicative is used in all ITR contexts and for complements to immediate perception predicates. The subjunctive codes DTR contexts, while the nominal is restricted to backgrounded contexts. Three-member systems, especially of the first type, are fairly common.

Another sort of three-member opposition is illustrated by Modern Hebrew. Hebrew contrasts an indicative with an infinitive, and there is also a participle used only in immediate perception contexts. The infinitive is used only in DTR contexts, but since raising-to-object is not possible in Hebrew, the infinitive is used only when its notional subject is equi-deleted under identity with either the matrix subject or direct object.

Four-member systems typically include indicative and subjunctive complement types, and two non-s-like complement types. Catalan is typical of this sort of system, with an indicative used in assertive contexts, a subjunctive used in non-assertive contexts, an infinitive in DTR contexts where its notional subject has been equi-deleted under identity with the matrix subject, and a participial complement used for immediate perception complements. This sort of system is typical of the Western Romance languages. Another sort of four-member system is found in Lango, where the indicative codes ITR contexts, with the other three complement types used in DTR contexts: the paratactic complement is used where the complement is taken as expressing a realized situation, the subjunctive is used in unrealized situations, and the infinitive replacing either when the subject is equi-deleted. This sort of system is found in other Nilotic languages. With the effective loss of the subjunctive, most dialects of English have only a four-member system, contrasting an indicative which occurs only in ITR contexts with an infinitive used primarily in DTR contexts (some exceptions have been noted above). The nominalized complement is used for backgrounded information, and the participles occur mainly as complements to immediate perception predicates.

Systems of more than four members are rather uncommon. These systems typically include a contrast of more than two s-like complement types. Classical Greek, for example, contrasted an indicative, a subjunctive, and an aptative, all s-like complement types, with an infinitive and a participial complement type. Conservative forms of English manage a five-way contrast with just two s-like complements, contrasting an indicative, a subjunctive, an infinitive, a nominalization, and a participle.

5 A note on noun complementation

Many grammarians have distinguished ordinary complementation from noun complementation (e.g. Quirk *et al.* 1972, and Huddleston 1971). Noun complements are sometimes referred to as 'appositive clauses'. In fact, the structure of noun complements differs from other instances of complementation only in that the CTP is a noun and not a verb or an adjective. Many of the structures that we have considered in the preceding sections were in fact instances of noun complementation.

Some languages show a marked propensity for rendering predicates as nouns. In Irish, for example, predicates with experiencer arguments are typically nouns, the experiencer assuming an associative relation to the nominalized predicate:

(420)   Tá *súil* agam go   bhfaighidh tú   é
        COP hope at me COMP get(FUT)   you it
        'I hope that you'll get it'

(421)   Tá a *fhios*   agam gur   tháinig sé
        COP its knowledge at me COMP(PAST) came   he
        'I know that he came'

(422)   Tá *aifeála* orm   go   mbuailfear   é
        COP regret on me COMP beat(FUT IMPRS) him
        'I regret that he'll be beaten'

(423)   Tá *amhras* orm   an dtiocfadh sé
        COP doubt on me Q come(FUT) he
        'I doubt whether he'll come'

There is no verbal counterpart of *súil* in Modern Irish, even though other languages, for example English, can express this predicate verbally as well as nominally. But this is not just a peculiarity of Irish. English also has predicates that can function as noun heads of complement constructions, for example *fact*, *idea*, that have no verbal counterpart in the language. Most heads of noun complement constructions in English, however, have verbal counterparts, for example *ability* (be able), *decision* (decide), *hope* (hope), *belief* (believe), *command* (command), *desire* (desire) and *suggestion* (suggest). Though all these nominals are related to verbs, their semantic relations to them may be quite idiosyncratic as the following pairs of nominals show: *continuity* and *continuation* (continue), *referral* and *reference* (refer).

Complements to noun heads typically exhibit the same range of complement types as complements to other sorts of heads, as the following examples show:

(424)   Walt's ability to chew gum and tie his shoes at the same time impressed everyone
        Walt is able to chew gum and tie his shoes at the same time
                                                              (Infinitive)

(425)   Andrea's belief that Max is the King of Greenland annoyed Sally
        Andrea believes that Max is the King of Greenland
                                                              (Indicative)

(426)   Queen Zelda's command that Zeke be shot drew cries of protest

Queen Zelda commanded that Zeke be shot

(Subjunctive)

The distribution of these complement types is dependent on the same set of semantic and pragmatic factors that determine the distribution of complements with other sorts of heads. Complements to noun heads occasionally may have to assimilate to the internal structure of NPS (see chapter III:7 for some discussion of this).

6 Obtaining information about complement systems

Most published grammatical descriptions are inadequate sources for data about the organization of the complement system. One reason for this is that complementation has not, until fairly recently, been considered a single topic for discussion in grammars. What information is available is usually scattered in various places throughout the grammar and at best may be adequate only for the reconstruction of the broad outlines of the system. A useful adjunct to the grammar when no native speaker informants can be found is a good dictionary with a generous supply of illustrative sentences. By making a list of CTPS and checking their dictionary entries, much useful information can be gleaned. Unfortunately, not all dictionaries are helpful in this way, and it is usually only dictionaries of the better-studied languages (with more helpful grammars available in any case) that provide large numbers of illustrative sentences.

It goes without saying that the best technique for obtaining data about complement systems is elicitation from native speaker informants. One should only attempt to elicit data about complementation (or any other types of complex sentences) after a basic sketch of verbal and nominal morphology and syntax has been obtained from the examination of simple sentences.

A useful procedure for obtaining an overview of the system is outlined as follows: First, prepare a list of CTPS. Use the classes of CTPS given in section 3.2 as the basis for the list. Next, select a simple transitive sentence to use as the complement proposition. It is useful to elicit complement types initially with one constant complement proposition, varying it only where the sense or the opportunity to examine certain semantic or syntactic possibilities would suggest a change. In this way, changes in the form of the complement are more easily observed and comparisons more easily made. Now, create sentences from your list of CTPS using the simple transitive sentence as the complement and ask your informant to translate. For instance, you might begin with utterance predicates as CTPS and create sentences like:

(427)   a. The woman said that the boy stole the chicken
        b. The woman asked the man if the boy stole the chicken
        c. The woman told the man that the boy stole the chicken

Be sure to check out the various semantic and grammatical possibilities suggested in the subsections of 3.2. For example, in gathering data about utterance predicates, check out the difference between direct and indirect discourse, as in

(428)   a. The woman said, 'I stole the chicken'
        b. The woman said that she stole the chicken
        c. The woman said that I stole the chicken

After going through your list of CTPS with your basic transitive sentence, vary the predicate in the complement and see if other predicates exhibit the same range of morphological categories in complementation. Be sure to include in your sample the predicates that are most likely to be irregular, for example *be* (if such a predicate exists in the language), *come*, *go*, etc., since these predicates may retain vestiges of categories no longer productive in the system as a whole.

At this stage you should have adequate data to permit you to identify complement types and to begin to speculate on their semantic range *vis-à-vis* the set of CTPS. Make some hypotheses and check them out. A useful way to check out hypotheses of this sort is to find some predicates (like *remember*, in English) that can occur with more than one complement type and try to discover what the semantic difference is in choosing one complement type over the other. Bear in mind also that the grammatical forms representing the complement types in your language are probably not restricted in use solely to the complement system, but are used elsewhere in the grammar. Your hypotheses about the function of these forms within complementation should be compatible with their use elsewhere.

NOTES

1 Headless relatives, as illustrated in
    Wanda knows *what Boris eats*
  are likewise not considered to be complements even though they are, technically, arguments of predicates.

2 See Anderson (1971) and Washabaugh (1975) for discussion of the development of complementizers from adpositions, and Lord (1973) for development from verbs.

3 The differences and similarities are discussed in some detail in Noonan and Bavin (1981) and are briefly summarized in section 2.4.

4 It is important to emphasize that these constructions are complement constructions and not relative constructions (see Kirsner and Thompson 1976 and section 3.2.12 for discussion of this point).

5 In this section all raised arguments are in italics.

6 See section 2.5 and Johnson (1977) for more discussion of this phenomenon. The syntax of raising in English is discussed in Postal (1974). Steever (1977) discusses the semantic consequences of raising in English.

7 Factitive objects are found with three-place, manipulative predicates, where they represent the state or action brought about by the subject's activity on the direct object.

8 It may be that some languages make no use of grammatical relations (Schachter 1976, Noonan 1977). Even among the great majority that do, IO and FO may not function as distinct grammatical relations. See chapter I:2.

9 See, however, Gary and Keenan (1977) for a discussion as to whether there can be more than one direct object.

10 See Comrie (1976), Johnson (1977), and Aissen and Perlmutter (1976) for more discussion of this phenomenon. For a discussion relevant to all aspects of CU and lexical union, see chapter III:6.

11 See Shibatani (1976) for discussion of the syntax and semantics of LU.

12 Discussed in Noonan and Bavin (1981). Serial constructions are discussed in Stahlke (1970), Bamgboṣe (1974), George (1976), and Lord (1973).

13 Exceptions have been noted by Bamgboṣe (1974:27).

14 Examples are from Grosu and Thompson (1977), which should be consulted for more discussion of this phenomenon in English and other languages.

15 Urmson (1963); discussed also by Wittgenstein (1953) and Hooper (1975).

16 *fuil*, 'nasalized' to *bhfuil* after *go*, is the subordinate clause version of the copula *tá*.

17 See R. Lakoff (1970) and Riddle (1975b) for some discussion of the semantics of tense copying in English.

18 Negative raising has been referred to by a number of names in the literature: negative attraction (Jespersen 1964), negative transportation (R. Lakoff 1969), and negative absorption (Klima 1964). Horn (1978) reviews the literature on and current status of negative raising.

19 Sentences like (213b), it should be noted, seem to be ambiguous between a negative raising interpretation and a true negation of the CTP, corresponding to a commitment/non-commitment interpretation of the speaker's evaluation of the complement proposition (Jackendoū 1971). These two interpretations are similar to Lyons' negation of the phrastic versus negation of the neustic, respectively (Lyons 1977).

20 Discourse-dependent complements have the property of being pragmatically presupposed (Kempson 1975).

21 See Lyons (1977) for a discussion of the distinction between denial and assertion of negative propositions.

22 See Lockwood (1968) for discussion of the reduction of the former role of the subjunctive in German.

23 The parenthetical analysis of sentences with *believe* + infinitive only applies, of course, to sentences with first person singular subject.

24 The status of these verb phrases has been the subject of much debate in the transformational literature (e.g. Schachter 1974, Bamgboṣe 1974). A possible diachronic connection between parataxis and serialization is discussed in Noonan and Bavin (1981).

25 But see the discussion of this issue in Kirsner and Thompson (1976) and section 3.2.12.

26 Many of these verbs can also be manipulative predicates (section 3.2.8). The difference between these uses involves whether there is a simple transfer of information (utterance predicates) or a direct attempt to influence or manipulate the addressee (manipulative predicates). The distinction may be a fine one in some cases, but the syntactic consequences are considerable, as in English the difference between an s-like complement and an infinitive.

27 Predicates like *be evident* in

It's evident to George that Ron frequently blunders

seem to allow for two holders of propositional attitude, George and the speaker, since if this sentence is said sincerely (not ironically) the speaker is committed to the truth of the complement proposition.

28 There is a considerable literature on these predicates, for example Kiparsky and Kiparsky (1970), Morgan (1969), Karttunen (1971b), Kempson (1975).

29 Kiparsky and Kiparsky (1970), but see, for example, Kempson (1975), Rosenberg (1975).

30 For some speakers, *persuade* is like *force*, not *press*.

31 Notice that with epistemic interpretations, complements have ITR:

It must be that Arnold owns an Edsel

32 Some discussion of this issue can be found in Jenkins (1972).

33 The use of participles with immediate perception predicates was discussed in section 3.1.5. The relative clause constructions, quite rare cross-linguistically, probably have a similar explanation, due to the functional similarity of participles and relative clauses. These relative clause constructions have been discussed by Kayne (1975), Mathias (1978), and Seaver (1978), who note the differences between these and ordinary relative clauses (which are simply the product of pragmatic factors).

3 Relative clauses

EDWARD L. KEENAN

0 Introduction

Our purpose here is to characterize the types of relative clauses which the languages of the world present. In section 1 below we give a classification of the types of basic restrictive relative clauses with which we shall be concerned. In sections 2 and 3 we discuss the properties of these types and relate them to other properties of the languages in which they occur. In section 4 we discuss *corelatives*, a widespread functional equivalent of restrictive relative clauses. And in section 5 we conclude with a brief mention of other types of relative clauses and relative-like structures.

1 Types of restrictive relative clauses

The typology of restrictive relative clauses (RCs for short) we present is based on the works mentioned below, ones from which we shall often draw examples and terminology, and to which we refer the reader for much more extensive discussion of particular points than can be attempted here: Andrews (1975), who provides a typology for both RCs and corelatives; Keenan and Comrie (1977), who discuss the formation of RCs in fifty-odd languages and present several generalizations concerning which NP positions can be relativized; C. Lehmann (1979), probably the most thorough typology of RCs in the current literature; Peranteau *et al.* (1972), a valuable source book containing twenty-one articles on relativization in different languages; and Schwartz (1971), an early study which relates the form of RCs to the word order types of languages.

We shall regard RCs here as full noun phrases (NPS) of the sort italicized in (1–3) below from English:

(1)   I picked up *two towels that were lying on the floor*

(2)   John gave a check to *the farmer whose cows Bill stole*

(3)   *Every student who Mary advised* passed the exam

Such NPS consist of a determiner (*two, the, every* above), a common noun (*towels, farmer, student* above), and a restrictive clause (*that were lying on the floor, whose cows Bill stole, who Mary advised* above). Semantically the common noun determines a class of objects, which we shall call the *domain* of relativization, and the restrictive clause identifies a subset of the domain, those elements which satisfy the condition given by the restrictive clause. We shall refer to the common noun in an RC which expresses the domain of relativization as the *domain noun*, and the restrictive clause as S_{rel} (since it has in general the syntactic properties of a sentence, though one which lacks to varying extents documented below an NP position).

We take the presence of an S_{rel} to be the defining feature of RCS; NPS such as *two towels, every student*, etc. which lack anything identifiable as a restrictive clause will not be considered RCS. On the other hand there are structures we consider RCS which lack a domain noun, in which case the domain of relativization is the class of objects of which it makes sense to assert the restrictive clause. (4b) below from Malagasy (Malayo-Polynesian) is illustrative.

(4)   a. ny olona mbola tsy tonga
           the people still   not came
           'the people who still haven't come'

       b. ny mbola tsy tonga
           the still   not came
           'those who still haven't come'

We note that *ny* in Malagasy functions only as definite article and can never stand alone as a demonstrative pronoun, in contrast, for example, to *those* in English. So (4b) clearly consists of a determiner *ny* and a restrictive clause *mbola tsy tonga* and does not present overtly a domain noun.

Furthermore the presence of determiners in RCS is also not necessary. In general across languages determiners occur in NPS which are not RCS, and their distribution in RCS is not significantly different from their distribution in NPS in general. Example (5) below from Latin (Justus 1977) illustrates an RC which presents neither a determiner nor a domain noun.

(5)   Qui primus ad funus   venerit   ei   heres meus X
       who first   to funeral come(FUT) to him heir my   ten

       milia   dato
       thousand let him give
       '(He) who comes first to my funeral, let my heir give him ten thousand'

We shall base our classification of RCS on those which do present a domain noun, leaving it to the field worker to notice cases like (4b) above in which the domain noun is absent; and for each type of RC we distinguish, we shall discuss the positions in which determiners may be presented.

Returning now to the English RCS in (1–3), notice that the domain noun (*towels*, etc.) occurs outside the S_{rel}. We shall refer to such RCS as *external* or *headed* relatives. Since S_{rel} occurs to the right of the domain noun in these examples we shall refer to them more specifically as *postnominal external* relatives. Correspondingly, RCS in which the domain noun is outside of S_{rel} and the latter occurs to the left of the domain noun will be called *prenominal external* relatives. (6b) below from Japanese (McCawley 1972:205) is illustrative:

(6) a. Yamada-san ga   sa'ru   o ka't-te   i-ru
         Yamada-Mr SUBJ monkey DO keep-PART be-PRES
         'Mr Yamada keeps a monkey'

     b. Yamada-san ga   ka't-te   i-ru   sa'ru
         Yamada-Mr SUBJ keep-PART be-PRES monkey
         'the monkey which Mr Yamada keeps'

Clearly in (6b) the domain noun *sa'ru* 'monkey' occurs outside and to the right of S_{rel} *Yamada-san ga ka'tte iru*.

External relatives, whether pre- or postnominal, contrast as a class with *internal* relatives in which the domain noun occurs within S_{rel}. Example (7) below from Navajo (Hale and Platero, n.d.) illustrates an internal relative.

(7) Tl'eedaa' hastiin yałti'-ee ałhosh
     last night man   spoke-REL sleep
     'The man who spoke last night is sleeping'

Clearly here both *tl'eedaa'* 'last night' and *yałti'* 'spoke' belong to S_{rel} and the domain noun *hastiin* 'man' occurs between them and is thus properly embedded within S_{rel}. So the subject NP of *ałhosh* 'sleep' is an internal RC.

Our basic classification of RCS then consists in a primary distinction between external and internal relatives, and among the external relatives we distinguish prenominal from postnominal ones.

2 External (headed) relative clauses

2.1 *Distribution*

There is a general tendency across languages to favor postnominal as opposed to prenominal RCS. More specifically, postnominal RCS are almost the only type attested in verb-initial languages (ones which present the verb leftmost in syntactically simple pragmatically unmarked sentences). A partial exception here is Tagalog (Malayo-Polynesian) and possibly other Philippine languages which present both prenominal and postnominal RCS. And even here the postnominal position seems favored when S_{rel} is at all complex.

Further, in verb-medial languages of the svo sort, postnominal RCS are the overwhelming norm and are to our knowledge always the dominant or most productive form of RC. Compared with verb-initial languages however it is more common in svo languages to find both prenominal and postnominal RCS. Examples (8) and (9) below from Finnish and German (Keenan and Comrie 1977:64) respectively are illustrative, the (a) sentences in each case presenting the prenominal forms, the (b) ones the postnominal forms.

(8)   a. Pöydällä tanssinut   poika oli sairas
          on table having danced boy   was sick
          'The boy who danced on the table was sick'

       b. John näki veitsen jolla   mies tappoi kanan
          John saw knife   which with man killed chicken
          'John saw the knife with which the man killed the chicken'

(9)   a. der in seinem Büro arbeitende Mann
          the in his   study working   man
          'the man who is working in his study'

       b. der Mann, der in seinem Büro arbeitet
          the man   who in his   study works
          'the man who is working in his study'

We note that the postnominal forms can be used to relativize any main clause NP in these languages whereas the relativizable positions using the prenominal forms are much more constrained. In German for example only main clause subjects can be relativized using the prenominal strategy. It is in this sense that we claim the postnominal forms to be dominant or more productive.

Finally it is only in verb-final languages that prenominal RCS are the only or most productive form. This is so for example in Japanese, Korean, and Tibetan. However, verb-final languages commonly present any of the other types of RCS as dominant. Thus Yaqui (Uto-Aztecan; Lindenfeld 1973) is verb final as illustrated in (10a) below and presents postnominal RCS as the dominant type, illustrated in (10b).

(10)   a. Wepul oʔoo hu-ka   maso-ta meʔa-k
          one   man this-DEF deer-DEF kill-PERF
          'One man killed this deer'

       b. Hu kari   in acai-ta   hinu-k-aʔu   wece-k
          this house my father-DEF buy-PERF-REL fall-PERF
          'The house which my father bought fell down'

Similarly in verb-final Navajo, while prenominal headed RCs are possible, it is the internal RCs illustrated in (7) above which are the dominant
form. Moreover we may note here (see section 4.1 for discussion) that
corelatives are a functional equivalent of RCs and are common in
verb-final languages. Thus while prenominal RCs are dominant only in
verb-final languages other forms of relativization are common in such
languages.

2.2 Position of the determiner

In headed RCs with a determiner we might expect that the determiner
could occur at either end of the RC or else between the domain noun
and s_{rel}. And in fact all logically possible orders are attested, both
in postnominal and in prenominal RCs. For postnominal the
Det + Head + s_{rel} order is attested from English; the Head + Det + s_{rel}
order is illustrated in (11) below from Urhobo (Kwa, Nigeria); and the
Head + s_{rel} + Det order is illustrated in Yoruba (Kwa, Nigeria) in (12)
below.

(11)   oshale na l-aye   na teye ǫ
       man   the that-woman the hit   him
       'the man that the woman hit'

(12)   isu ti   mo ra lana   naa
       yam REL I buy yesterday that
       'that yam which I bought yesterday'

As regards prenominal RCs, the Det + s_{rel} + Head order has been
illustrated in (9a) from German; the s_{rel} + Det + Head order is illustrated in (13) below from Korean; and the s_{rel} + Head + Det order in
(14) from Basque (Keenan and Comrie 1977:72).

(13)   chaki-ij la-ka   chongmy ngha-n ki salam
       he-of   dog-SUBJ smart-REL   the man
       'the man whose dog is smart'

(14)   gizon-a-k   liburu-a eman dio-n   emakume-a
       man-the-SUBJ book-the give has-REL woman-the
       'the woman that the man has given the book to'

Having noted that all possible orders of Det, Head, and S_{rel} are attested it is perhaps fair to remark that the orders in which the Det is adjacent to the head and thus not separated from it by S_{rel} are more common than the orders in which the Det is separated from the Head by S_{rel}.

2.3 *Marking the position relativized*

Let us use the notation NP_{rel} to refer to the position in S_{rel} which refers to the elements in the domain of relativization. For example in *the men who I know* NP_{rel} is in the direct object (DO) position of S_{rel}; in *the man who I took the money from* it is the object of the preposition *from*; in *the man who left early* it is the subject of the predicate *left early*.

It is an interesting question to consider how languages mark which position in S_{rel} is the NP_{rel} one. For example how do languages in general signal the meaning difference between *the man who John saw*, where NP_{rel} is the DO of *saw*, and *the man who saw John*, where NP_{rel} is the subject of *saw*? There appear to be four ways of presenting NP_{rel}: it may be an ordinary personal pronoun, a special pronominal form peculiar to RCS (in which case it is called a *relative pronoun*), a full NP, or nothing at all, a gap. We consider these possibilities in turn.

2.3.1 NP_{rel} *is a personal pronoun*

In postnominal RCS it is quite common to find NP_{rel} expressed by an ordinary personal pronoun. Example (15) below from Modern Hebrew is illustrative.

(15)   ha-sarim   she-ha-nasi   shalax otam la-mitsraim
        the-ministers that-the-President sent   them to Egypt
        'the ministers that the President sent to Egypt'

Keenan and Comrie (1977) present a dozen-odd languages in which NP_{rel} is typically presented as such a personal pronoun. We may note here that these languages include verb-final languages such as Turkish and Persian which present postnominal RCS. Example (16) below from Persian is illustrative:

(16)   Man zan-i   râ ke John be u   sibe zamini dâd
        I   woman-the DO that John to her potato   gave
        mishenasam
        know
        'I know the woman that John gave the potato to (her)'

We should note that the possibility of presenting NP_{rel} as an ordinary personal pronoun is not independent of which position in S_{rel} NP_{rel} is.

Thus if NP_{rel} is the subject of S_{rel} it is not at all common to find it expressed as a personal pronoun. Thus (17) below from Hebrew is ungrammatical.

(17)   *ha-ish   she-hu makir oti
          the-man that-he knows me
          'the man who knows me'

Somewhat exceptionally, however, if the main predicate of S_{rel} is a predicate adjective then the subject pronoun must be present:

(18)   a. ha-ish   she-hu meod xaxam
           the-man that-he very smart
           'the man who is very smart'

        b. *ha-ish   she-meod xaxam
           the-man that-very smart

The only languages we know of which regularly present subject NP_{rel}s as pronouns are Urhobo and Yiddish. (19) below from Urhobo is illustrative:

(19)   a. Ọ vbere
           she sleep
           'She is sleeping'

        b. John mle aye   l-ọ   vbere
           John saw woman that-she sleep
           'John saw the woman who is sleeping'

On the other hand, if NP_{rel} is the direct object of S_{rel} it is much more common to find it expressed by a personal pronoun. The Hebrew example in (15) above is illustrative, and further examples can be found in colloquial Czech, Genoese, and Persian. And commonly enough here the presence of direct object pronouns is optional. Thus the DO *otam* 'them' in (15) may be omitted and the result is fully grammatical.

And if NP_{rel} is the indirect object or the object of a pre- or postposition in S_{rel} it is even more common to find it expressed by a personal pronoun. (16) above from Persian is illustrative. And to consider a last case, if NP_{rel} is the possessor of an NP in S_{rel} it is even more common to find it expressed by a personal pronoun, even, as is the case in Indonesian, where other NP positions in S_{rel} do not present such pronouns. These facts may be summarized in what Keenan and Comrie (1977) call the Accessibility Hierarchy below:

(20)   Subject > Direct object > Indirect object > Object of pre-
        or postposition > Possessor

The generalization is that the lower NP$_{rel}$ is on the Hierarchy the more common it is to find it expressed by a personal pronoun.

A further Hierarchy generalization also holds here: If a given language presents NP$_{rel}$ as a pronoun for any position in the Hierarchy then it presents NP$_{rel}$ as a pronoun for all lower positions on the Hierarchy. So the presence of pronouns for subject NP$_{rel}$s in Urhobo guarantees that all lower positions on the Hierarchy may be relativized in Urhobo and in all cases pronouns may be present in the NP$_{rel}$ position. Similarly the presence of direct object pronouns in NP$_{rel}$ in Hebrew guarantees the relativizability of all lower positions on the Hierarchy in Hebrew and guarantees that in each case pronouns may be present in NP$_{rel}$.

There is a final generalization here which the field worker should note: namely, RCS which express NP$_{rel}$ as a personal pronoun typically allow a greater range of positions to be relativized compared with RCS which do not use such pronouns (though they may use specifically relative pronouns). For example some languages, such as N. Frisian and Basque, do not easily relativize possessor NPS at all, but possessors are always relativizable in 'pronoun retaining' RCS. Similarly NPS in sentence complements of verbs of thinking and saying are sometimes not relativizable directly in non-pronoun retaining languages such as German and Russian but always are in pronoun retaining languages such as Hebrew, Arabic, and Welsh. (21) below illustrates such non-relativizability in German (Keenan 1975:419), and (22) the corresponding well formed relative in Hebrew.

(21)   a. Du glaubst, dass Fritz das Mädchen liebt
           you think   that Fritz the girl   loves
           'You think that Fritz loves the girl'

        b.*Das Mädchen, das   du glaubst dass Fritz liebt
           the girl   whom you think   that Fritz loves
           'the girl who you think that Fritz loves'

(22)   ha-baxura she-atah xoshev she-Fritz ohev ota
        the-girl   that-you think   that-Fritz loves her
        'the girl that you think that Fritz loves'

We refer the reader to Keenan (1975) for a discussion of many other embedded NP positions which are commonly relativizable using pronoun retaining RCS.

The reader may have noticed that all our examples of RCS expressing NP$_{rel}$ as a personal pronoun were postnominal ones. This is not an accident of illustration. It very rarely happens that prenominal RCS regularly retain personal pronouns in the NP_{rel} position. The only clear counterexample we know to this claim is Mandarin, as illustrated in (23) below:

(23) a. wo da-le   (ta) yidum de neige nanhaizi
         I hit-PERF him once REL that boy
         'the boy that I hit once'

      b. wo bei ta   da-le   yidum de neige nanhaizi
         I by him hit-PERF once REL that boy
         'the boy by whom I was hit once'

(The pattern of pronoun retention in Mandarin is like that of Hebrew: not normal for NP_{rel} the subject of S_{rel}, optional if NP_{rel} is the direct object of S_{rel}, and generally obligatory otherwise.)

   Aside from the Mandarin example however, the only other examples of personal pronoun NP_{rel}s we know of are the occasional use of such when NP_{rel} is a possessor. (13) above from Korean in fact illustrates such a case.

2.3.2 NP_{rel} is a relative pronoun

Relative pronouns are pronominal elements occurring in S_{rel} which are distinct from the ordinary definite personal pronouns which occur in simple declarative sentences. They are nominal in that they mark nominal properties such as gender, number, and case. They are pronominal in that they are drawn from a small closed class; in fact they are typically the same as, or morphologically related to, the demonstrative pronouns or the interrogative pronouns in the language. (24) below from German illustrates the relative pronouns *den/die/das*.

(24) a. der Mann, den   Marie liebt
         the man   who(MASC SG ACC) Mary loves
         'the man who Mary loves'

      b. die Frau, die   er liebt
         the woman who(FEM SG ACC) he loves
         'the woman who he loves'

      c. das Mädchen, das   er liebt
         the girl   who(NEUT SG ACC) he loves
         'the girl who he loves'

Let us note first that relative pronouns (RPROS) are limited to postnominal RCS; we know of no prenominal relatives in any language which clearly present relative pronouns. We turn now to a more detailed consideration of the properties of RPROS.

Note first from the German examples above that the RPRO marks the
case of NP$_{rel}$ and agrees with the domain noun in features such as number
and gender. Such case coding and agreement in number and gender are
completely typical properties of RPROS, though we may note that there
are occasional cases cited in the literature where the case marking on the
RPRO assimilates to that independently given on the domain noun. Latin
and the dual RPROS in Classical Arabic are examples here.

Furthermore the RPRO can normally be constructed with the prepositions or postpositions used independently for full NPS in the language.
(25) below from French is illustrative:

(25)   la femme avec qui   j'ai   parlé
        the woman with whom I have spoken
        'the woman with whom I spoke'

Secondly, RPROS are commonly related to demonstratives, interrogatives, or both. In the German examples in (24) above the RPROS are
identical to the definite article, which itself still functions independently
as a demonstrative pronoun, though normally reinforced by an independent deictic such as *da* 'there'. For example:

(26)   Ich habe den-da   gekauft
        I   have that (one)-there bought
        'I bought that one'

The use of interrogative pronouns as relative pronouns is well known
from French and English. (27) from Indonesian is a further example.

(27)   a. Kapada siapa yang Ali memberi ubi kentang itu?
           to   who that Ali give   potato   this
           'To whom did Ali give the potato?'

        b. perempuan kapada siapa Ali beri ubi kentang itu
           woman   to   who Ali gave potato   this
           'the woman to whom Ali gave the potato'

RPROS formed from combinations of demonstrative and interrogative
pronouns are cited for Classical Nahuatl (Uto-Aztecan; Rosenthal 1972)
and Georgian (Caucasian; Aronson 1972). (28) below from Tzeltal
(Mayan) is illustrative.

(28)   a. Mač'a la   smah te   anze?
           who PAST hit DEM woman
           'Who hit the woman?' (Or, 'Who did the woman hit?')

        b. te winike te   mač'a la   smah te   Ziake
           DEM man   DEM who PAST hit DEM Ziak
           'The man who Ziak hit' (Or, 'the man who hit Ziak')

It appears clear here that the combination of the demonstrative *te* 'this' and the interrogative *mac'a* 'who?' function together to form an RPRO.

Third, note that the RPRO almost always occurs leftmost in S_{rel}. To our knowledge this is always the case, as noted in Schwartz (1971), if the RPRO is independently an interrogative pronoun. But this may sometimes fail to be the case if the RPRO is not independently an interrogative. For example in (296) below (Keenan 1972:186) from Luganda (Bantu), the RPRO prefixes to the main verb and is thus not clause initial when the direct object is NP_{rel} (Luganda, like most Bantu languages, has svo as its basic word order).

(29)   a. Omukazi ya-kuba omusajja
        woman she-hit man
        'The woman hit the man'

        b. omusajja omukazi gwe-ya-kuba
        man   woman   RPRO-she-hit
        'the man who the woman hit'

It has however been pointed out by Givón (1973) that in several Bantu languages, for example Dzamba, relativization on the direct object triggers the postposing of the subject NP with the result that the RPRO is leftmost in its clause.

We have already noted that RCs formed with personal pronouns and ones formed with relative pronouns for NP_{rel} are similar in distribution in that both are largely limited to postnominal RCs (relative pronoun types being entirely limited to postnominal RCs). It is perhaps not surprising then to find languages which present RCs formed in both ways. Modern Czech, Modern Greek, and Slovenian all present both ways of forming RCs. (30) below from Czech is illustrative:

(30)   a. Jan viděl toho muže, co ho to   děvče uhodilo
        John saw that man   REL him that girl   hit
        'John saw the man that the girl hit (him)'

        b. Jan viděl toho muže, kterého to   děvče uhodilo
        John saw that man   whom   that girl   hit
        'John saw the man whom the girl hit'

Similarly, Modern Hebrew is probably counted among the languages presenting both types of postnominal RCs. For note that alongside of (15), repeated below as (31a), we also have (31b) in which the retained pronoun *otam* 'them' has been fronted to form a single phonological word with the morphologically invariant complementizer *she-*.

(31)   a. ha-sarim   she-ha-nasi   shalax otam la-mitsraim
            the-ministers that-the-President sent   them to Egypt
            'the ministers that the President sent to Egypt'

        b. ha-sarim   she-otam ha-nasi   shalax la-mitsraim
            the-ministers that-them the-President sent   to Egypt
            'the ministers whom the President sent to Egypt'

Treating *she-otam* 'that-them' as a single word we can reasonably call it
an RPRO. It agrees in number and gender with the domain noun *sarim*
'ministers' (the gender distinction being neutralized in the plural but
morphologically distinctive in the singular) and codes the case of NP_{rel},
namely accusative. And let us note in any event that the attraction of the
retained personal pronoun to the clause-initial or complementizer
position is not peculiar to Hebrew; it is also illustrated in (30a) from
Czech.

2.3.3 NP_{rel} is a full NP

If NP_{rel} occupies a major position in S_{rel}, for example subject, or object,
or even object of a simple adposition (i.e., a preposition or a postposition), we do not find it expressed by a full (non-pronominal) NP in either
prenominal or postnominal RCS. We have however found a few cases in
prenominal RCS where NP_{rel} is embedded within another NP and is
expressed by a full NP. We have an example of this in (32b) from Tibetan
(Mazaudon 1976). (32a) illustrates the more usual form of RCS in
Tibetan.

(32)   a. Peemɛ   khii-pa   thep the   nee   yin
            Peem(ERG) carry-PART GEN book the(ABS) I(GEN) be
            'The book Peem carried is mine'

        b. Peemɛ   coqtsee   waa-la   kurka
            Peem(ERG) table(GEN) under-DAT cross(ABS)

            thii-pe   coqtse the   na   noo-qi yin
            write-PART GEN table   the(ABS) I(ABS) buy-PRES be
            'I will buy the table under which Peem made a cross'

We have a comparable example from Quechua, but the scarcity of
examples leaves it open as to whether this should be considered a
regular way of forming complex prenominal RCS or else merely an
artifact of the complexity of the example. (We may note that while our
Quechua example was elicited, the Tibetan example is taken from
spontaneous discourse.)

    On the other hand we have found no such RCS among our very large
corpus of postnominal RCS, so there may be some regular difference here

between prenominal and postnominal external RCs. This difference may be somewhat mitigated by the following two observations, however. First, we do have cases of postnominal RCS in which S_{rel} contains a repetition of the domain noun, but these are cases where S_{rel} is separated from the domain noun by material in the sentence extraneous to the RC properly speaking. (33) from Latin (Greenough 1903) is illustrative:

(33)   Loci   natura erat haec quem locum nostri
        of the ground nature was this which ground our   (men)

        delegerant
        chose
        'The nature of the ground which (ground) our men had chosen
        was this'

And second we also find cases where S_{rel} repeats (or nearly repeats) the domain noun, but where the entire RC seems to have a non-restrictive interpretation, that is, S_{rel} does not seem to function to restrict the domain of relativization but merely to make an additional assertion about its elements. (34) below from Serbo-Croatian (Browne 1973) is perhaps illustrative:

(34)   roman o   ratu, koje delo prevodim
        novel about war, which work I am translating
        'A novel about war, which work I am translating'

2.3.4 NP_{rel} is not present at all

Here we consider RCs in which there is no element in S_{rel} which expresses NP_{rel}. RCS in English such as *two students I saw*, *the man I gave the money to*, etc. illustrate this sort. Note that in such RCS S_{rel} may be introduced by a complementizer which is not a nominal (or pronominal) element. (35) below from Hebrew, as well as its English translation, is illustrative:

(35)   ha-nashim she-ani makir
        the-women that-I   know
        'the women that I know'

The complementizer *she-* in Hebrew serves to introduce a great variety of subordinate clauses, such as complements of verbs of thinking and saying (see example (22)) and is thus a general complementizer, not a pronominal element of any sort. In particular it never functions alone as a noun or pronoun, does not mark gender and number, and does not code the case of NP_{rel}.

When no element in S_{rel} expresses NP_{rel}, as in the examples above, we shall say that NP_{rel} has been *gapped* and sometimes refer to such RCs as

being formed by *gapping*, noting that the term *gapping* is used differently in the literature on generative grammar.

We can offer here a few generalizations concerning the use of gapping
strategies in the formation of RCs. First, while both prenominal and
postnominal RCs may be formed by gapping, we should note that
gapping is the overwhelmingly dominant mode of RC formation in
prenominals, which, as we have seen, never use relative pronouns and
only sporadically present NP_{rel} as a personal pronoun or (even more
rarely) as a full NP. On the other hand, the use of personal pronouns,
and to a slightly lesser extent relative pronouns, is very common in
postnominal RCs.

Second, with respect to NP positions given on the Accessibility
Hierarchy, (20), we find the distribution of gapping strategies to be
roughly the opposite of pronoun retaining strategies. More specifically,
if a given language can relativize a position low on the Hierarchy by
gapping then it can generally relativize all higher positions by gapping
(see Keenan and Comrie (1977) for a more detailed statement). Thus
NP_{rel} is most likely to be gapped if it is the subject of S_{rel}, next most likely
if it is the direct object, etc. And at the bottom of the Hierarchy we find
that possessors are very rarely relativized by gapping (though we do
occasionally find such, as in older forms of English where we could say
things like *the village that I walked down the main street*).

Moreover the possibility of gapping the object of an adposition is an
interesting one and distinguishes somewhat between prenominal and
postnominal relatives. We may sometimes, though not commonly, gap
the object of a preposition in a postnominal RC, as in English *the man I
took the money from*. English is unusual in the freedom with which it
allows prepositions to be stranded by gapping in RCs, though some
related languages such as N. Frisian and Swedish also permit it (with
somewhat less freedom). (36) below from Swedish is illustrative:

(36)   Han är en man, som jag kan lita på
        he   is a man, that I   can rely on
        'He is a man that I can rely on'

On the other hand we have no clear cases where a prenominal RC gaps
the object of a postposition leaving the postposition itself stranded in
S_{rel}. Thus the norm here, in English paraphrase, is to say *the stick I hit
the dog* and not *the stick I hit the dog with*. The closest thing we have as
an exception to this claim is given by (37b) below from Quechua (Weber
1978). Note first that in (37a) the subject NP is nominative as expected
and triggers verb agreement. The head of the RC subject however, *roopa*
'clothes', functions as a comitative in S_{rel}, and as expected, the comita-

tive postposition *-wan* is not present in (37a). However, in (37b) it is present, though not stranded in S_{rel}. It appears to have floated up to the head of the RC, apparently putting the subject of the main verb in the comitative case. Note that the subject NP still behaves like a subject; in particular it triggers verb agreement on *drying*.

(37)   a. Yaku-man yayku-shal roopa-ø   chakikuykan
          water-GOAL enter-REL   clothes-NOM they are drying
          'The clothes with which he entered the water are drying'

       b. Yaku-man yayku-shan roopa-wan   chakikuykan
          water-GOAL enter-REL   clothes-COMITATIVE they are drying
          'The clothes with which he entered the water are drying'

(We should note that (37a) is actually ambiguous, semantically, the preferred reading being 'The clothes which entered the water are drying'. Nonetheless the translation given in (37a) is a reading of it.)

2.4 *Which NP positions can be relativized?*

The question of which positions in a clause may function as NP_{rel} has been a central concern of much recent work in generative grammar. We cannot attempt to summarize that extensive literature here but will content ourselves with a few broad generalizations useful for the field worker. We refer the reader to Ross (1967) for a broad and insightful statement of many positions in English which cannot function as NP_{rel}s, and we refer the reader to Chomsky (1981) for a current statement of these facts (and many others) within the framework of contemporary generative grammar.

Let us note first, as pointed out in the previous sections, that the question of which positions in a language can be relativized is not independent of the RC forming strategy used. Other things being equal, more positions can be relativized if personal pronouns are presented in the NP_{rel} position than if they are not. Ross (1967) for example observed that NPS in single branches of a coordinate structure cannot be relativized in English. Thus from (38a) below we cannot form (38b).

(38)   a. The boy and the girl left early

       b. *the girl that the boy and left early

Similarly, NPS within complex NPS (ones headed by a noun) are unrelativizable in English. From (39a) we cannot form (39b).

(39)   a. I know the man who left the hat on the table

       b. *the hat which I know the man who left on the table

However, these positions are not uncommonly relativizable using pronoun retaining strategies. Thus (40) below is a grammatical translation of (39b) above in Welsh (Keenan 1975:407).

(40)   ... 'r het y   gwn   y dyn a' i gadewodd ar y   ford
        the hat that I know the man that it left   on the table
        'the hat that I know the man who left it on the table'

And (41) below illustrates relativization into a coordinate structure in Egyptian Arabic (not quite comparable with (38b) above, though the comparable English relative is still staggeringly ungrammatical).

(41)   al-rajul allathi hua wa ibna-hu thahabu ille New York
        the-man that   he and son-his went   to New York
        'the man that he and his son went to New York'

Similarly, current work in generative grammar generally rejects relativization in embedded questions (*wh*-islands) as ungrammatical in English, as indicated in (42) below. Yet its translation into the pronoun retaining Hebrew in (43) is completely natural.

(42)   *?the crimes that the police don't know who committed

(43)   ha-pshaim she-ha-mishtara lo yodat mi   bitsea   otam
        the-crimes that-the-police not know who committed them
        'the crimes that the police don't know who committed (them)'

Having noted that pronoun retaining strategies are more effective means of forming RCs than RPRO or gapping strategies, we must hasten to add that, holding the strategy constant, there are still very great differences among languages. Thus of the twelve pronoun retaining languages studied in Keenan (1975) many did not accept relativization into complex NPS (and many did). Similarly, while many languages which form RCs by gapping do not permit relativization into complex NPS, some such as Japanese (McCawley 1972), Korean, and Scandinavian languages often do.

We have seen then that some languages are very generous in their RC forming possibilities. Conversely, and of somewhat greater relevance to the field worker who at least initially need not be concerned with relativization into complex NPS, some languages have very restrictive means of forming RCs. Among these are Malagasy and the Philippine languages, where by and large only main clause subjects can be relativized. That is, NP_{rel} is always understood to be the subject of S_{rel}. Thus compare (44b) and (44c) from Malagasy (cf. Keenan 1972:171):

(44)   a. Manasa ny lamba ny vehivavy
           wash   the clothes the woman
           'The woman is washing the clothes'

       b. ny vehivavy (izay) manasa ny lamba
           the woman   that wash   the clothes
           'the woman who is washing the clothes'

       c.*ny lamba (izay) manasa ny vehivavy
           the clothes that wash   the woman
           'the clothes that the woman is washing'

(44b) is a straightforward postnominal RC in which NP$_{rel}$ is the subject of S$_{rel}$. *izay* is a morphologically constant form which introduces S$_{rel}$ and whose occurrence is optional. (44c) would appear to be an RC in which NP$_{rel}$ is the direct object of *manasa* 'wash', but it is ungrammatical on the intended reading. It can only mean 'the clothes that are washing the woman', which informants reject as nonsense. And if *ny vehivavy* in (44c) is replaced by the nominative form of the personal pronoun (*izy*) then there is no way of construing the result as grammatical at all. Conclusion: NP$_{rel}$ is always understood to function as the subject of S$_{rel}$.

How then in such languages do we manage to talk about the clothes that someone is washing? The answer is that we must avail ourselves of the highly developed voicing systems in these languages to present as a subject the NP position we want to relativize. Thus if we passivize (44a) above we obtain (45a) below in which *ny lamba* 'the clothes' is the subject, and the corresponding RC in (45b) is fully grammatical.

(45)   a. Sasan'ny vehivavy   ny lamba
           washed by the woman the clothes
           'The clothes are washed by the woman'

       b. ny lamba (izay) sasan'ny   vehivavy
           the clothes that washed by the woman
           'the clothes that are washed by the woman'

Similarly, if we want to relativize on the instrumental NP *ny savony* 'the soap' from (46a) below we must first present the sentence in the instrumental voice in (46b) in which the instrumental NP is the subject (it occurs sentence finally and without a preposition as do subjects generally in Malagasy) and then relativize it as in (46c).

(46)   a. Manasa lamba amin'ny savony Rasoa
           wash   clothes with the soap Rasoa
           'Rasoa is washing clothes with the soap'

b. Anasan-dRasoa   lamba ny savony
   wash with-by Rasoa clothes the soap
   'The soap is being washed clothes with by Rasoa'

c. ny savony (izay) anasan-dRasoa   lamba
   the soap   that wash with-by Rasoa clothes
   'the soap that Rasoa is washing clothes with'

Formally, as we have characterized RC forming strategies above, the Malagasy relatives are formed straightforwardly by gapping, subject to the condition that the NP gapped is the subject of the clause. In order to determine the semantic role that NP_{rel} bears to S_{rel}, however, we must check the voice on the main verb of S_{rel}. If it is active then NP_{rel} is both a surface and an underlying subject of S_{rel}. If the verb is in a direct object passive form then NP_{rel} is the underlying direct object of the verb; if it is in the instrumental passive then it is an underlying instrumental, etc. Malagasy has four voices in terms of which underlying semantic roles of NP_{rel} may be coded. Philippine languages typically have more, often six, and on some analyses even more. We refer the reader to Keenan (1972) for more detailed treatment of the Malagasy type relatives, and to Schachter and Otanes (1972) for a detailed description of the voicing system in Tagalog.

The Malagasy data above illustrates a useful generalization concerning the possibilities of RC formation across languages: namely, if a language has a restricted set of positions which can be relativized, these will always include subjects. If they include only subjects then the language will provide some means for presenting patients, instrumentals, etc. as subjects enabling them to be relativized. Thus subjects are universally the most relativizable of NPs, and in fact all languages to our knowledge permit RCs in which NP_{rel} is the subject of S_{rel}.

Moreover this generalization can be extended in two directions. In the first place, recalling the Accessibility Hierarchy given in (20), one might wonder whether there are languages which restrict the relativizable positions to subject and direct object, providing means of presenting oblique NPs like instrumentals, locatives, benefactives, etc. as either subjects or objects, whence they would be relativizable. And in fact many Bantu languages appear to fall into this category. Thus from an active sentence like (47a) below from Luganda (Keenan 1972:186) we cannot directly relativize the instrumental NP *ekiso* 'knife', as illustrated in (47b).

(47)   a. John yatta enkonko n'-ekiso
       John killed chicken   with-knife
       'John killed the chicken with the knife'

b. *ekiso John (na)   kye-yatta enkoko (na)
knife John with REL-killed chicken with
'the knife with which John killed the chicken'

However, Luganda and Bantu languages quite generally have very productive means for presenting oblique NPS as surface direct objects. Thus in (48a) below the verb *yatta* 'killed' takes a non-final suffix *-is-* putting it in an instrumental form in which the instrumental NP *ekiso* 'knife' is presented as a surface direct object, whence it can be directly relativized as in (48b) (TA stands for 'Tense–Aspect').

(48)   a. John yatt-is-a   ekiso enkoko
John kill-INSTR-TA knife chicken
'John killed with a knife the chicken'

b. ekiso John kye-yatt-is-a   enkoko
knife John REL-kill-INSTR-TA chicken
'the knife with which John killed the chicken'

We refer the reader to Keenan and Comrie (1977) for further discussion of Hierarchy generalizations in RC formation.

Returning now to the claim that subjects are always relativizable we should note that not all subjects are equally relativizable. Specifically subjects of intransitive verbs are more relativizable than subjects of transitive ones in the sense that some languages do not permit relativization on transitive subjects but do on intransitive ones, in which case of course they provide a means of detransitivizing transitive verbs in such a way that the original transitive subject is now the intransitive subject, whence it can be relativized. Languages which illustrate this strategy are K'ekchi (Mayan; Berenstein 1977), Dyirbal and Yidiɲ (Australia; Dixon 1972), and Eskimo (Creider 1977). All these languages are ergative as regards either verb agreements, case marking, or both. (49) below from K'ekchi is illustrative. (49a) gives an active transitive sentence in the most usual vos order (the subject can be fronted yielding an svo order with some topicalization effect). (49b) shows the ungrammaticality of attempting to directly relativize on the transitive subject of (49a). (49c) presents (49a) in the so-called antipassive (ANTIPASS) form in which the main verb has become intransitive, taking only subject agreement but no object agreement as in the active transitive form. The subject *li kwi:nq* 'the man' is fronted. (49d) indicates the grammatical RC formed by relativizing *li kwi:nq* 'the man' from (49c).

(49)   a. S-ø-s-sak'   li   isq   li kwi:nq
PAST-3SG ABS-3SG ERG-hit the woman the man
'The man hit the woman'

b. *li kwi:nq li   s-∅-s-sak'   li isq
   the man   that PAST-3SG ABS-3SG ERG-hit the woman
   'the man who hit the woman'

c. Li kwi:nq s-∅-sak'-ok   re li isq
   the man   PAST-3SG ABS-hit-ANTIPASS PREP the woman
   'The man hit to the woman'

d. li kwi:nq li   s-∅-sak'-ok   re li isq
   the man   that PAST-3SG ABS-hit-ANTIPASS PREP the woman
   'the man who hit the woman'

2.5 The form of s_{rel}

We shall consider here the various ways in which s_{rel} differs from a main clause declarative sentence. We have already discussed the most obvious difference, namely the various ways in which NP_{rel} is marked. We have also remarked in passing that postnominal relatives may be preceded by a morphologically invariant complementizer. Similarly, prenominal relatives may be followed by a morphologically invariant form as illustrated in (23) above from Mandarin (where the particle *de* is invariant) and in (14) from Basque (the particle *n*). Our impression is that the use of such clause-final complementizers in prenominal RCs is less common than the use of clause-initial complementizers in postnominal RCs. Moreover we know of no cases where the clause-final complementizer in RCs is identical to the clause-final complementizer used with sentential objects of verbs of thinking and saying. However, this may merely reflect an absence of knowledge on our part and not a regularity concerning prenominal RCs.

A more regular difference between prenominal and postnominal RCs concerns the form of the main verb of s_{rel}, which we shall denote by v_{rel}. In prenominal RCs, v_{rel} is almost always in some sort of non-finite form, that is a form different from the one it would have as the main verb of a simple declarative sentence. Typically v_{rel} exhibits a reduction in tense–aspect marking and in verb agreement morphology compared with main clause declarative verbs. We have often above called such verb forms participles; we have examples in (8a) from Finnish, (9a) from German, and (32) from Tibetan. (50) below from Turkish is another example, which illustrates the common enough property of such s_{rel}s that the subject (when it is not NP_{rel}) may be put in the genitive or possessor case.

(50)   John-'un Mary-ye ver-dig-i   patates-i yedim
   John-GEN Mary-IO give-VN-his potato-DO I ate
   'I ate the potato that John gave to Mary'
   (lit: 'I ate the potato of John's giving to Mary')

We may note that the prenominal RCs in Japanese do not put v_{rel} in a non-finite or specifically relative form, but the Japanese case appears to be the exception among prenominal RCs here.

By contrast postnominal RCs most typically present v_{rel} in the form it would have as the main verb of a declarative sentence though this is certainly not always the case. For example in (10b) above from Yaqui, v_{rel} takes some sort of subordinate suffix *-aʔu* which we glossed simply as REL though we do not know if this suffix is specific to RCs or has a more general subordinating function. Another example is given by Swahili (Bantu), where v_{rel} takes a concord marker agreeing with the head noun in addition to subject and object concord markers. Similarly in Dyirbal (Dixon 1977) v_{rel} takes a specifically relative suffix. And in certain Bantu languages, such as Kinyarwanda (Kimenyi 1976) and Haya (Duranti 1977) v_{rel} takes a tone marking distinct from that it would have as a main clause declarative verb.

This completes our discussion of external (headed) relative clauses. We turn now to internal relatives.

3 Internal relative clauses

Internal RCs, recall, are ones which present a domain noun internal to S_{rel} and are thus syntactically headless. Our knowledge of the syntactic properties of such RCs is much more limited than in the case of external RCs so our discussion of them will be limited to a variety of examples and some comments on their obvious properties.

First let us establish that internal RCs are indeed NPs, a point which in some cases at least is not immediately obvious since the domain noun occurs in a normal NP position in S_{rel} and consequently S_{rel} may appear to be simply some sort of subordinate clause rather than an NP. In the examples which follow, however, it seems best to treat S_{rel} as a clause which has been sufficiently nominalized to take determiners, case markings, and adpositions, all properties which are characteristic of NPs. Thus consider (51) below from Tibetan.

(51) Peemɛ   thep   khii-pa   the   nee   yin
      Peem(ERG) book(ABS) carry-PART the(ABS) I (GEN) be
      'The book Peem carried is mine'

In this example S_{rel} is *Peemɛ thep khii-pa* which looks rather like a simple sentence except that its main predicate *khii* 'carry' is in a 'participial' (or 'nominal') form. And it appears that S_{rel} is sufficiently nominal to take the determiner *the* 'the' (this is not a misprint) in the absolutive case, the case required by the predicate *nee yin* 'is mine'.

Similarly consider the internal RC functioning as the subject of (52c) below from Diegueño (Hokan, Amerindian; Gorbet 1972). (52a) and (52b) are simple declarative sentences in Diegueño. Note that in (52a) the noun ʔəwa: 'house' takes a definiteness marker -pu and a locative postposition -Lʸ.

(52) a. ʔəwa:-pu-Lʸ ʔciyawx
         house-DEF-in I will sing
         'I will sing in the house'

      b. Tənay   ʔəwa:-ø ʔəwu:w
         yesterday house-DO I saw
         'I saw the house yesterday'

      c. Tənay   ʔəwa:ø ʔəwu:w-pu-Lʸ ʔciyawx
         yesterday house-DO I saw-DEF-in   I will sing
         'I will sing in the house that I saw yesterday'

Note here that the subject of (52c) is identical to sentence (52b) except that it takes the definiteness marker -pu and the locative postposition Lʸ.

Example (53) below illustrates an internal RC from Wappo (Amerindian; Li and Thompson 1977) where S_{rel} takes a non-zero case marker.

(53)   ʔi čhuya-ø   tumt-i   šoýikhiʔ
       me house-DO bought-SUBJ burned down
       'The house I bought burned down'

We note here that the subject ʔi 'me' of S_{rel} is in the direct object case form, it being a peculiarity of Wappo that subjects of subordinate clauses quite generally take this case form.

As a final example note (54b) below from Bambara (W. Africa; Keenan and Comrie 1977:45 and cf. Bird 1968) where the internal RC occurs as the object of the verb *san* 'buy'. (We have bracketed the internal RC as the example is visually hard to parse.) (54a) is a simple declarative sentence.

(54) a. ne ye so   ye
         I PAST horse see
         'I saw a horse'

      b. tye ye [ne ye so   min ye] san
         man PAST I PAST horse REL see buy
         'The man bought the horse which I saw'

Additional examples of internal RCs may be found in Quechua.

On the basis of the relatively few examples of internal RCS we have cited we may tentatively advance only a few generalizations concerning their distribution and internal syntactic properties. Concerning distribution, it appears that clear cases of internal RCS are present only in languages whose basic word order is SOV. At least, all the examples cited satisfy this condition, though we might note that Bambara has SOVX as a basic word order (i.e. NPS other than subject and direct object follow the verb). Moreover we may note that many of the languages cited above for internal RCS also present prenominal RCS, for example Tibetan, Quechua, and Navajo.

Second, contrasted with external RCS it appears that NP_{rel} in internal RCS is in general not distinctively marked. Only in the Bambara example do we have any marker on NP_{rel} (*min*). As a result such RCS could appear to be open to a high degree of ambiguity according to which NP in S_{rel} is semantically regarded as defining the domain of relativization. And it does in fact appear that such relatives are ambiguous in just this way. (55) below from Diegueño is illustrative:

(55) Xatəkcok-∅ wi:-m   ʔtuc-pu-c   nʸiLʸ
      dog-DO   rock-COMITATIVE I hit-DEF-SUBJ was black
      'The rock I hit the dog with was black' or
      'The dog I hit with the rock was black'

Third, to judge from our limited sample it appears that S_{rel}, considered independently of whatever nominal markings it takes, may occur either in the same form it would have as a main clause (Diegueño) or show various markings of subordinate clauses (non-finite V_{rel} in Tibetan, case change in Wappo).

Finally, we note that our data is insufficient to judge the range of NPS relativizable by internal RCS. All examples we have are ones in which a major NP of S_{rel} has been relativized; we don't know whether, for example, NPS within complex NPS may be relativized in this way.

4.0 Corelatives

In addition to external and internal RCS, translations of English relative clauses into many languages commonly elicit a structure which we call *corelatives* (COREL). These are not NPS and thus *a fortiori* not RCS on our definition, but they are the functional equivalent of RCS in many languages, so the field worker interested in RCS should be aware of their existence. In their most widespread form corelatives have a form which we may diagram as follows:

(56)

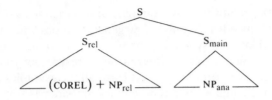

S_{main} above indicates a main clause. It can stand alone as a well formed sentence. S_{rel} above is a subordinate clause which cannot stand alone as a complete sentence. In contrast to internal RCs, however, S_{rel} here does not take nominal markings such as determiners, case markers, and adpositions and is thus best thought of as a sentence rather than an NP. It presents a noun, which we have called NP_{rel} above, which is normally accompanied by a distinctive marker called COREL above. It is typically only the presence of this marker which is responsible for the subordinate status of S_{rel}. Otherwise (there are some exceptions) S_{rel} looks like a main clause. In particular it has its full complement of NPs and its verb is normally finite. Basically the presence of COREL in S_{rel} tells us that the NP so marked will be referred to by some NP in the following clause, S_{main}. That NP has been designated as NP_{ana} above, for anaphoric NP. (57) below from Hindi illustrates the corelative structure:

(57) Jis   a:dmi ka kutta bema:r hai, us   a:dmi ko mai ne
      COREL man GEN dog   sick   is, that man DO I   ERG
      dekha
      saw
      'I saw the man whose dog is sick'
      (lit: 'Which man's dog is sick, that man I saw')

We note that the COREL marker *jis*, in various case forms, is specific to these structures and does not occur independently as an interrogative pronoun, as our 'literal' translation into English might suggest. Note further that the corelative NP in S_{rel} and its anaphor in S_{main} both occur initially in their clause. This is the most common pattern; other patterns in which NP_{rel} or NP_{ana} are not clause initial are possible.

4.1 Distribution of corelatives

Downing (1973), the most thorough treatment of corelatives we know of, notes that corelatives are limited to verb-final languages, and, in fact, are largely limited to 'loose' verb-final ones, namely ones which permit some NPs, especially 'heavy' ones to occur to the right of the verb without any special effect of foregrounding or backgrounding. For example corelatives are not attested in rigid verb-final languages such as

Japanese and Turkish. Nor are they attested in rigid SVO or verb-initial languages. On the other hand they are attested in languages such as Warlpiri with exceedingly free word order as well as in early forms of Indo-European languages such as Sanskrit and Medieval Russian. Since corelatives are like internal RCs in being limited to verb-final languages it is perhaps unsurprising to find languages which present both corelatives and internal RCs. (58) below from Wappo is arguably a corelative (compare with the internal RC in (53) from Wappo).

(58) ʔi čhuya-∅ ʃumta cephi šoýikhiʔ
      me house-DO bought it(SUBJ) burned down
      'The house I bought burned down'

Note that, analyzing (58) as a corelative, it is exceptional in that NP_{rel}, *čhuya* 'house', is not marked by a marker specific to corelatives. It is not obvious in fact that (58) should not be analyzed simply as a left-dislocated internal RC on the pattern of *My father, he's out of work again* in English. However, two properties of (58) argue that it is a corelative. First, the main verb of s_{rel} is in its main clause form, and second, s_{rel} is not treated as an NP as it is in (53); specifically it does not take the subject case marker -*i*.

4.2 *Marking NP_{rel}*

We have already noted that NP_{rel} is normally accompanied by a marker COREL. This marker may be used as an NP_{rel} marker in whatever other sorts of RCs the language presents. Thus in (59) below from Bambara (Bird 1968:43) the COREL marker is the same *min* which showed up in internal RCs (example (54b)).

(59) Ne ye tye min ye, o ye fini fere
      I PAST man COREL see, that PAST cloth the sell
      'The man that I saw sold the cloth'

In distinction to the Wappo case cited above we cannot justify with our limited knowledge of Bambara that (59) is anything other than a left-dislocated internal RC. To justify our distinction we would have to show that there are nominal markings which s_{rel} above cannot take. I don't know enough about Bambara to support such a claim, but even if it is so, it is clear from the example that in practice the distinction between corelatives and (dislocated) internal RCs is not always easy to make.

Example (60) below from Medieval Russian (Payne 1974) illustrates a case where the COREL marker also functions as the relative pronoun in RCs. The example also illustrates a non-trivial case of fronting of NP_{rel} as we would have more naturally expected it to follow its governing verb *videt'* 'see'.

(60)   I   kotoruju   zvezdu potrebno bylo nam videt',
        and which(ACC) star   necessary was to us to see,

        tu   zvezdu zaslonilo   tucheju
        that star   was covered by cloud
        'The star we needed to see was covered by cloud'

Note that the COREL marker *kotoruju* is marked accusative as is NP$_{rel}$, giving evidence that the COREL marker forms a constituent with the noun it marks. Further examples of this sort are attested in Sanskrit, Gujarati, and Mabuiag (Australian).

Warlpiri is like a number of Australian languages in not having a relative clause construction *per se*, but rather a more generally useful subordinate clause construction which can function in a way equivalent to a relative clause when it contains an argument coreferential to an NP in the main clause. In Warlpiri a common way of achieving the functional equivalent of a relative clause is with the subordinator *kuja* which basically means 'when'. If the clause introduced by *kuja* contains an argument coreferential with an NP in the main clause, then the 'when' clause can be translated either as a temporal clause or as a relative clause. If this coreferentiality is not present, then the subordinate clause can only be translated as a temporal adverbial. Compare (61a) with (61b) (cf. Hale 1976). (Warlpiri uses zero anaphora for coreferential NPS):

(61)   a. Ngarrka-ngku ka   marlu   luwa-rni   kuja ka
           man-ERG   AUX kangaroo shoot-NONPAST when AUX

           marna nga-rni
           grass eat-NONPAST
           'The man is shooting the kangaroo which is eating grass' or
           'The man is shooting the kangaroo while it is eating grass'

        b. Ngarrka-ngku ka   marlu   luwa-rni   kuja ka
           man-ERG   AUX kangaroo shoot-NONPAST when AUX

           wardapi palkamani karnta-ngku
           goanna catch   woman-ERG
           'The man is shooting the kangaroo while the woman is catching the goanna'

The field worker should always investigate whether a form that looks like a COREL (such as *kuja*) does not in fact have other functions. If it does, then the proper analysis is not to call it COREL but to point out that under certain conditions it can be the functional equivalent of a COREL.

4.3 *Marking NP$_{ana}$*

The anaphoric NP in the main clause of corelatives can be any overt nominal which is elsewhere in the language used anaphorically: a personal pronoun, a demonstrative pronoun, a demonstrative adjective + common noun, or any other anaphoric determiner + common noun. (62) below illustrates from Medieval Russian the use of *such* as an anaphoric determiner. It also illustrates a non-trivial case of fronting of NP$_{ana}$.

(62) A   kotorye devitsy byvajut uvechny i   stary i
      And which   maidens are   crippled and old   and

      zamuzh   ikh   vzjati za sebja   nikto   ne khochet, i
      in marriage them to take for himself no-one not wants,   and

      takikh devits   ottsy i   materi   postrigajut v
      such   maidens fathers and mothers send   to

      monastyrekh, bez   zamuzhestva
      monasteries, without marriage
      'Those maidens which are crippled and old and which no-one wants to take in marriage, such maidens fathers and mothers send to monasteries without marriage'

4.4 *Which positions may function as NP$_{rel}$?*

We have insufficient data to assess whether in general a large variety of NP positions may function as NP$_{rel}$ or not. Keenan and Bimson (1975) compare the possibilities for NP$_{rel}$ in Hindi and Bambara. It appears that in Hindi NP$_{rel}$ is largely limited to major NPs (i.e. unembedded ones) in S$_{rel}$, while in Bambara most of the complex positions discussed earlier can be relativized in this way. (63) below from Medieval Russian gives one case where a single NP in a coordinate structure may function as NP$_{rel}$.

(63) A   kotorye de   mesta i   bashni delali frjanchiki
      And which   (it is said) towns and towers made the Franks

      izdavna, i   te   de mesta krepki
      long ago, and those   towns are strong
      'Which towns and towers the Franks made long ago, those towns are strong'

4.5 *Language-internal distribution of corelatives*

Almost all the examples we have of corelatives are ones where they occur as complete sentences in discourse. We have no examples where they are nominalized and embedded as arguments of verbs of saying or thinking for example, and we suspect that in general corelatives do not productively nominalize or embed. However we do have one example where a corelative structure itself functions as S_{rel} in a 'higher' corelative, namely (64) below from Bambara (Bird 1968:44):

(64)   Fini min   ka di   n ye, muso min   be   o   fere, a
        cloth COREL is nice to me, woman COREL PAST that sell, he

        ye   o   furu
        PAST that marry
        'He married the woman that sells the cloth that I like'

Somewhat more literally we might render (64) as 'Which cloth I like, which woman sells that cloth, he married that woman'.

4.6 Marking S_{rel}

We have already noted that S_{rel} normally occurs initially in corelatives and usually has the form it would have as a main clause with the exception of the presence of the COREL marker and the fronting of NP_{rel}. Here we merely note that S_{rel} may sometimes occur to the right of the main clause, illustrated in (65) below from Hindi (compare with its paraphrase in (57)).

(65)   Mai ne us   a:dmi ko dekha jis-ka   kutta bema:r hai
        I   ERG that man DO saw who-GEN dog   sick is
        'I saw the man whose dog is sick'

Note that here S_{rel} contains only the COREL marker *jis* in the genitive case but does not contain a repetition of NP_{ana} *a:dmi* 'man'. Thus (65) could also be analyzed as the rightward extraposition of S_{rel} from an ordinary postnominal RC.

5 Conclusion: other relative-like structures

In addition to corelatives, languages may present a variety of other structures similar in one or another respect to RCs. We shall attempt no general discussion of these structures here beyond merely pointing out their existence.

Perhaps the most obvious case is that of non-restrictive RCs mentioned briefly earlier. Contrast (66a) and (66b).

(66)   a. The Japanese who are industrious now outcompete W. Europe

b. The Japanese, who are industrious, now outcompete W. Europe

The subject NP of (66a) is a straightforward postnominal external RC in English. The subject of (66b) is a non-restrictive RC, one in which S_{rel} (*who are industrious*) does not function to constrain the domain of relativization as in (66a). Thus (66b) for example logically implies that the Japanese now outcompete W. Europe, whereas (66a) does not; it only claims that the industrious Japanese outcompete W. Europe.

In English and a few other languages, for example Hebrew, non-restrictive RCs differ from restrictive ones in having a comma, or parenthetical intonation, which separates S_{rel} from the head, and indeed from the rest of the sentence. Otherwise, however, the construction of S_{rel} seems largely parallel to that for S_{rel}s in restrictive RCs, though there are some small differences. For example *that* does not introduce non-restrictive RCs in English but can introduce restrictive ones.

Similarly in French the syntax of non-restrictive S_{rel}s is largely similar to that of restrictives, with again a few small differences. For example the RPRO *lequel* may function as a subject NP_{rel} in non-restrictives but not in restrictives.

It rather seems then the syntax of non-restrictives in a language will be largely similar to that for restrictives, modulo some small differences, plus of course the fact that non-restrictives modify fully specified, definite NPS such as proper nouns. Thus we expect that non-restrictives will not be formed with indefinite determiners such as *no*. For example **No student, who was sitting on the steps, said hello*.

We should note as well that the use of comma intonation to mark non-restrictives is not universal. Both Malagasy and Japanese form such RCs without such intonation.

A second type of RC discussed in generative grammars for English are *infinitival relatives* of the sort illustrated in (67).

(67)   a. *The man to see* is Fred

b. *The first man to cross the line* will get a prize

Such relatives in English have a kind of modal, generic interpretation and are of quite limited distribution. We have no idea whether other languages present such structures and if so whether they have the modal interpretation they have in English.

Third, let us note that in many languages, such as Yoruba, in which the superficial syntax of RCs and constituent questions is quite distinct, we find that the embedded question complements of verbs like *know*, *remember*, etc. are constructed like RCs and not like questions. In fact

English illustrates this possibility to some extent. Thus alongside (68a), where the complement of *know* looks basically like a question (without subject–auxiliary inversion) we also have (68b) where the complement of *know* looks straightforwardly like an RC.

(68)   a. John always knows which horse will win

         b. John always knows the horse that will win

Finally, we note that in some languages, such as English and French, focused or cleft structures exhibit a syntax very similar in surface to that of RCs:

(69)   C'était Jean qui a   parlé
         It was John who has spoken
         'It was John who spoke'

On the other hand, in languages like Malagasy in which RCS and constituent questions have a quite distinct superficial syntax we find that clefts pattern on the form of questions and not that of RCS. (70) below illustrates this:

(70)   a. Niteny ny lehilahy
            spoke the man
            'The man spoke'

         b. ny lehilahy izay niteny
            the man   who spoke
            'the man who spoke'

         c. Iza   no niteny?
            Who PCL spoke
            'Who spoke?'

         d. Ny lehilahy no niteny
            the man   PCL spoke
            'It was the man who spoke'

4 Adverbial clauses

SANDRA A. THOMPSON and ROBERT E. LONGACRE

PART I A TYPOLOGY OF ADVERBIAL CLAUSES

1 Introduction

It appears that all languages have a set of two-clause constructions in which one clause can be said to modify the other in a way similar to the way in which an adverb modifies a proposition.

Just as with adverbs which are single words or phrases, adverbial clauses can be labeled and categorized with respect to the semantic roles they play. For example, in the English sentences in (1), the italicized expressions can all be called 'time adverbials'; that in (1a) is a 'time adverb'; those in (1b) and (1c) are 'time adverbial phrases'; while in (1d) we have a 'time adverbial clause':

(1)   a. She mailed it *yesterday*
       b. He eats lunch *at 11:45*
       c. She has chemistry lab *in the morning*
       d. I get up *when the sun rises*

In Part I of this chapter we examine the various structural types of adverbial clauses found in languages of the world, while in Part II we treat the adverbial clause from its discourse perspective. Part I has been primarily Sandra Thompson's responsibility, while Part II has been that of Robert Longacre.

The remainder of Part I is organized as follows: section 2 characterizes the notion 'adverbial subordinate clauses', while section 3 examines the adverbial subordinate clause types which languages typically manifest. In section 4 we describe 'speech act' adverbial clauses, and in section 5 we raise the issue of subordinators being borrowed from one language into another. Section 6 recapitulates and summarizes the findings of Part I.

2 Characterization of adverbial clauses

We can distinguish three types of subordinate clauses: those which function as noun phrases (called complements), those which function as modifiers of nouns (called relative clauses), and those which function as modifiers of verb phrases or entire propositions (called adverbial clauses).

An adverbial subordinate clause, then, is one which modifies a verb phrase or a sentence.

There are three devices which are typically found among languages of the world for marking subordinate clauses, all of which are found with adverbial clauses. They are:

    (a) subordinating morphemes
    (b) special verb forms
    (c) word order

(a) Subordinating morphemes. There are two types of subordinating morphemes: (1) grammatical morphemes with no lexical meaning (e.g. English *to*, as in *to buy beer*); (2) grammatical morphemes with lexical content (e.g. English *before, when, if*).

(b) Special verb forms. A special verb form is one which is not used in independent assertions. In languages with subject–verb agreement, the special verb form may be a non-finite form which lacks one or more agreement categories. In Latin, for example, in independent assertions the verb must agree with its subject in person and number:

(2)   Dux   scrib-it   epistol-as
       leader(NOM SG) write-PRES 3SG letter-ACC PL
       'The leader writes letters'

But in an adverbial subordinate clause, the verb may take an ending which signals nothing about the person or number of the subject.

(3)   Ter-it   temp-us   scrib-*endo*   epistol-as
       spend-PRES 3SG time-ACC SG write-GERUND letter-ACC PL
       'He spends time writing letters'

In a language without agreement, a special subordinate verb form may still be identifiable. In Wappo, a California Indian language, for example, the verb in an independent sentence ends with a glottal stop (even when it is not sentence final), but this glottal stop is dropped in subordinate clauses of all types:

(4)   a. Cephi   šawo paʔ-*ta*ʔ
          he(NOM) bread eat-PAST
          'He ate bread'

b. Te   šawo paʔ-*ta*-wen,   ah
he(ACC) bread eat-PAST-when/because I(NOM)
naleʔiš-khiʔ
angry-NONFUTURE
'When/because he ate the bread, I got angry'

c. Ah   te   šawo paʔ-*tah* haṭis-khiʔ
I(NOM) he(ACC) bread eat-PAST know-NONFUTURE
'I know that he ate the bread'

(c) Word order. Some languages have a special word order for subordinate clauses; German is a well-known example, where the finite verb (here, *habe*) appears at the end of the subordinate clause (but for some discussion, see Ebert 1973):

(5)   Wir wohn-ten auf dem   Lande, *wie ich dir   schon*
we   live-PAST on ART(DAT) land   as I you(DAT) already

gesagt habe
told   have(SG)
'We lived in the country, as I have already told you'

Compare:

(6)   Ich *habe*   dir   schon   gesagt
I   have(SG) you(DAT) already told
'I have already told you'

In sentence (5), the finite verb *habe* 'have' in the *wie* 'as' clause appears at the end, while in the independent simple sentence, (6), it appears in its standard second position. This distinction between verb-final and verb-second order for subordinate and main clauses respectively is fairly regular in German.[1]

A slightly different example of a word-order difference between main and subordinate clauses comes from Swedish, where a number of adverbial morphemes, including *kanske* 'perhaps', *ofta* 'often', and the negative marker, come after the finite verb in main clauses, as in (7a), but before it in subordinate clauses, as in (7b) (see Andersson 1975):

(7)   a. Vi *kunde inte* öppna kokosnöten
We could not open   coconut
'We could not open the coconut'

b. Vi var   ladsna därfor   att vi *inte kunde* öppna
We were sorry because that we not could open

kokosnöten
coconut
'We were sorry because we couldn't open the coconut'

A characteristic of adverbial subordinate clauses in some languages is their position. For example, in Mandarin, Ethiopian Semitic, Turkish, and many other languages, adverbial clauses must precede the main clause. Here is an example from Mandarin:

(8)   *Suiran   wo xihuan ta*, keshi ta bu-xihuan wo
        although I   like   he but   he NEG-like   I
        'Although I like him, he doesn't like me'

In many languages, however, the position of the adverbial clause is determined by its role in linking the main clause which it modifies to the preceding discourse. This phenomenon is discussed in detail in Part II of this chapter.

Before going on to a detailed discussion of the various types of adverbial clauses that languages have, it is crucial to point out that, although we have tried to identify the major types of adverbial clauses which we have found in the languages we have looked at, we are by no means claiming that a relationship which may be signaled by an adverbial subordinate clause in one language must be so signaled in every other. For example, where one language may signal consecutivity by means of time adverbial clauses, another may do so by means of constructions involving not subordination but co-ordination or juxta-position.

The Otomanguean languages of Mexico provide good examples of languages in which juxtaposition of clauses with certain aspect markers is more commonly exploited as a signal of clause relationships than are subordinating constructions (see Bartholomew 1973 and Longacre 1966). (9a) is an example of two juxtaposed clauses in the Otomanguean language Otomi, which were translated into Spanish (see (9b)) by an Otomi bilingual using the subordinator *cuando* 'when':

(9)   a. Mí-zøni   ya kam-ta   bi-ʔyɔni   kha
          PAST-arrive (IMPERF) now my-father PAST-ask   Q

          ši-pati   kar-hmẹ
          PAST-heated(STAT) the-tortilla
          'My father had arrived, he asked if the tortilla were heated'

      b. *Cuando* lleg-o   mi papa, pregunt-o si ya
          when   arrive-PAST my father ask-PAST   if already

          hubiera   calenta-do   las tortillas
          have(IMPERF SJNCT) heat-PAST PART the tortillas
          'When my father arrived, he asked if the tortillas were heated'

Two further examples of the contrast between subordination and juxtaposition are shown in (10–11). English happens to be a language which makes relatively extensive use of the possibilities for subordinating one proposition to another. Thus, in English there is an adverbial subordinate clause type which we term 'substitutive' in section 3 below. An illustration is:

(10)   *Instead of studying*, he played ball

In Mandarin (and many other languages), however, this relationship is signaled not by a subordinate clause construction, but by a juxtaposition of a negative and a positive proposition:

(11)   Ta mei nian shu, ta da qiu le
        he NEG study book he hit ball ASP
        'He didn't study, he played ball'

A similar example can be found by comparing a language in which a purpose clause is expressed by a subordinate clause with one in which a serial verb construction is used for this function. As an example of the first type of language, let us take Literary Arabic, where the subordinate clause is marked with the subjunctive -*a*:

(12)   ðahab-tu ?ila s-su:q-i   li-?-aštariy-*a*
        go(PERF)-I to the-market-GEN for-I-buy(IMPERF)-SJNCT

        samak-a-n
        fish-ACC COLLECTIVE-INDEF
        'I went to the market to buy fish'

Nupe, a Kwa language of Nigeria, however, like most Kwa languages, expresses purpose by means of a serial verb construction in which the second verb phrase is not marked as being subordinate in any way (see George 1975):

(13)   Musa bé   lá   èbi
        Musa came took knife
        'Musa came to take the knife'

A somewhat different sort of situation can be found in 'chaining' languages, such as those of the New Guinea Highlands or the Semitic languages of Ethiopia. In a chaining language, a clause is marked as being either final or non-final in a sequence of clauses. Thus, whereas in English a subordinate clause might be used to express one event in a sequence (e.g. with *when, before, after*, etc.), a chaining language would use a non-final clause followed by a final one. Here is an example from

Managalasi, a language of the New Guinea Highlands. (Longacre 1972:38):

(14)   Naumijaho apej-u-jine   'aiju nunijaho ape-na va-'e. Ijí
       string   got-PAST-when knife my   got-and go-ss then

       'osa   tua-ma   i-ne   'Pu'a vuicha kuna-huna-'e
       sugarcane break-and eat-ss trap door   close-FUT-SS

       'osanana-ma hin-ana,' 'uí-i   mih-ume.   Ape-na ro-a
       trap-and   stay-and say-as gave-me-DS get-and come-and

       va-'e osanana-ma hij-uta
       go-ss trap-and   stay-PAST

       'I took the string and I took my knife and went. And then I
       broke some sugarcane and ate it. "Close the trap door (with the
       knife) and stay trapping birds", he said as he gave me (the
       knife). And I took (the knife) and came and went. And I stayed
       trapping birds.'
       (ss = same subject; DS = different subject.)

In this paragraph -ne and -'e are morphophonemic alternants which signal that the subject of the verb they are attached to is the same as the subject of the following verb, while -ume signals that the following subject is different. These are both non-final clause markers; only the last verb in the chaining sentence is marked as an independent final verb with a tense marker. For various reasons, however, linguists working on these languages have not been inclined to view these constructions as involving subordination, the most important reason being the fact that in chaining sequences, each clause relates to the one preceding it and the one following it, but not necessarily to the final clause (Olson 1973:4). With subordination, on the other hand, the subordinate clause must be subordinate to a main clause. For more discussion of chaining see Healey (1966), Hetzron (1969, 1977), Longacre (1972), Olson (1973), McCarthy (1965), and Thurman (1975).

Thus, it is advisable to keep in mind that both chaining and juxtaposition may occur in some languages to signal clause relationships which other languages use subordination for. For a more thorough discussion of these clause-relating devices, see Longacre's chapter on interclausal relations, II.5 in this volume.

As a final note of caution, it must be mentioned that in some languages the same morpheme can be used for both co-ordination and subordination. (Gaelic appears to be such a language, with the morphemes *ach* 'but' and *agus* 'and' performing both functions; see Boyle 1973). Naturally, to show that this is indeed the case, the linguist must specify precisely what the distinguishing criteria are for that language between subordination and co-ordination.

Thus, it should be borne in mind that in outlining the functional types of adverbial subordination which languages manifest, we are simply making no claim about a language which happens not to use subordination for a given function.

In the next section we examine twelve adverbial clause types in detail. Before we begin, however, we must make explicit a very important point about formal similarities. We will assume with Haiman (1978) 'that superficial similarities are reflections of underlying similarities in meaning'. Thus, in the discussion of adverbial clause types we will emphasize similarities in form between various types of adverbial clauses as well as between certain adverbial clause types and other constructions. This will not only reveal what semantic categories languages tend to code in their adverbial clause systems, but it will also highlight the types of formal similarities the field worker is likely to encounter in a new language.

3.0 The types of adverbial subordinate clauses

The adverbial clauses which have been reported for languages around the world can be divided into twelve basic types, which are:

(i)   Clauses substitutable for by a single word:
        time
        location
        manner

(ii)   Clauses not substitutable for by a single word:

purpose	concessive
reason	substitutive
circumstantial	additive
simultaneous	absolutive[2]
conditional	

The distinction between group (i) and group (ii) is that, in general, languages have monomorphemic non-anaphoric adverbs expressing the time, location, and manner relationships, but they do not have such adverbs expressing purpose, reason, concession, etc.

3.1 *Clauses that are substitutable for by a single word*

In this category are clauses expressing time, locative, and manner relationships. To illustrate the replaceability of clauses in this group by single non-anaphoric words, let us look at some examples from Isthmus Zapotec, another Otomanguean language of Mexico (from Velma Pickett, personal communication, and Pickett 1960):

(15)   *Time*

    a. Kundubi bi   *yánaji*
       is blowing wind today
       'It's windy today'

    b. *Ora geeda-be*   zune   ni.
       when (POT)come-he (FUT)do I it
       'When he comes I'll do it'

(16)   *Locative*

    a. Nabeza Juan *rarí'*
       dwells John here
       'John lives here'

    b. *Ra   zeeda-be-ke*   nuu ti dani
       where is coming-he-that is   a hill
       'Where he was coming along, there was a hill'

(17)   *Manner*

    a. *Nageenda* biluže-be
       quickly   finished-he
       'He finished quickly'

    b. Gu'nu   *sika ma*   *guti-lu'*
       (POT)do you like already (COMPL)die-you
       'Act as if you're dead'

From these examples, it is clear that in claiming that a clause can be substituted for by a word, we are not claiming that the word necessarily occurs in the same position as the clause does. What we are claiming is that the *semantic relationship* between the adverbial clause and the main clause is exactly the same as that between the adverbial word and the main clause. That is, either a (non-anaphoric) word or an entire clause can express the time, locative, and manner relationships. As we will see, this is not the case for any of the other adverbial clause types we will be considering.

In addition to the fact that these clause types are semantically equivalent to single word adverbs, there is another interesting typological fact about such clauses: they tend to take the form of, or share properties with, relative clauses. This is because time, locative, and manner clauses can always be paraphrased as relative clause sentences in which the relative pronoun referring to the head noun plays the same role in the relative clause as the entire noun phrase (the noun plus the relative clause) plays in the main clause. Let us exemplify this point with English:

(18)   a. *Time*
          We'll go *when Tom gets here*
       b. *Locative*
          I'll meet you *where the statue used to be*
       c. *Manner*
          She spoke *as he had taught her to*

Each of these sentences can be paraphrased with a relative clause with a generic and relatively semantically empty head noun: *time*, *place*, and *way/manner*, respectively:

(19)   a. *Time*
          We'll go at **the time** *at which Tom gets here*
       b. *Locative*
          I'll meet you at **the place** *at which the statue used to be*
       c. *Manner*
          She spoke in **the way** *in which he had taught her to*

Looking at just (19b), then, for example, we can see that the relative pronoun referring to the *place* functions as the location in the relative clause, and the noun phrase *the place at which the statue used to be* functions as the location in the main clause. In other words, time, locative, and manner clauses state that the relationship between the time, place, or manner of the event in the main clause and that of the subordinate clause is the same. And it is precisely for this reason that they often share properties with relative clause constructions.

In contrast, the other adverbial clause types which we will be looking at do not express that two events have something in common, but that one event *modifies* the other, as in the reason or conditional clause sentences, (20) and (21):

(20)   *Because it was raining*, I stayed in

(21)   *If you like spinach*, you'll love the salad I made

Since these sentences express a reason and a condition, respectively, for the main clause event, but not that two events have a reason or

condition in common, they cannot be paraphrased as relative clauses
and hence do not appear in relative clause form.[3]

In what follows we will examine time, locative, and manner clauses in
more detail.

3.1.1 Time clauses

3.1.1.1 *Temporal sequence clauses.* The morphemes signaling 'succession' (see chapter II:5, following), or temporal sequence relationships
between clauses, are typically either independent morphemes on the
order of the English *when, before, after*, etc. or verbal affixes. In the
languages of Papua New Guinea, the latter strategy is very common;
here is an example from Barai (Olson 1973), where *-mo* is a past
sequence marker (PAST SEQ), one of several sequence markers:

(22)   Bae-*mo*-gana   e   ije   bu-ne   ke
        ripe-PAST SEQ-DS people these 3PL-FOCUS take
        'When it was ripe, these people took it'

English has a rich array of subordinating morphemes introducing
temporal sequence clauses, including *when, while, as, before, after,
since, until, now that, once, as soon as*, etc. But English also has the
option of allowing the time clause to be in the form of a relative clause
with a head noun such as *time, day, week*, etc.

(23)   a. By *the time we got back*, the steaks were all gone.

        b. *The week that we spent in Big Sur*, it rained every day.

In Hausa, time adverbial clauses have all the surface characteristics of
relative clauses. For example, they contain the relative subordinator,
which is *da*, and the aspect marker is the same as that which appears in
relative clauses. Head nouns such as *locaci* 'time' and *baya* 'back' are
used to make clear distinctions in time and location. Relative clauses
may also be used as time adverbials without a head noun, in which case
the meaning is the one understood with the noun *locaci* 'time'.

(24a)   Yara-n   sun   ga sarki (locaci-n) *da suka*
         kids-the they(COMPL) see king time-the REL they(REL COMPL)

         shiga birni
         enter city
         'The kids saw the king when they visited the city'

(24b) Yara-n sun   fita *baya-n da suka*   *ci*
kids-the they(COMPL) go out back-of REL they(REL COMPL) eat
abinci
food
'The kids went out after they had eaten'
(*sun* = completive aspect pronoun for main clauses;
suka = completive aspect pronoun for relative clauses)

(For an excellent discussion, see Bagari 1976.)
In Mandarin, 'when' clauses are simply relative clauses on a head
noun such as *shihou* 'time' or *neitian* 'that day':

(25) *Ta lai   de shihou*, women dou zou   le
he come REL time   we   all leave ASP
'When he arrived, we all left'

The evidence in Swahili for time clauses being relative clauses is
particularly interesting: in relative clauses, the relative clause marker is
prefixed to the subordinate clause verb and agrees with the head noun in
number and noun class. In time clauses, the relative marker is *po*, which
agrees with abstract nouns of place and time, though such a head noun
does not appear when the clause functions adverbially:

(26) Baba a-na-*po*-pika   chakula, kuna   pilipili sana
father SUBJ-PRES-REL-cook food   there is pepper plenty
'When father cooks, there is plenty of pepper'

Other languages in which time clauses have the form of relative clauses
include Hungarian and Turkish.

3.1.1.2 *Time/cause.* In some languages which simply use a subordinating morpheme like *when* for time clauses, this morpheme may signal
cause as well. It is easy to see why: two events which are mentioned
together as being simultaneous or adjacent in time are often inferred to
be causally related. Consider an English example such as:

(27) When he told me how much money he lost, I had a fit

The natural inference here is that the telling *caused* the fit. Wappo is a
language in which one subordinator is neutral between a time and a

cause interpretation. Consider again example (4b):

(4)   b. Te   šawo paʔ-ta-*wen*,   ah
          he(ACC) bread eat-PAST-when/because I(NOM)
          naleʔiš-khiʔ
          angry-NONFUTURE
          'When/because he ate the bread, I got angry'

3.1.1.3 *'Before' clauses.* 'Before' clauses are different from 'when' and 'after' clauses in that it is always the case that the event named in the 'before' clause has not happened yet by the time of the event named in the main clause. Thus there is a sense in which 'before' clauses are conceptually negative from the point of view of the event in the main clause. Languages may deal with this semantic fact in different ways. Some languages have no equivalent to 'before' clauses at all. In others, the 'before' clause interacts with negation in interesting ways. In Mandarin, a negative marker is optional in a past time 'before' clause with no change of meaning:

(28)   Ta (*mei*) lai   *yiqian*, women yijing hui   jia   le
        be NEG come before we   already return home ASP
        'Before he arrived we had already gone home'

In Lakhota, 'before' clauses must take the negative marker, which is *śni*, in the past tense (Buechel 1939:251):

(29)   T'e śni *it'okab* c'inca-pi kin wahokon-wica-kiye
        die NEG before child-PL the admonish-3PL PATIENT-admonish
        'He admonished his children before he died'

Turkish has the same constraint: 'before' clauses must contain a negative marker.

Many languages, including Tolkapaya Yavapai, Quechua, Bauan Fijian (Lynn Gordon, personal communication), and Ethiopian Semitic (Robert Hetzron, personal communication), are different from both of these two cases in that there is no morpheme meaning 'before'; in Yavapai (30), the prior event is signaled by a negative verb which has the simultaneity suffix (SIM) together with the irrealis (IRR) form of the verb (Hardy 1977). Its literal meaning is then something like 'when X hasn't happened, Y happens'.

(30)   Kmun-v-ch   vaa-h   '*um-t-m*   tyach-va   '-yoo-ch-a
        frost-DEM-SUBJ come-IRR NEG-SIM-SS corn-DEM I-gather-PL-IRR
        'Before the frost sets in, we'll gather corn'

Similarly, in Quechua (31), the negative adverb *mana-raq* 'not yet' is
used (David Weber, personal communication).

(31)   *Mana-raq* šamu-r   armaku-y
        not-yet   come-ss bathe-IMP
        'Bathe before you come'
        (lit.: 'not yet coming, bathe')

In English, although 'before' clauses cannot occur with the negative *not*,
they can occur with negative polarity items such as *any* and *ever*:

(32)   a. *Before any* shots were fired, a truce was declared
        b. *Before* he *ever* went to UCSD, he had heard of 'space
           grammar'

The semantic fact that the event in the 'before' clause is always
incomplete with respect to the main clause event, then, is reflected in
many languages in the way negation shows up in the 'before' clause. The
details may differ, but the principle is the same.

3.1.2 *Locative clauses*

Locative clauses in English and other languages are introduced by the
subordinator *where*, as in:

(33)   I'll meet you *where the statue used to be*

But, as with time clauses, locative clauses in some languages have the
shape of relative clauses. In Turkish, for example, locative clauses can
only be expressed with a head noun meaning 'place' and a prenominal
relative clause (Eser Erguvanli, personal communication):

(34)   Sen Erol-un otur-duğ-u *yer*-e   otur
        you Erol-GEN sit-OBJ-POSS place-DAT sit
        'You sit where Erol was sitting'

3.1.3 *Manner clauses*

A manner clause, as illustrated by the Isthmus Zapotec sentence in
(17b) above, may be signaled by a subordinate clause marker, as in the

following English examples:

(35)   a. She talks *like* she has a cold
        b. Carry this *as* I told you to

Certain manner clauses in a number of other languages may also have the form of relative clauses, for example English:

(36)   Carry this *the way (that) I told you to*

In Swahili, the verb in the subordinate clause is marked with the relative marker *vyo*, which agrees with adverbial head nouns (though the head noun is not present, just as with Swahili temporal clauses; see (26) above):

(37)   Sema kama a-sema-*vyo* yeye
        say   as   SUBJ-say-REL he
        'Say it as he does'

In Quechua the relative marker appears in the manner clause (Weber 1978):

(38)   Noqa marka-kuna-chaw rika-*shaa*-naw yaykusuxhn
        I   town-PL-LOC   see-REL-man   we will enter
        'We will go in like I saw people do in the towns'

(39)   Manam kankipaqchu   kayku-*shayki*-naw-qa
        NEG   you will not be being-REL-man-TOP
        'You will not be like you are now'

(40)   Alista-pan   kuura ni-*shan*-naw
        prepare-BEN3 priest say-REL-man
        'They prepared it for him just like the priest said'

In line with what we said above, however, it seems clear that only those manner clauses in which the manner in the main clause is the same as that in the subordinate clause would look like relative clauses. Thus, while in (18c), the way she spoke is claimed to be the same as the way he taught her to, in (35a), the way she talks is *not* the way she has a cold. Thus sentences like (18c) have relative clause parallels, but those of the form (35a) do not.

3.1.4 Summary

So far we have seen, then, that clauses expressing time, location, and manner relationships are those which bear the same semantic relationship to the main clause as single adverbial words as *here*, *now* and *quickly*. They are typically introduced by subordinating morphemes, and may appear in relative clause form in some languages.

3.2 *Clauses not substitutable for by a single word*
While languages typically have adverbial words to modify a verb in terms of time, location, and manner, as we discussed just above in section 3.1, the semantic relationships to be discussed below are generally not renderable with a single non-anaphoric lexical item. For example, the conditional relationship is by its semantic nature one which cannot be expressed by a single adverb.

3.2.1 *Purpose and reason clauses*
Many languages use the same morphology for purpose and reason clauses. Ngizim, a Chadic language, is one such language. The subordinating morpheme for both types of clauses is *gàadà* (see Schuh 1972:380):

(41) *Reason*
      A ta   abən *gáadà* aci ngaa
      eat(PERF) food   he well
      'He ate food because he was well'

(42) *Purpose*
      Vəru   *gàadà* dà   ši   səma
      go out(PERF)   SJNCT drink beer
      'He went out to drink beer'

The semantic explanation for the fact that one morpheme can serve these two functions is that both purpose and reason clauses can be seen as providing *explanations* for the occurrence of a given state or action (see Chapter II:5, section 2.4.2). They differ in that purpose clauses express a motivating event which must be *unrealized* at the time of the main event, while reason clauses express a motivating event which may be *realized* at the time of the main clause event. In most languages, even those that share morphology signaling purpose and reason, then, there will be different marking to signal the unrealized status of the purpose clause versus the realized status of the reason clause.

For example, in the Ngizim sentences in (41-2) above, the purpose clause, but not the reason clause, shows the subjunctive morpheme *dà*, which signals that the proposition is unrealized. Similarly, Kanuri, a Nilo-Saharan language of Africa (see Hutchison 1976), shows the same morpheme *ro* in both types of clauses. Here is an interesting near-minimal pair (Hutchison 1976:147):

(43)   *Purpose*
       Biska   Monguno-ro lete-*ro*   tawange ciwoko
       yesterday Monguno-to go(VN)-*ro* early(1SG) get up(1SG PAST)
       'Yesterday I got up early to go to Monguno'

(44)   *Reason*
       Biska   Monguno-ro lengin-dǝ-*ro*   tawange
       yesterday Monguno-to go(1SG IMPERF)-DEF-*ro* early(1SG)

       ciwoko
       get up(1SG PAST)
       'Yesterday I got up early because I was going to Monguno'

In Kanuri, there are two morphological correlates to the realized/unrealized distinction. First, the verb in the purpose clause is a non-finite verbal noun with no person or tense marking, while the verb in the reason clause is a fully inflected finite verb. Second, the presence of the definite marker -*dǝ*- preceding -*ro* in the reason clause signals that the reason for which the main clause event happened is asserted as a fact. The purpose clause, representing an unrealized proposition, has no definite marker.

3.2.1.1 *Datives.* In some languages, the case ending expressing the idea of 'to' or 'for' used for datives, benefactives, or allatives ('direction to') is used for purpose clauses (Matthew Dryer, personal communication). Thus, in Tamil, the case ending for indirect objects and allatives is found suffixed to the purpose clause:

(45)   Avan poo-R-atu-*kku*   kutu-tt-en
       he   go-NONPAST-NOM-'to' give-PAST-1SG
       'I'll give in order that he can go'

The Kanuri examples in (43–4) above provide yet another illustration; the purpose/reason marker -*ro* is the allative suffix which is also used in these sentences for '*to* Monguno'.

   In Kinyarwanda, the similarity between purpose clauses and benefactives is signaled in a slightly different way: since case relations are marked on verbs rather than on nouns in Bantu languages, what we find is that a verb is marked by the same suffix when it takes a benefactive argument as when it takes a purpose clause (Kimenyi 1976):

(46) Abaantu bi-iig-*ir*-a   ku-menya ubwéenge
      people SUBJ PRON-study-BEN-ASP INF-know knowledge
      'People study in order to learn'

Compare the benefactive sentence:

(46') Umugóre a-rá-kor-*er*-a   umugabo
       woman SUBJ PRON-PRES-work-BEN-ASP man
       'The woman is working for the man'

3.2.1.2 *Same and different subjects.* Many languages have distinct
syntax for purpose clauses whose subject is the same as the main clause
subject as opposed to those whose subject is different. In fact, for
same-subject purpose clauses, it is most common to find an infinitive if
the language has one; English is like this, and so is Kinyarwanda:

(47) Tuagiiya muli parika *ku*-reeba uiyamasure
      we went in zoo   INF-see   animals
      'We went to the zoo to see the animals'

For languages without an infinitive, verb forms in special moods or
aspects are typically found in purpose clauses, as well as in other
environments where a non-finite verb is called for (such as with 'want').
Consider these two examples from Godié, a Kru language (see Marchese 1976) (VOL = volitive):

(48) -A yɛlʌ ɔ 'kʌ   Godié walɩ ki
      we want he VOLITIVE Godié word talk
      'We want him to speak Godié'

(49) ɔ sʌ   ɲʉkpa blɔ-'kw ɔ 'kʌ   pʉlʉ
      he clear(INCOMPL) men   road-on he VOLITIVE pass
      'He clears men from the road in order to pass'

Luiseño is interesting here since purpose clauses have verbs with the
same form as in one of the future tenses. For same-subject clauses it is
-lut:

(50) Nó·n má·kina sá·msa-*lut*
      I   car   buy-FUT
      'I'm going to buy a car'

(51) Ya?ášpil ?uwó?a-quʂ   má·kina sá·msa-*lut*
      man   work-PROG PAST car   buy-PURPOSE
      'The man was working in order to buy a car'

Different-subject purpose clauses, however, use -*pi*, one of the future tenses used in relative clauses (Davis 1973:236, 299):

(52)   *Relative*
        Nawítmal ?éxŋi   ?u-qáni-*pi*   pilék yawáywis
        girl   tomorrow your-meet-FUT/REL very pretty
        'The girl you're going to meet tomorrow is very pretty'

(53)   *Purpose*
        Ya?áš ŋé·ŋi   ʂuŋá·l kí·š   pu-wá·qi-*pi*
        man   leave/remote woman house(ACC) her-sweep-PURPOSE
        'The man left in order for the woman to sweep the house'

Finally, some languages, like Wappo, have a special form for same-subject purpose clauses, which is only used to express purpose:

(54)   Isi   celahaya čaphahaw-ta? olol-*ema*
        we(NOM) things   put away-PAST dance-PURPOSE
        'We put away things in order to dance'

3.2.1.3 *Negative purpose clauses.* Before leaving the discussion of purpose clauses, we should point out that some languages have a special negative subordinator for negative purpose clauses. In English, it is *lest*; in Daga, a language of Papua New Guinea (Murane 1974:156), this morpheme is *tawa*:

(55)   Enu-nege-pi   *tawa* tarep war-an
        spear-me-3SG MEDIAL lest   dance get-ISG PAST
        'Lest he spear me, I dance about'

3.2.2 *Circumstantial clauses*

Clauses expressing the circumstances by which a given state of affairs comes to be can be introduced by either affirmative or negative morphemes. In English these are *by* and *without*, both of which take the participial form of the verb:

(56)   He got into the army *by* lying about his age

(57)   She carried the punch into the living room *without* spilling a drop

3.2.3 *Simultaneity clauses*

Simultaneity clauses code the relationship called 'overlap' in the next chapter. In marking that two events occurred simultaneously, it appears to be universally the case that languages allow one of the simultaneous events to be signaled as providing the context or background for the other, or foregrounded, event. The choice of which clause serves as the background is, of course, determined essentially by the nature of the discourse (see Hopper 1979 for an important discussion of the relationship between discourse and grammar in the expression of background/foreground information).

There are two common ways of marking a backgrounded clause as simultaneous with its main clause: either a marker explicitly signaling simultaneity is used, or a continuative, durative, or imperfective aspect marker is used. An example of the first strategy can be found in Tolkapaya Yavapai (Hardy 1977):

(58)   Kwawa '-chkyat-a-k vak '-unuu-*t*-m   swach'skyap-ch
        hair   I-cut-IRR-SS   here I-INCOMPL-SIM-DS scissors-SUBJ

        vqaov-k yuny
        break-SS TNS
        'As I was cutting my hair, the scissors broke'

For an example of the second strategy, the use of an aspect marker which functions in simple sentences to mark 'ongoingness', we cite Yessan-Mayo of Papua New Guinea (Foreman 1974). Here the suffix *-men* is a progressive aspect marker:

(59)   Ti Wiywek ti-*men*-im   ti   ak   sam
        she Wewak be-PROG-FAR PAST she then died
        'While she was in Wewak, she died'

English is a language in which both strategies are used: not only does *while* explicitly signal simultaneity, but the verb in a *while* clause may also be marked by the progressive marker *-ing*:

(60)   *While* (we were) eat*ing*, we heard a noise outside the window

Another construction uses just the latter type of marking for simultaneity:

(61)   He woke up cry*ing*

Similarly, in Mandarin, the durative (DUR) aspect marker *-zhe* occurs in clauses with such a function:

(62)   Ta ku-*zhe* xinglai
        he cry-DUR wake up
        'He woke up crying'

And Swahili uses its imperfective aspect marker *-ki-* for clauses functioning in this way (Tom Hinnebusch, personal communication).

(63)   A-li-amka   a-ki-lia
        he-PAST-wake up he-PROG-cry
        'He woke up crying'

A third, somewhat less common, strategy for signaling simultaneity is that found in Warlpiri and other Australian languages: what Hale (1976) calls the 'adjoined relative clause'. With this strategy, two clauses are juxtaposed, one of which is marked as subordinate, but not signaling simultaneity or aspect in any way. Here is an example from Warlpiri (Hale (1976:78));

(64)   ŋatjulu-ḷu ø-ṇa yankiri pantu-ṇu kutja-lpa ŋapa ŋa-ṇu
        I-ERG   AUX emu   spear-PAST COMP-AUX water drink-PAST
        'I speared the emu while it was drinking water'

The subordination marking in this sentence is the complementizer *kutja*.

3.2.4 *Conditional clauses*

Before beginning our discussion of the semantics and structure of conditional sentences, let us agree on the term 'if'-clause for the clause which names the condition, and the term 'then'-clause for the main clauses. These terms are not intended to imply anything about the order in which the two clauses occur with respect to each other, nor about the obligatoriness of the morphemes which signal these clauses.

3.2.4.1 *The semantics of conditionals.*

A basic semantic distinction between types of conditionals which is signaled by most languages is the distinction between *reality* conditionals and *unreality* conditionals.[4] Reality conditionals are those which refer to 'real' present, 'habitual' (or 'generic') or past situations. Examples from English are:

(65)   *Present*
        If it's raining out there, my car is getting wet

(66)   *Habitual/generic*
        If you step on the brake, the car slows down

(67)   *Past*
        If you were at the party, then you know about Sue and Fred

The term 'unreality conditionals' is used for conditionals which refer to 'unreal' situations. There are two types of unreal situations: those in which we *imagine* what might be or what might have been, and those in which we *predict* what will be. We can label these two types of unreality *imaginative* and *predictive*, respectively. Examples from English:

(68)   *Imaginative*
       If I saw David, I'd speak Barai with him (what might be – hypothetical)

(69)   If you had been at the concert, you would have seen Ravi Shankar (what might have been – counterfactual)

(70)   *Predictive*
       If he gets the job, we'll all celebrate

As can be seen from these examples, among the imaginative conditionals, a further distinction can be made. Some imaginatives refer to situations which might happen, as in (68) above, while some refer to situations which *didn't* happen or which *couldn't* happen, as in (69). Those which might happen we can call 'hypothetical', those which *didn't* or *couldn't*, we can call 'counterfactual'.

The semantic types of conditionals, then, can be summarized as follows:

> *Real*
> 1 present
> 2 'habitual'/'generic'
> 3 past
> *Unreal*
>   *Imaginative*
>   1 hypothetical
>   2 counterfactual
>   *Predictive*

In the next subsection. we will see that languages divide up this semantic space in slightly different ways.

3.2.4.2 *The syntax of conditionals.* Most languages, as mentioned above, signal conditionals by means of subordinating morphemes such as *if.* Gwari, a Kwa language of Nigeria (Hyman and Magaji 1970), for example, uses the subordinator *ńgyē*:

(71)   Ńgyē hō sī   shnamá, ho kū   gyĭ
       if   you buy yams   you COMP eat
       'If you buy yams, eat them up'

Ngizim, a Chadic language (Schuh 1972), on the other hand, although it has an 'if'-word, makes much more extensive use of a clause-final marker *nən* (allophonically -*n*):

(72)   Ká rɗə-naa   aci bii-*n* dà   kii'ya-naa   tluwii-gu
       you stop-TRANS him not SJNCT eat-totality meat-the
       'If you don't stop him, he'll eat up the meat'

nən, according to Schuh, is best viewed as an indefinite determiner
which marks the conditional clause as not yet realized or of 'general
relevance', as in (73):

(73)   Akər ika   miya-k   sau darəpta-*n*, aa   tfa
       thief see(PERF) mouth-ASSOC hut open   IMPERF enter
       'If a thief sees the door of a hut open, he will enter'

   In imaginative conditionals, it is very common to find special marking. In English this marker is *would*; in Hausa (Bagari 1976), it is *daa*,
which occurs in both the 'if'-clause and the 'then'-clause.

(74)   If he were sick, he *would* call us

(75)   In *daa* sarki za-i   ziyarce ni, *daa* naa   baa shi tuwo
       if IMAG king FUT-he visit   me IMAG I(COMP) give him tuwo
       'If the king visited me, I'd give him tuwo'

In both languages, the imaginative marker (IMAG) also shows up in
non-conditional imaginative sentences, which is common in other
languages as well:

(76)   *Would* that he were here now! (a bit archaic, = 'I wish that he
       were here now')

(77)   *Daa* naa   sanii
       IMAG PERF(1SG) know
       'Had I only known!'

In some languages, conditional clauses are marked as nominalizations
or relative clauses. Ngizim, as we saw above, is marked with what may
be plausibly argued to be an indefinite determiner. Welmers (1973:433–
4) points out that in 'verifiable' conditionals in Efik, a Kwa language,
the word *èdyékè* is used followed by relative clauses, where *èdyékè*
seems to be derived from a noun phrase meaning something like 'the
indefinite circumstance'. Furbee (1973:15) suggests for Tojolabal, a
Mayan language, that conditional clauses may be like relative clauses in
that both may be marked with the definite determiner *ha*.

3.2.4.3 *Conditionals and time clauses.* In some languages, including Indonesian and certain languages of Papua New Guinea, there is no distinction between 'if'-clauses and 'when'-clauses. In many of these languages, the neutralization holds, however, only for *predictive* conditionals and *future* time clauses. Vai, a Mande language of Liberia (Welmers 1976), is a good example (where the discontinuous *à–'èè* is the conditional marker):

(78)   Á *à* ná   *'èè í–ì*   à   fé'έ-'à
       he come   you-FUT him see-FUT
       'If he comes, you will see him' or
       'When he comes, you will see him'

That is, the distinction between English *when* and *if* clauses is simply one of degree of expectability, and is a distinction which many languages do not code.

A slightly different kind of relationship between predictive conditionals and temporal clauses can be found in a language like Kanuri (see Hutchison 1976): the marker *ga* marks a predictive conditional clause (among other things), while *dəgo* (the definite marker plus *ga*) signals a reason clause in the future:

(79)   Ishin-*ga*   shi-ga jengin
       come(3SG IMPERF)-*ga* he-DO wait for(1SG IMPERF)
       'If he is coming I'll wait for him'

(80)   Ishin-*də-ga*   shi-ga jengin
       come(3SG IMPERF)-DEF-*ga* he-DO wait for(1SG IMPERF)
       'Since he's coming I'll wait for him'

3.2.4.4 *Predictive clauses: 'real' or 'unreal'?* Though predictive conditionals are semantically 'unreal', languages differ as to whether predictive conditionals are grouped *syntactically* with the imaginary conditionals, i.e., are coded together with them as 'unreal', or with the 'real' conditionals. Swahili and Chagga, another Bantu language (Saloné 1977), are languages of the first type. In both languages, the 'then'-clauses in predictive conditionals may be marked with either an imaginative marker (Swahili: *-nge-*; Chagga: *-we-*) or a future tense marker (Swahili: *-ta-*; Chagga: special verb forms). Let us look at three Chagga examples:

(81)   *Hypothetical*
       a. John a-wé-icha   inú   ngí-*we*-korá machalári
          John SUBJ PRON-IMAG-come today I-IMAG-cook bananas
          'If John came today, I would cook bananas'

b. John k-a-cha   inú   ngé-*kora*   machalári
   John if-SUBJ PRON-come today I-cook(FUT) bananas
   'If John came today, I would cook bananas'

Predictive
c. Kokóya John na-icha   inú   ngé-*kora*
   If   John SUBJ PRON-come today I-cook(FUT)

   machalári
   bananas
   'If John comes today, I will cook bananas'

Sentences (81a) and (81b) are both imaginative hypotheticals; the verb in (81a) is marked with an imaginative marker, while that in (81b) is a future verb form, exactly like the main verb in the predictive conditional in (81c).

English and Haya, another Bantu language (Saloné 1977), on the other hand, are both languages in which predictive conditionals are never marked by the same morphology as imaginative conditionals, but have the same verb morphology as 'real' conditionals. Looking at an example in Haya, we see that predictive conditionals are marked with future tense markers in both 'if'- and 'then'-clauses; imaginative conditionals, on the other hand, may never be so marked, but must contain a past or perfect marker in both clauses:

(82)   *Predictive*
       K-á   *la*-ijá   n-*da*-mu-bóna
       if-he NEAR FUT-come I-NEAR FUT-him-see
       'If he comes I'll see him'

(83)   *Imaginative*
       Ká n-*a*-ku-bona   efarasy' ein'   ámabába
       if I-NEAR PAST-UNREAL-see horse   having wings

       ti-ni-*á*-ku-amini
       NEG-I-NEAR PAST-UNREAL-believe
       'If I saw a horse with wings, I wouldn't believe it'

The semantic explanation for the fact that languages differ as to whether predictive conditionals are marked in the same way as imaginative conditionals, i.e., as 'unreal', or in the same way as 'real' conditionals is clearly that predictive conditionals can be seen semantically as either 'unreal' or as 'real'. That is, a future prediction is about something that hasn't yet happened, so it is 'unreal', as are sentences about what didn't happen or what might happen. But it is also 'real' in that it is making a prediction about a state of affairs in the 'real world'.

3.2.4.5 *Imaginary conditionals: hypothetical and counterfactual.* The semantic distinction between hypothetical and counterfactual conditionals is typically not matched one-to-one by a morphological distinction. There seem to be two kinds of ways in which the two planes fail to be precisely isomorphic. English is an example of the first way: the same morphology is used for both hypotheticals and those counterfactuals which express *not* what *didn't* happen, but what we know *couldn't* happen. Thus the form

'if'-clause	*'then'-clause*
'present subjunctive'	*would* and uninflected verb
(=past tense, except with *be*)	

is used in the following situations:

(84)   *Hypothetical (what might happen)*
       If I *saw* Jimmy Carter, I *would faint*

(85)   *Counterfactual (expressing what couldn't happen)*
       If I *were* you, I *would write* a book

For counterfactuals expressing what *didn't* happen, on the other hand, only the following morphology is found:

'if'-clause	*'then'-clause*
had and past participle	*would* and uninflected verb

(86)   If we *had wanted* a quiet evening, we *would have left* you at home

The second way in which meaning and morphology may diverge in imaginary conditionals is for the language to make *no* morphological distinction between hypotheticals and counterfactuals. Isthmus Zapotec is like this: all imaginative conditionals (hypothetical and counterfactual) are marked with the unreality aspect (Velma Pickett, personal communication).

(87)   *Hypothetical*
       Pa ñuuya   ti elefante ra skwela ñate'
       if see(UNREAL 1SG) an elephant at school die(UNREAL 1SG)
       'If I saw an elephant at school, I'd die'

(88)   *Counterfactual (what couldn't happen)*
       Pa ñaka   lii ke ninie   zaka
       if be(UNREAL 1SG) you not talk(UNREAL) thus
       'If I were you I wouldn't talk that way'

(89)   *Counterfactual (what didn't happen)*
        Pa ño-be   ni ñaka   wara-be
        if eat(UNREAL)-he it be(UNREAL) sick-be
        'If he had eaten it he would be sick'

Luiseño is another such language in which hypothetical and counterfactual conditionals are not distinguished.

3.2.4.6 *Negative conditionals*. Many languages have a morpheme to signal a negative condition. In English it is *unless*:

(90)   *Unless* you get there by 6:00, we're leaving without you

(91)   We'll go to Chicago *unless* the airport is snowed in

Mandarin is another example; its negative conditional marker is *chufei*:

(92)   *Chufei* pianyi (yaoburan) wo bu mai
        Unless cheap   otherwise I   not buy
        'Unless it's cheap I won't buy it'

What these conditionals signal is that the proposition in the main clause depends on a certain condition *not* obtaining. In languages with a special negative conditional morpheme, they may sometimes have the same truth value as a sentence whose 'if'-clause contains the conditional marker and a negative marker, but the implications are not the same.[5] Consider the following pair in English as an example:

(93)   a. *Unless it rains*, we'll have our picnic

        b. *If it doesn't rain*, we'll have our picnic

While (93b) is neutral with respect to how likely the speaker thinks it is to rain, (93a) implies that the speaker thinks it is likely *not* to rain. Negative conditionals are typically like the ordinary conditionals of the language both syntactically, in that they manifest the same restrictions on verb forms, and semantically, in the way the reality/unreality and hypothetical/counterfactual distinctions are expressed.

3.2.4.7 *'Concessive conditionals'*. The term 'concessive conditional' has been used to refer to clauses analogous to 'even if' clauses in English, coding the relation 'frustrated implication' discussed in Chapter II:5, section 2.9.2.

(94)   *Even if* it rains we'll have our picnic

(95)   He wouldn't have passed *even if* he had turned in his term paper

Mandarin has a subordinator which is morphologically distinct from any of its 'if' morphemes for this relationship:

(96)   *Jiushi* ta song gei wo wo dou bu   yao
         even if he give to I   I   still NEG want
         'Even if he gave it to me I wouldn't take it'

Like negative conditionals, concessive conditionals in a given language are typically similar to ordinary conditionals in that language in terms of verb forms and the expressions of reality/unreality and hypotheticality/counterfactuality. However, concessive conditional clauses do carry additional presuppositions not signaled by ordinary conditionals, which match quite closely those carried by such contrary-to-expectation morphemes as the English *even*.[6]

Let us consider just one example from English to illustrate how these presuppositions operate. If we let X and Y stand for the propositions underlying the *even if*-clause and the main clause respectively of a sentence like (97):

(97)   Even if it rains, we'll have our picnic

then we can give the meaning of concessive conditionals roughly as follows:

(98)   asserted: Y
         presupposed: there is an expectation that the proposition
                      [If X, then Y]
                      would *not* be true
         presupposed: there is a belief that the proposition
                      [If not X, then Y]
                      is likely

Filling in the formula for sentence (97), we get:

(99)   asserted: we'll have our picnic
         presupposed: there is an expectation that the proposition
                      [If it rains, we'll have our picnic]
                      would *not* be true
         presupposed: there is a belief that the proposition
                      [If it doesn't rain, we'll have our picnic]
                      is likely

A concessive conditional declarative sentence, then, is like an ordinary conditional sentence in that it may be talking about some 'unreal' event, either predictive or hypothetical, but it is like a concessive sentence (see next section) in that its main clause is asserted *in spite of* assumptions to the contrary.

3.2.5 *Concessive clauses*

'Concessive' is a general term for a clause which makes a concession, against which the proposition in the main clause is contrasted. There are two types of concessive clauses, those which we might label 'definite' and those which we might label 'indefinite'. 'Definite' concessive clauses are simply those marked by a concessive subordinator like 'although'. Examples from English include:

(100)   *Although* she hates Bartók, she agreed to go to the concert

(101)   *Even though* it's still early, we'd better find our seats

(102)   *Except that* we ran out of money, we had a great vacation

Tagalog (Schachter and Otanes 1972:479) is a language which has a rich variety of 'definite' concessive clause subordinators. Here is one example:

(103)   *Bagaman at* hindi sila mag-aaral, umaasa silang   pumasa
         although   not   they will study   expect   they(LINK) to pass
         'Although they aren't going to study, they expect to pass'

Evidence of the semantic definiteness of these clauses is that they can always be paraphrased with the complex introducer 'in spite of *the fact that* . . .'

The presuppositional and assertional structure for concessive sentences is similar to that which we discussed above for concessive conditionals. Let us again take one English example to illustrate. If X and Y stand for the propositions underlying the concessive and the main clause respectively in a sentence like

(100)   Although she hates Bartók, she agreed to go to the concert

then the meaning of definite concessive sentences can be roughly characterized like this:

(104)   asserted: Y (she agreed to go to the concert)
         presupposed: there is an expectation that [If X, then Y] (If she
                        hated Bartók, then she would agree to go to the
                        concert) would *not* be true

'Indefinite' concessive clauses, on the other hand, are those which signal a meaning like 'no matter what' or 'whatever'; these contain some unspecified element, typically an indefinite pronoun or question word.

Examples from English include such sentences as the following:

(105)   *No matter what* he said, she still refused to go out with him

(106)   *Whoever* he is, I'm not opening that door

In Mandarin, indefinite concessives are introduced by *wulun* or *bulun* and have the form of indirect questions:

(107)   *Wulun*   *ta shi shei,* wo haishi bu qu
        no matter he be who I   still not go
        'No matter who he is I still won't go'

(108)   *Bulun*   *ta lai   bu lai,* women ye dei   zuo
        no matter he come not come we   still must do
        'Whether he comes or not, we'll still have to do it'

(For further discussion, see Haiman 1974.)

3.2.6 *Substitutive clauses*
Some languages have subordinating markers for signaling the replacing of an expected event by an unexpected one. English uses such forms as *instead of* and *rather than* for this purpose (see Thompson 1972 for some discussion):

(109)   We barbecued chicken *instead of* going out to eat

(110)   Harry decided to eat the salad *rather than* send it back to the kitchen

In Isthmus Zapotec, a morpheme of Spanish origin *lugar de* 'in place of' is found in the analogous construction:

(111)   *Lugar de* nuni-be   ni zaka nuni-be   ni sikari'
        place of do(UNREAL)-he it thus do(UNREAL)-he it this way
        'Instead of doing it that way, he should have done it this way'

An examination of the verbs in the substitutive clauses in these two languages reveals interesting parallels, which may be shared by a wider range of languages: both the form and the interpretation of the subordinate clause verbs are predictable. In Zapotec, example (111), the subordinate clause always comes first, and the first verb must be in the unreal aspect because the action never gets realized. In English, the verb must be a non-finite form, the participial *-ing* form with *instead of* and either the participial or the uninflected verb form with *rather than*. In both languages, the *interpretation* of the time reference of the substitutive clause verb depends on that of the main clause verb. For example, the interpretation of the time reference of a clause like

(112)   Instead of going out to eat . . .

can be seen to depend entirely on that of the main clause. Each of the following three possible continuations of (112) imposes a different interpretation of the tense/aspect of (112):

(113)   a. . . . we barbecued chicken

         b. . . . we're barbecuing chicken

         c. . . . we'll barbecue chicken

As was the case with 'before'-clauses, substitutive subordinate clauses, because of their negative meaning, interact with negation in interesting ways. In English, both substitutive and 'before' clauses can occur with negative polarity items like *any* and *ever*:

(114)   Instead of doing *any* homework, he just sits around watching TV

3.2.7 'Additive' clauses
Some languages have subordinating morphemes which express one state of affairs in addition to another. In English, *besides* and *in addition to* serve this function; both require that their verbs be in the participial forms, which provides evidence that they are subordinate in this language:

(115)   *In addition to* having your hand stamped, you must show your ticket stub

(116)   *Besides* missing my bus, I got my feet all wet

In Tagalog, the additive subordinating morpheme is *bukod sa*:

(117)   Nag-aalaga siya ng hayop, *bukod sa* nagtatrabaho siya sa
         raise   he ART animals besides work   he ART
         bukid
         field
         'He raises animals, besides working in the field'

3.2.8 'Absolutive' clauses[7]
'Absolutive' here is a cover term for a subordinate clause type in which the following conditions hold:

         (i) the clause is marked in some way as being subordinate;

    (ii) there is no explicit signal of the relationship between the
        main and subordinate clause; thus
    (iii) the interpretation of this relationship is inferred from the
        pragmatic and linguistic context.

There are essentially two ways to mark a clause as subordinate without
signaling the precise subordinating relationship; one is to mark the verb
in a special way, often by nominalizing it, and the other is to use a
general subordinating morpheme. English, Latin, and Ngizim are
languages in which the first type of strategy is used. English uses a
non-finite verb form:

(118)   a. *Having* told a few bad jokes, Harvey proceeded to introduce
        the speaker

       b. *Seeing* me, Jamie hid behind his mother's skirt

In Latin (Greenough *et al.* 1903) and in Classical Greek, the verb in the
absolutive clause appears in its participial form and is then case-marked
according to the following convention: if the subject of the participial
subordinate verb and the subject of the main clause verb are understood
to be the same, the participial verb agrees with that subject in case,
number, and gender; if the subject of the participial subordinate verb is
not the same as that of the main verb, then the participial verb and the
nouns dependent on it appear in the ablative case (Matthew Dryer,
personal communication). Here is an example of each of these two
situations from Latin:

(119)   Ab   oppid-o   *duct-a*   femin-a   prope
       from town-ABL lead(PAST PART)-NOM woman-NOM near

       templ-um   *habita-ba-t*
       temple-ACC live-IMPERF-3SG
       'Having been brought from the town, the woman lived near the
       temple'

(120)   Caesar,   *accept-is*   *litter-is*,   nuntium
       Caesar-NOM receive(PAST PART)-ABL letter-ABL messenger-ACC

       misit
       send-3SG PERF
       'The letter having been received, Caesar sent a messenger'

In Ngizim (Schuh 1972), a clause may be nominalized by postposing its
subject, deleting its auxiliary, and replacing the finite verb with a verbal

noun, which is marked by the possessive suffix. It can then function as an absolutive clause:

(121)   Kalaktayi-gaa   ná   təfə-n-gaa   ii
         return-1SG POSS 1SG PERF enter(PERF)-totality-ASSOC to
         mənduwa
         house
         'Having returned, I entered the house'

Languages illustrating the second strategy for marking an absolutive clause as subordinate, using a multifunctional subordinating morpheme, include Luiseño and Yaqui, in the Uto-Aztecan family, and Godié from the Kru subgroup of Niger-Congo. First, some examples from Luiseño, illustrating the subordinator *qala* (Davis 1973):[8]

(122) a. ʔó:nu-pil   ney   wultúʔ-ya   ʔi:k   nu-htíʔa-*qala*
           he-REMOTE me(ACC) angry-REMOTE there(DAT) my-go-SUBORD
           'He got angry at me when/because I went there'

       b. ʔári-n-up   póy   ʔóy   pu-ʔári-*qala*
           kick-FUT-IMPERF him(ACC) you(ACC) his-kick-SUBORD
           'Kick him when/if he kicks you'

       c. Wámʔ-ta   nó naxánmal ʔi:qal pumó:m-i tów-ma
           now-CONTRAST I old man   just   they-ACC look-HABIT
           pum-péla-*qala*
           their-dance-SUBORD
           'Now that I'm old I just watch them while they're dancing'

In Godié (Marchese 1976), the general subordinator is *nʌ*, which can appear with clauses which are introduced by an initial subordinator, as well as by itself in absolutive constructions (more on *nʌ*, in section 4 below):

(123)   ɔ yi   mɔ Dakpaduu' *nʌ*   gbesi ɔ tla a
        he came to Dakpadu   SUBORD traps he set recent
        'Having come to Dakpadu, he set some traps'

The interpretation of the relationship between the clauses in an absolutive relationship is entirely determined by inference, and may not be very specific. Greenough *et al.*'s Latin grammar (1903:264) for example, lists five types of clauses which the ablative absolutive can 'take the place of':

    1 a temporal clause (='when')
    2 a causal clause (='because')

    3 a concessive clause (= 'although')

    4 a conditional clause (= 'if')

    5 a 'clause of accompanying circumstance'

Absolutive constructions are used, then, when there is no need to specify more than that the clauses are related.

3.3 *Summary*

In this section, we have provided a survey of the types of adverbial clauses which can be found in languages of the world. We have discussed the types of semantic relationships which adverbial clauses signal, and we have indicated and attempted to explain some of the structural regularities which are found in certain of these clause types.

4 'Speech act' adverbial clauses

Some adverbial clauses in any language can be seen to relate not to the main clauses, nor to the preceding discourse, but to the fact that the act of communication is taking place. Examples from English would include such clauses as the italicized one in the following sentence:

(124)   *As I'm sure you're aware*, bananas have doubled in price since last year

Speech act adverbial clauses, although identical in form to the clauses we have been discussing, need to be recognized as a separate category because their function is not to modify or qualify the main clause in any way, but to modify or qualify, as it were, the speech act which the speaker is performing in uttering the main clause. A particularly clear illustration of this fact is an English sentence such as:

(125)   *If you're interested*, the Lakers just won

The *if*-clause in (125) in no way sets a condition on the Lakers winning; in fact, it is clear that they won whether or not 'you' are interested. Instead, this clause sets a condition on the hearer's appreciating the main clause, and might be paraphrased as: 'If you're interested, then consider the message that the Lakers just won.' Another example from English is:

(126)   Harry will be late, *because I just talked to his wife*

If the reason for Harry's being late is that I just talked to his wife, then the *because*-clause is a reason clause like those discussed above in section 3.2.1. The more likely interpretation, however, is that in which the *because*-clause gives my reason for being able to make the assertion that Harry will be late; that is, I know he will be late because I just talked to his wife, who told me so.

Illuminating discussions of speech act adverbial clauses in English can be found in Rutherford (1970) and Kac (1972).

5 Borrowed subordinators

In the description of the adverbial clause systems of certain languages, it is quite evident that the majority of subordinators are borrowed. Two striking examples are Yaqui (see Lindenfeld 1973) and Isthmus Zapotec (Velma Pickett, personal communication, and Pickett 1960). It will be recalled that Yaqui is a Uto-Aztecan language spoken in Arizona and Sonora, Mexico, while Isthmus Zapotec is an Otomanguean language spoken in Oaxaca, Mexico. The majority of speakers of both languages are bilinguals, and both languages have borrowed a number of subordinating morphemes from Spanish. For example:

Yaqui

kwando	'when'
si	'if'
paraka/pake	'in order to'
porke	'because'

Isthmus Zapotec

ora	'when'
dede	'until'
kada	'each time'
ante	'before'
para	'in order to'
kumu	'since'
modo	'the way'
sinuke	'but rather'
lugar de	'instead of'
sin	'without'

While no hard and fast conclusions can be drawn about the nature of subordination or of syntactic borrowing from these two examples, this phenomenon does suggest a basic question which further research might seek to resolve. That question is, of course: Why would a language borrow a number of subordinating morphemes from another language?

There are several factors to be considered in attempting to answer this question. One is the socio-political fact of language dominance. In the case at hand, we would want to consider to what extent the sheer fact of the dominance of Spanish speakers over Indian populations contributed to the borrowing of these subordinators into Yaqui and Zapotec. We might also hypothesize that influence from the more prestigious language might be greater in the area of complex sentence use, where there is somewhat greater opportunity for planning and exercising options in the presentation of information than in simple sentence use.

A second factor has to do with the semantic structure of the borrowing language itself. In Otomanguean languages less influenced by Spanish, such as Otomi and Trique, as mentioned above in section 2 (see Bartholomew 1973 and Longacre 1966), and therefore quite possibly in Zapotec as well, the 'basic' clause-connecting strategy is one of juxtaposition, with the semantic relationship between the clauses inferred rather than signaled explicitly. We might hypothesize, then, that when such a language comes into contact with one in which there are a number of clause-connecting morphemes which explicitly signal the relationship between the two clauses, there will be a tendency for a bilingual speaker to transfer the explicit signals into the language which uses the less explicit strategy whenever a specific message is intended. Such an explanation for the borrowing of subordinating morphemes, though appealing, is less satisfying for Uto-Aztecan: both Yaqui and Luiseño, on which studies of adverbial clauses are available (Lindenfeld 1973 and Davis 1973), have a fairly rich set of native subordinating morphemes.

Finally, a third factor may be a tendency ön the part of bilinguals to create patterns in one of their languages which are structurally parallel to those found in the other. Thus, since in Spanish, subordinating morphemes occur clause-initially, it would be natural for a Luiseño/Spanish bilingual to use a Spanish subordinator in creating an analogous subordinator-initial adverbial clause in Luiseño.

Clearly, much more research needs to be done on the parameters of syntactic borrowing before firm answers to these questions can be provided.

6 Summary and conclusions

In Part 1 of this chapter on adverbial subordinate clauses, we have shown how adverbial subordinate clauses can be distinguished from co-ordinate clauses and from other types of subordinate clauses. We have discussed in detail the twelve types of adverbial subordinate clauses which we have found in surveying a number of unrelated languages, attempting to relate patterns of correlations between form and meaning from one language to another.

In Part II we will look at the function of adverbial clauses in discourse.

PART II ADVERBIAL CLAUSES BEYOND THE SENTENCE

1 Introduction

In chapter 11:5, where he presents various models of sentence structure found around the world, Longacre mentions that for many languages sentences can be considered to consist of a *nucleus* with structural units called *sentence margins* draped around the edges. Sentence margins are considered to be functional slots whose fillers are typically adverbial clauses but which may be embedded sentences of complex internal structure. Positing such sentence margins is most useful when we find structures that are maximally detachable and occur with many different sorts of sentence nuclei – as in English and other Indo-European languages, Philippine languages, and many languages of Mesoamerica. In some parts of the world, noticeably in the northern part of South America, we find structures similar to what Longacre calls sentence margins but restricted to the structure of a unit which we might call the complex sentence; i.e., they occur essentially with only one sort of sentence nucleus. In still other parts of the world where chaining languages are found, we find that, although the model is initial link, medial link, and final link, the initial link is very often specialized to do jobs much like that of a sentence margin in Indo-European languages.

Part of the usefulness of setting up sentence margins is seen on the sentence level itself, i.e., we assume that there are essentially fewer sentence types, because not every margin–nucleus combination constitutes a new sentence type. It simply reflects a further distribution of a given sentence margin. Sentence margins, however, are of much greater usefulness than simply in reference to the internal structure and description of sentences themselves. We hope to show in this part of the chapter that, as sentence margins, adverbial clauses have considerable relevance to the structure of paragraphs and discourse.

2 Adverbial clauses and discourse movement

Adverbial clauses may be used to provide cohesion for an entire discourse by assisting to maintain the discourse perspective and by helping to articulate the sections of the discourse.

We will use for illustration a travel book on Mexico (Castillo 1939). While the material in this discourse is essentially descriptive, it is given in pseudo-procedural form, i.e., the discourse is given as if one were on a guided tour through the regions and towns mentioned. Thus, after a section of the discourse which describes Cuernavaca, a further section begins, *Leaving charming, tourist-ridden Cuernavaca* ... Here an absolutive clause, filling a time margin, serves to connect two sections of the discourse.

The portion of the discourse that we will be looking at in particular in this chapter has to do with the trip from Cuernavaca to Taxco, including an aside to see the caverns of Cacahuamilpa, and some description of the town of Taxco itself.

By skilful use of adverbial clauses in various functions, the author of this discourse is constantly reminding the reader of the you're-on-a-journey perspective of the entire discourse. Thus, in the middle of the visit to the caverns a paragraph begins, *As you walk through these huge chambers decorated with the great icy-looking columns* ... This, of course, has the function of binding the paragraph which it introduces to the previous paragraph, which describes stalactites, stalagmites, and columns. It seems, however, that an overriding function of the adverbial clause just cited is to maintain the discourse perspective.

After the section concerning the caverns, there occurs a paragraph which acts as aperture to the section which deals with the trip to Taxco. This aperture consists of a one-sentence paragraph which begins, *After seeing this underground fairyland* ... The balance of the sentence tells us, *you get back into your car again, travel back to the main highway, and start for Taxco, the most picturesque village in central Mexico.* Here the adverbial clause serves to separate the part of the discourse that deals with the caverns from the part of the discourse that deals with the trip to Taxco.

After a paragraph about reaching the town of Taxco itself and one which tries to picture one's initial impression of the town, there's a paragraph which begins, *As your car moves on* ... This adverbial clause seems again to function in maintaining discourse perspective. A few paragraphs on, a paragraph begins with, *In a few seconds (you reach)* ... There follows a series of five paragraphs in which reminders of discourse perspective are absent. Then comes a paragraph which begins, *Wherever you go in Taxco* ... which is an adverbial clause (locative margin) which again serves to maintain the discourse perspective. The following paragraph continues in the same vein in that it begins, *As you browse about the village* ... Two paragraphs following, one finds a similar phrase which begins a paragaph, *As you prowl up and down the narrow streets.* . . . Somewhat more subtle is the clue in the opening of the next paragraph where we find the sentence:

But you will enjoy Taxco most, if you sit under the famous laurel trees in its colorful plaza drinking in its superb scenery and studying the faces of the passing Indians.

Here the 'if'-clause seems to be crucial in maintaining the discourse perspective. This is further maintained in the balance of the paragraph by picturing various people as coming or going with reference to the tourist who is seated under the laurel tree in the plaza.

Thus, we see that what is essentially a descriptive discourse is given a pseudo-procedural perspective and this perspective is maintained through the discourse largely by use of adverbial clauses in the first sentences of various paragraphs. Such clauses also occasionally function to delineate portions of the discourse from each other.

Another device which is used to maintain discourse perspective in the Mexican travel discourse, in addition to the use of adverbial clauses, is the use of the pronoun *you*. In purely descriptive parts of the discourse both devices are dropped. The overall framework of the discourse can be readily seen in compiling an abstract of the parts which couple the pronoun *you* with various motion verbs. I submit the following abstract of this discourse to show the importance of adverbial clauses in the overall picture:

Leaving charming, tourist-ridden Cuernavaca, you continue your journey south-westward ... Then, after a time, your guide suggests that you leave the main road and go to see the famous caverns of Cacahuamilpa ... *After seeing this underground fairyland,* you get into your car again *to go back to the main highway,* and start for Taxco ... Now your upward climb grows more exciting ... Your driver is taking a series of curves ... *Although he sounds his horn at every turn* ... Meanwhile your road winds upward ... You take another sharp curve or so; and suddenly, you see before you the quaint, picturesque village of Taxco ... *As your car moves on,* you see ... Your driver takes the narrow, rough streets on high *as he drives by* ... In a few seconds you reach the level, well-shaded plaza ... *Wherever you go in Taxco* ... *As you browse through the village,* you will visit a number of shops ... *As you prowl up and down the narrow streets* ... But you will enjoy Taxco most *if you will sit under the famous laurel trees* ...

3 Cohesion between successive paragraphs

By 'paragraph', we mean a coherent stretch of discourse which is usually larger than a sentence and smaller than the whole discourse; the term can be used for either spoken or written language.

Now, a further function of adverbial clauses is to provide cohesion between successive paragraphs of a discourse. Notice that this is a more specific relation than that referred to above, where the function of the adverbial clause is to maintain discourse perspective relative to the discourse as a whole. Here the function is narrower, simply that of relating successive paragraphs. A very frequent device used here is what might be referred to as *tail–head linkage*, i.e., something mentioned in the last sentence of the preceding paragraph is referred to by means of back-reference in an adverbial clause in the following paragraph. Thus, one paragraph may end with *So saying, Rutherford gave up the struggle and went home for the night*. The next paragraph can begin, *When he reached his front door* ...

Since Longacre first noted this in material from the Philippines, we quote here some earlier work (Longacre, 1968:1.8–9) in which *tail–head linkage* through adverbial clauses and related elements is described. Notice that he posits devices which separate one paragraph from the other. Nevertheless, these devices are accompanied by those which also provide cohesion among the successive paragraphs of the discourse:

The first device (Tail–head linkage), with S_n of paragraph$_i$ linking to S_l of paragraph$_j$, is the same device used for intraparagraph narrative linkage. This device is reported in Atta by Claudia Whittle. The narrative in question recounts in first person a man's story of his wife's death by drowning. In the first main paragraph of the discourse, the story is told of the wife and son getting in the boat, crossing the river, and returning – with the boat overturning in the water. The paragraph concludes with 'When the boat had overturned with them, the mother and child were then swimming in the middle of the water'. The next paragraph reintroduces the woman's proper name (not mentioned since the first sentence of the preceding paragraph) and follows with a gerund construction *pakanunnuk* 'swimming' which recapitulates the verb *mannunnunnuk* 'they were swimming' of the concluding sentence of the preceding paragraph: 'Therefore (as far as what Ikenia was doing) (as they swam), the child swimmer was exhausted from carrying his mother.' The new paragraph is clearly distinguished from the former by the portion of the sentence which mentions the proper name Ikenia but is linked to the preceding paragraph by the next portion of the sentence (which repeats the verb 'swim'). Similarly, in Botolan Sambal, Harriet Minot reports the use of tail–head linkage several times in a text about a monkey and a turtle. Thus, one paragraph concludes with 'They both planted'. The next paragraph begins with a particle which often functions as a paragraph marker 'Now', followed by a recapitulatory phrase 'when they had both planted ...'. Thus, both paragraph boundary and paragraph linkage are secured. In other cases where linkage of this sort is found, paragraph boundary is covert, i.e., the typical slot class structures into which the sentences fall require separate paragraphs.

Similarly, in Ilianen Manobo (Narrative Discourse II. paragraphs 3 and 4) one paragraph ends with '(Ukap) he returned to his mother', and the following paragraph contains the recapitulation 'When the mother of Ukap saw that her child had returned home . . .'. Nevertheless, a paragraph boundary is signaled by the particle complex *hune ve su* 'and then ended' which precedes the recapitulatory stretch and which progress from episode to episode.

Very similar to tail–head linkage is *summary–head linkage*, i.e., the first sentence of a successive paragraph has a clause which summarizes the preceding paragraph. Thus, we may have a paragraph involving description of a variety of activities. The next paragraph may begin, *When he had done all this*, or something to that effect.

Tail–head linkage and summary–head linkage are characteristic not only of narrative (i.e., telling a story), but also of procedural discourse (i.e., telling how something is done). We adapt here from earlier materials (Longacre 1968:1.25) a diagram (Diagram 1) which shows graphically the use of time clauses, conditional clauses, and concessive clauses in interparagraph linkage in a procedural text from Botolan Sambal, spoken in the Philippines.

Diagram 1 Interparagraph linkage in Botolan Sambal

Sentence no.	Margin	Nucleus
1	Rice farmer	. . . his work
3		. . . go to work
4		. . . his work
5		. . . he must be tired in what he does
6	First thing he does	. . .
8		. . . he scatters *his seed* . . .
9	(Time) While his seedlings grow	. . .
12	(Condit) If his seedlings have grown	. . .
15	. . . if he's *finished planting* his paddy	He is happy
16	(Concess) But even tho he's *finished* and has his *planting* done	he still has work
19	. . . if *rice heads* are appearing	
20	(Time) When *rice heads* have become a little yellow	
22	. . . if he tastes the fruit of his tiredness	He is happy
23	(Condit) if the *rice heads* are mature	it can be *harvested*
27	When the rice is all *harvested*	. . .
32		That is the story of the rice farmer

The material in the margin column, which can be seen as the 'ground' against which to view the nucleus, or 'figure', is typically old information, i.e. what is given, while the material in the nucleus column is the new event or state which ensues.

Not all sentences of the component paragraphs are given, but only the first and the last, which are relevant to the linking mechanism. In some cases in the diagram the linkage is a further type of linkage, *head–head*; thus, sentence 20 seems to relate to sentence 23 and both are related by virtue of initial adverbial clauses.

4.0 Cohesion within the paragraph

Cohesion within the paragraph by means of adverbial clauses and similar elements is so important that we are convinced that a theory of paragraph structure could be centered around such phenomena. We state here in germ such a theory and then proceed in the balance of this chapter to talk more particularly of intraparagraph connections via adverbial clauses.

(1) Thesis

Lexical overlap is the primary mode of intersentential connection, i.e., a sentence$_j$ may include in it part of sentence$_i$ or a paraphrase of all or part of sentence$_i$ may occur within sentence$_j$.

This overlap may be via sentence margin filled by adverbial clause. Typical introducers of such clauses are the elements *when, while, after, although, because, in that, since, in order to, if, even if.* A sentence margin (especially time margin) may, however, be filled by a noun phrase or a temporal phrase of some sort.[9]

(2) Corollary 1

In some parts of the world verbs of highly generic meaning such as 'do' and 'be' (and sometimes 'say') are used as back-reference via adverbial clauses in a highly stylized and reduced manner so that they become in effect conjunctival elements. This is seen in Cayapa, Paez, Guanano, Inga (all in South America) and to some degree in Kosena, a language of New Guinea. See 4.4 immediately below.

(3) Corollary 2

Instead of a sentence margin or a conjunctival element as described above in (1) and (2), a language may use a true conjunction (i.e., a particle without verbal or nominal structure). See 4.5 below.

(4) Corollary 3

A conjunction may be an affix. We will not feature this corollary in the present chapter but will confine ourselves to (1–3) as outlined above.

4.1 *Linkage via adverbial clauses in sentence margins*

4.1.1 *Adverbial clauses in prior-time margins*

This is the standard linkage in narrative and procedural paragraphs in a typical Philippine language. The units so linked are sentences or embedded paragraphs. Instances involving the latter are a more complex variation of relatively simpler structures of the sort illustrated here in which each successive 'build-up' of the paragraph is a separate sentence which carries forward the event line. In such simpler structures sentence$_j$ has an initial time clause or a time phrase that is a back-reference to sentence$_i$ – much as described as tail–head linkage under section 3 of Part II above. Note the schema presented in Diagram II where A, B, C, and D represent successive events (or event complexes), and BU = build-up. Such a structure could be either narrative or procedural and might better be termed somewhat more neutrally a SEQUENCE PARAGRAPH.

Diagram II Linkage via preposed temporal elements in sequence paragraphs

Margin	Nucleus	
	he A'd	BU$_1$
having A'd		
when he had A'd	he B'd	BU$_2$
after A-ing		
having B'd		
etc.	he C'd	BU$_3$
having C'd		
etc.	he D'd	BU$_n$

The form of the back-reference or recapitulation differs considerably from language to language.[10] The commonest form is a nominalized construction (a non-focus verb). This construction prefixes *pag-/pag-ka-/*or *ka-/* or a phonological variety of one of these prefixes. Back-reference may, however, be via an adverbial clause (much as in English) with an introducer meaning something on the order of 'when' or 'after'. In some Manobo dialects a special tense form (irrealis or dependent tense) characterizes clauses in this function (Longacre 1968:1.61). Finally, all the Philippine languages contain certain conjunctions or conjunctive complexes that supply narrative movement and, in effect, are substitutes for the occurrence of a back-reference margin.

It is also important to note the relations which occur between the element in the preceding sentence and the related element (back-reference) in the following sentence. We may have simple repetition or paraphrase (often contracted) of the element of the preceding sentence. Thus, a preceding sentence can have a clause, 'And he chopped down five trees.' The next sentence may begin with a back-reference, 'After chopping (them) ...' On the other hand, the relation between the repeated part of the preceding sentence and the back-reference of the following sentence may be one of 'reciprocal coupling'. Thus, the preceding sentence may be, 'They said, "Why not let us be the ones to build it?"' And the following sentence may begin, 'When they heard this ...' in which 'A says to B' and 'B hears A' are reciprocals. Just as frequently a back-reference may proceed along an expectancy chain so that the action which is referred to in a back-reference is really an action which would naturally succeed on the action which is referred to in the preceding sentence. Thus, the preceding sentence might have, 'They killed a wild pig, cut it up, and cooked it' and the next sentence could begin, 'After eating it ...'

Back-reference of this sort is endemic for many Philippine languages. Thus, the following short paragraph from Itneg (Walton, in Longacre 1972) shows a regularity which would be difficult to duplicate in English, and, if duplicated, would probably be considered to be stylistically ineffective (see Diagram III).

Diagram III Sequence linkage in an Itneg paragraph

Margin	Nucleus	
	He went	BU_1
When he arrived in the forest	he chopped the trees.	BU_2
When he had chopped them	he shaped them.	BU_3
When he had shaped them	he went home again.	BU_n

Such regularity of back-reference is also characteristic of many structures in New Guinea. It is, of course, more characteristic of the oral style than of the written style. In the written style there is sometimes a certain reluctance to write in back-reference with this frequency, a reluctance especially observable in the new literates. Nevertheless, once literacy and writing are firmly established in a community, people frequently return to the resources of the oral language to enrich the written style. Consequently, we suspect that extensive back-reference will probably not be confined to oral style, but also, in at least some languages, will characterize written literature as well.

English, which has a wealth of conjunctions, does not use back-reference nearly as often as do the languages of the Philippines and New Guinea. Nevertheless, examples of the sort illustrated in Diagram IV (Tolkien 1969:20) can be found and appear to be stylistically effective.

Diagram IV Sequence linkage in an English paragraph (with BU_2 expounded by an embedded paraphrase paragraph)

It was a good cake, and no one had any fault to find with it, except that it was no bigger than was needed.		Setting
Margin	**Nucleus**	
When it was all cut up	there was a large slice for each of the children, but nothing left over: no coming again.	BU_1
		BU_2
	The slices soon disappeared, and every now and then a trinket or a coin was discovered.	Paraphrase paragraph: Text
	Some found one, and some found two, and several found none; for that is the way luck goes, whether there is a doll with a wand on the cake or not.	Paraphrase
But when the cake was all eaten	there was no sign of any magic star.	BU_n

The first sentence functions as setting to the entire paragraph, introducing the cake and giving some idea of its adequacy. The first build-up reported in sentence two simply tells us that the cake is cut up and passed out among the children. The third sentence (which initiates a short embedded paragraph which here fills the slot of the second build-up) is a co-ordinate sentence, the first conjunct of which is, *The slices soon disappeared.* The fourth sentence, as the second sentence of an embedded paragraph, simply expands on the material found in the former sentence. In this sentence the event line of the paragraph does not move forward. The final sentence of the paragraph, however, tells us of the outcome of it all and, therefore, can be regarded as the final and climactic outcome of the whole paragraph (BU_n). It begins with, *But when the cake was all eaten . . . When the cake was all eaten* seems to be clearly a paraphrase of *The slices soon disappeared.* As such, this back-reference binds the end of the paragraph to the preceding material.

Another such example from English is from the travelogue discourse which we referred to earlier (Castillo 1939). There is a paragraph which begins, *Even more interesting is the guide's story of the Empress*

Carlota's visit to Cacahuamilpa. The next sentence begins, *When she visited the caves in 1866, she wrote on one of the walls 'Maria Carlota reached this far'.* The clause at the onset of the second sentence is a recapitulation and back-reference to material in the previous sentence.

4.1.2 *Adverbial clauses in concurrent-time margins*
A rather clear example of this device is from our Mexican travelogue discourse (Castillo 1939). The entire paragraph from which this example is taken consists of four sentences, the first of which is:

As you prowl up and down the narrow streets, you must not fail to see the public washing basin, which looks more like a small outdoor swimming pool than anything else.

This introduces the topic of the paragraph, namely *the public washing basin*. The paragraph likewise ends with an element which refers back again to the topic, *Even though you cannot understand a word that is said, you will find the public washing place a fascinating spot.* In between occur two sentences which apparently express simultaneous actions:

Here the women and girls of the village come to wash their family clothing on the concrete washboards built along the basin's four sides. As they dip the water from the basin in their colorfully painted gourd bowls, these native housewives chatter among themselves combining their gossip with their work.

The initial adverbial clause in the second of these two sentences is a back-reference to the preceding sentence. While the former sentence simply refers to washing the family clothing on the washboards, the adverbial clause in the second sentence refers to an inevitable concomitant activity of that process, namely dipping the water from the basin and pouring it over the clothes. Therefore, the former sentence and its recapitulatory back-reference in the adverbial clause of the second sentence constitute a generic-specific paraphrase, i.e., the whole process of washing clothes is referred to in the former sentence and part of the process is referred to in the recapitulation of the latter sentence. The recapitulation serves to tell us (by use of the subordinator *as*) that the activity of the former sentence is to be construed as simultaneous with the activity reported in the balance of the latter sentence, namely, *these native housewives chatter among themselves.* Lest we fail to get the point, the last phrase of the second sentence says, *combining their gossip with their work*.

The above example encodes the notion of coterminous overlap. The situation is somewhat different when an adverbial clause and the balance of the sentence encode continuous–punctiliar overlap, i.e., a span of activity during which an event takes place. Note the example from Tboly (Doris Porter, in Longacre 1968:1.59) in Diagram v.

Diagram v Continuous–punctiliar overlap in Tboly

Margin	Nucleus	
When it was almost the middle of the morning then	I returned and stopped by to eat some young coconut on the path.	BU$_1$
While (igò) I was still eating the young coconut	I just saw Awey coming from downstream carrying a small bag over his shoulder.	BU$_2$

In continuous–punctiliar overlap as illustrated in Diagram v, the events reported in the sentence *nuclei* are really successive, i.e., we're told that, 'I returned and stopped by to eat some young coconut on the path' and then, presumably after the 'stopping', occurs a further event,'I just saw Awey coming from downstream carrying a small bag over his shoulder'. We're given, however, the additional information in the adverbial clause at the onset of the second sentence that the speaker was still eating the coconut when he saw someone coming. For a similar Tboly example note Diagram vi (Doris Porter, in Longacre 1968:1.59).

Diagram vi Further example from Tboly

Margin	Nucleus	
Old Man arrived up in the house and then	he cooked it, he cooked it in a big kettle.	BU$_1$
While (igo) what Old Man was cooking was boiling	one of Big Spirit's children said, 'Hey, that looks like Father's feet.'	BU$_2$

4.1.3 *Adverbial clauses in reason margins*

Within a single sentence a reason margin may express efficient cause relative to a result which is expressed in the nucleus of the sentence. Thus, in the sentence *I went downtown because I was bored*, the reason margin *because I was bored* expresses efficient cause relative to the nucleus *I went downtown*. If we have a two-sentence sequence in which the reason margin is paraphrased or is a paraphrase of one of the sentence nuclei, then there is an extrapolation of this relationship to the paragraph level. Thus, we may take the above sentence and add a further sentence which paraphrases the reason margin of the former: *I went downtown because I was bored. I just couldn't stand being around them anymore*. The reason–result relationship is now spread over the two sentences.

Thus, the sentence *I just couldn't stand being around them anymore* is a paraphrase of *because I was bored*. The structural possibilities include at this point, however, not one but two paragraphs, the first of which expresses reason in its .second sentence and the second of which expresses result in its second sentence. The two paragraphs can be called reason and result paragraphs respectively. Diagram VII summarizes these structures (the linear order of margins and nucleus is irrelevant).

Diagram VII Reason and result paragraphs

		Reason paragraph		
s_1	Reason margin			
		Nucleus$_1$		Text
s_2		Nucleus$_2$		Reason
		Result paragraph		
s_1	Nucleus$_1$			Text
s_2	Nucleus$_2$	Reason margin		Result

The two structures schematically sketched above are extremely common in Philippine languages. Note the example of a reason paragraph from Dibabawon in Diagram VIII (Janette Forster, in Longacre 1968:1.76) where the reason margin appears to come after the nucleus.

Diagram VIII A reason paragraph in Dibabawon

	Nucleus	Margin	
s_1	But it was the same as if he had recovered from his illness	because he became famous by riding in an airplane.	Text
s_2	There is no other old man who has ridden in an airplane; he's the only one.		Reason

Note that in the above example the reason margin of the first sentence is paraphrased as the nucleus of the second sentence, i.e., 'he became famous by riding in an airplane' is explained in more detail: 'There is no other old man who has ridden in an airplane; he's the only one.' Thus, while we might argue that we are told everything in the first sentence itself, the paraphrase of the reason margin in the second sentence serves to spread the relation over both sentences and thus results in an extrapolation of the result–reason relationship to the paragraph level.

That such examples are not limited to the Philippines, but occur in English, is readily deducible, not only from the fact that the translations of these paragraphs make good English, but also from examples readily documentable in English itself. This is seen in the example in Diagram IX (Schaeffer 1968:129)

Diagram IX Paraphrase of the reason margin in the second sentence

Nucleus	Margin	
Hell or any such concept is unthinkable to *modern man*	because he has been brain-washed into accepting the monolithic belief of naturalism which surrounds him.	Text
We of the West are not brain-washed by our State but we are brain-washed by our culture.		Reason

Note in Diagram IX that it is brain-washing that is paraphrastically expanded in the second sentence, and brain-washing belongs to the reason margin of the first sentence.

Since-clauses function in much the same way. The rather long and complex example in Diagram X is from a medical writer (Garn 1961).

Diagram X The use of a *since*-clause

Margin	Nucleus	
Since races are natural units reproductively isolated from each other and with separate evolutionary histories through time,	it is not surprising that they differ from each other in a great many gene-determined respects.	Text: Paraphrase paragraph Text
Considering the unique history behind each race, and the geographical and ecological uniqueness of its successive homelands,	lack of differentiation would be remarkable indeed.	Paraphrase
	Particularly in the random loss or chance acquisition of genes each race represents a cumulative succession of accidents that could never be duplicated in millions of years.	Reason

In the example in Diagram X the first sentence begins with a reason margin, *Since races are natural units reproductively isolated from each other and with separate evolutionary histories through time* ... This is paraphrased in the initial participial element of the second sentence, *Considering the unique history behind each race, and the geographical and ecological uniqueness of its successive homelands* ... All this is summed up rather skilfully in the nucleus of the third sentence – especially in the last part of that sentence, *each race represents a cumulative succession of accidents that could never be duplicated in millions of years.* Here *isolated* and *separate* in the first sentence, *uniqueness* in the second sentence, and *could never be duplicated in millions of years* in the third sentence all continue the same lexical chain. The first two sentences constitute an embedded paragraph, not only by virtue of the paraphrase relationship between their reason margins, but also by virtue of the paraphrase found in the nuclei themselves. Thus, we're told that *it is not surprising that they differ* in the first sentence, and in the second sentence that *lack of differentiation would be remarkable indeed.* This is a negated antonym paraphrase, i.e., *it is not surprising that they differ* is paraphrased by a stretch which in effect means 'It would be surprising if they didn't differ'. Therefore, the first slot of this paragraph is filled by an embedded paraphrase paragraph. The marginal elements in the two sentences of this embedded paragraph are paraphrased and developed yet once more in the nucleus of the third sentence. The third sentence fills a reason slot in respect to the two preceding sentences.

We have been looking at situations in which a reason margin in the first sentence in a paragraph is paraphrased as the nucleus of the second sentence. We can also have the opposite situation in which the nucleus of a *first* sentence is paraphrased in a reason margin of a *following* sentence. (Again questions of relative order of margin and nucleus within a sentence are not relevant here.)

We begin again with a Philippine example since structures of this sort are especially common in that part of the world. The example in Diagram XI is also from Dibabawon (Forster, in Longacre 1968:1.121):

Diagram XI Nucleus of a first sentence paraphrased in a reason margin of a second sentence in Dibabawon

	Nucleus	Margin	
S$_1$	Wow, what a beautiful place that is at Nasuli		Text
S$_2$	No wonder they chose to live there	because it is really a beautiful place there at Nasuli.	Result

Here the nucleus of the first sentence 'Wow, what a beautiful place that is at Nasuli ...' is closely paraphrased in the reason margin of the second sentence 'because it is really a beautiful place there at Nasuli'. Again we can note that the second sentence is a fairly self-contained unit and that the addition of the preceding sentence is what extrapolates the reason–result relationship from the sentence level to the paragraph level.

For an English example of this we turn again to the writings of the Christian apologist quoted above (Schaeffer 1969: 120). See Diagram XII.

Diagram XII An English example of a reason margin that paraphrases a preceding sentence

	Nucleus	Margin	
s_1	They are my kind; they are my people; they are not something else; they're that which I am.		Text
s_2	I can really understand them	because I am who they are	Result

In the example in Diagram XII, the reason margin, *because I am who they are*, is a succinct contraction paraphrase of the nucleus of the preceding sentence.

For an example of a reason clause with the relator *since* in the same function, we turn again to the medical writer (Garn 1961) quoted above. See Diagram XIII.

Diagram XIII A *since*-clause paraphrasing a preceding sentence

	Margin	Nucleus	
s_1		In the female the homozygote develops early Kuru whereas the heterozygote develops late Kuru.	Text: Parallel paragraph Parallel$_1$
s_2		Among the males the homozygotes die of early Kuru while the heterozygotes survive as do homozygous normals.	Parallel$_2$
s_3	Since most of the heterozygous females live through the reproductive period and even those homozygous for Kuru (married early in life) manage to have children,	the continuation of the abnormal Kuru gene is therefore assured.	Result

Note that in the example in Diagram XIII there is a text slot which is filled by an embedded parallel paragraph which includes the first two sentences, i.e., we have a parallel paragraph which compares female and male as to Kuru genes. Then in the third sentence (which expresses result), the reference is to the first sentence of the parallel, ignoring the data presented in the second sentence as parallel but largely irrelevant. Again the *since*-clause is a paraphrase of material found in the nucleus of the first sentence.

4.1.4 *Adverbial clauses in conditional margins*

There are several functions that *if*-clauses perform in paragraph structure. To begin with, *if*-clauses figure in a paragraph structure that is essentially a two-sentence or more enlargement of a conditional sentence, so that we have in effect a conditional paragraph. These clauses may also figure in successive sentences in stating alternatives, i.e., in a binary alternative paragraph. Finally, *if*-clauses may function in what may be called a counterfactual paragraph structure.

Thus, to return to the medical writer quoted above, we find the paragraph in Diagram xiv which illustrates the first function of *if*-clauses, i.e., enlargement of a conditional sentence into a conditional paragraph.

Diagram xiv The enlargement of a conditional sentence into a conditional paragraph

	Margin	Nucleus	
s₁		Carleton Gajdusek, the outstanding American authority on Kuru, observes that 'leprosy and yaws are less frequent here (in the Fore) than in many surrounding populaces who do not suffer from Kuru'.	protasis
s₂	Obviously, if the Kuru gene protects against either disease,	it could counteract the loss of genes due to Kuru.	apodosis

Note that in this example the first sentence broaches the possibility of some connection between the low incidence of leprosy and yaws and the incidence of Kuru. The *if*-clause of the second sentence makes this connection a bit more explicit by suggesting that maybe the Kuru gene actually protects against either disease. This is in keeping with the theory of paraphrase assumed elsewhere in this part of the chapter, namely, that paraphrase is not an exact semantic reproduction of the original material, but may involve loss or gain of information. Note that in this two-sentence paragraph structure a lot of the background for the *if*-condition within the conditional sentence proper is given in the previous sentence, and therefore, is not repeated in the *if*-clause of that sentence. Again, we conclude that the two-sentence sequence is essentially an extrapolation from the second sentence by the addition of a former sentence that gives extra background and explanation.

We can think of more colloquial, everyday examples which are parallel to the above, such as the following:

I'm wondering if you would be interested in coming to my house for supper Thursday night along with thrèe students from the National University. If you are, please let me know.

If-clauses may also be used to express alternatives on the paragraph level. The Tboly paragraph in Diagram xv (Doris Porter, in Longacre 1968:1.97) is an apt illustration.

Diagram xv 'If'-clauses expressing alternatives on the paragraph level

Margin	Nucleus	
	A well-loved person they put in a coffin so that his relatives can visit him.	Topic
If they make it long	the coffin stays in the house for 29 days.	Alternative step 1
If they make it short	it is only seven so that those who loved him can visit him.	Alternative step 2

In the example in Diagram xv, the 'if'-clauses in the margins express, along with the following nuclei, alternatives relative to the topic, 'viewing the dead in a coffin' that is expressed in the first sentence.

Such examples are not at all difficult to multiply for English, as in the following:

If you want to eat downtown, I'll meet you at Perkins Restaurant at 5:00. If you want to eat at home as usual, then we'd better delay supper until 6:30.

Still another use of 'if'-clauses on the paragraph level is to encode some kind of counter-consideration. The example from Atta Negrito in Diagram xvi (Claudia Whittle, in Longacre 1968:1.120) is apt.

Diagram xvi A counterfactual *if*-clause

Margin	Nucleus	
	Domi, the nephew of Uncle Inggie, he also came to visit.	Text
If Domi hadn't (come)	they wouldn't have known about the coming serenade.	Counter-consideration

The paragraph in Diagram XVI in some ways appears to be an extrapolation of a counterfactual sentence on the paragraph level. In the first sentence the information is given that Domi came to visit. This is put counterfactually in the second sentence, 'If Domi hadn't come', with the consequence stated 'they wouldn't have known about the coming serenade'. We display this paragraph a second time in Diagram XVII and supply in square brackets some material that is implied, but not stated.

Diagram XVII Material implied but not stated

Pre-margin	Nucleus	Post-margin	
	Domi, the nephew of Uncle Inggie, he also came to visit.	[so that they would know about the coming serenade]	Text
If Domi hadn't come to visit	they wouldn't have known about the coming serenade.		Counter-consideration

Note that as redone, the paragraph reveals the given and its consequence in the first sentence and the counterfactual condition and its consequence in the second sentence. It seems clear that such paragraphs are then extrapolations from counterfactual sentences whereby the first sentence gives extra information relative to the conditional element found in the second sentence.

It is evident that 'if'-clauses are rather versatile in their functions on the paragraph level in many languages.

4.1.5 *Adverbial clauses in purpose margins*

Adverbial clauses with *in order to* (or its equivalent *lest* in a negative clause) in a purpose margin may occur in sentence$_i$ and be paraphrased in the nucleus of sentence$_j$ thus providing a further variant of the text–reason structure which is illustrated above in respect to other sorts of sentence margins. The example from Schaeffer in Diagram XVIII (1968:129) is illustrative.

Diagram XVIII Text–reason structure

Nucleus	Margin	
It is unpleasant to be submerged by an avalanche, but we must allow the person to undergo this experience	in order that he realize that his system has no answer to the crucial questions of life.	Exhortation
He must come to know that his roof is a false protection from the storm of what is, and then we can talk to him of the storm of the Judgement of God.		Reason

In the example in Diagram XVIII the purpose margin is quite carefully paraphrased in the first base of the following co-ordinate sentence. Thus, we have in the purpose margin, *that he realize* which is parallel to, *He must come to know*. We have also the stretch, *that his system has no answer* which is parallel to *that his roof is a false protection*, and finally the stretch, *to the crucial questions of life* which is parallel to *from the storm of what is*. The co-ordinate sentence which is the second sentence of this paragraph goes on to add a further clause which brings in new material. This is a typical function of co-ordinate sentences, i.e., to attach an additional but parallel element to some systematic paraphrase which occurs in the regular development of a paragraph.

4.1.6 *Adverbial clauses in concessive margins*
The role of *although/though* clauses in paragraph structure is not clear at the present time. Two examples, however, in our present data have to do with incidental back-reference in the course of bringing paragraphs to a close. Perhaps some sort of summary or outcome is expressed. Perhaps all that is intended is a reiteration of the main topic of the paragraph.

Note the following example (again from the medical text, Garn 1961). We give the full text (with sentences numbered for ease of reference):

1 Mediterranean Fever is a 'periodic' disease.
2 Once the symptoms, the fever and malaise, have begun, they recur sporadically and unpredictably during the individual's lifetime.
3 At the least there is fever, lasting a day or two, joint pains, and chest and abdominal pain.
4 In advanced cases, there is a joint involvement, decalcification of the bone and kidney insufficiency.
5 Though most of the affected individuals are not permanently or seriously disabled, about 10% of cases studied to date succumbed to renal complications.

It appears in the above paragraph that the purpose of the first sentence is to introduce the topic *Mediterranean Fever*. The next sentence sounds somewhat like a fresh beginning in that the words, *Once the symptoms, the fever and malaise, have begun* begin that sentence. Sentences 3 and 4 express the course of the disease from light to heavy cases. Sentence 5, the sentence which interests us, begins with the adverbial clause, *Though most of the affected individuals are not permanently or seriously disabled*. This sentence seems to hark back two sentences to the sentence which says, *At the least there is fever, lasting a day or two, joint pains and chest and abdominal pain*. The remaining part of the last sentence of the paragraph, i.e., *about 10% of the cases studied to date succumbed to renal complications* seems to take off from the preceding sentence, i.e., *In advanced cases, there is joint involvement, decalcification of the bone and kidney insufficiency.* It appears, therefore, that this last sentence is some sort of summary which expresses the possible outcomes of the disease.

We now cite here the whole paragraph from the Mexican travelogue discourse which is cited in part in section 4.1.2 of this part.

As you prowl up and down the narrow streets, you must not fail to see the public washing basin, which looks more like a small outdoor swimming pool than anything else. Here the women and girls of the village come to wash their family clothing on the concrete washboards built along the basin's four sides. As they dip the water from the basin in their colorfully painted gourd bowls, these native housewives chatter among themselves combining their gossip with their work. Even though you cannot understand a word that is said, you will find the public washing place a fascinating spot.

It is evident that the last sentence is a reiteration of the topic which is stated in sentence one as the *public washing basin*, referred to briefly as *basin* in the next two sentences and now referred to as the *public washing place.* Also note that the word *you* occurs in the first and in the last sentence of this paragraph, but does not occur in the two intervening sentences. There is a return in the last sentence to the viewpoint of the reader as observer. It is, then, not unexpected that this last sentence begins with the adverbial clause, *Even though you cannot understand a word that is said.* This clause obviously refers back to the previous sentence, *these native housewives chatter among themselves combining their gossip with their work.* Apparently we have here an incidental reminder that the housewives are talking in a foreign language and the tourist (whose viewpoint is adopted here) cannot expect to understand them. In spite of the handicap, he will still find the public washing place a fascinating spot.

4.2 *Balanced or parallel clauses in successive sentences*

When-clauses in prior-time margins may be balanced in successive sentences to make an antithetical paragraph. In the medical text from which we have been quoting, the author quotes from someone else as follows (Garn 1961):

To quote Beutlar, Robson, and Buttenweiser, 57: 'When Primaquine was administered to non-sensitive subjects there was no change in their red cell GSH (reduced glutathione) level. When Primaquine was administered to a sensitive subject, there was an abrupt fall in the GSH content of the red blood cell to about one half of the original already abnormal value.'

The two sentences within this quotation clearly contrast with each other. An initial *but* or *however* (the overt sign of an antithetical paragraph) would clearly fit in the second sentence. In the parallel *when*-clauses the administration of Primaquine to *non-sensitive subjects* is balanced over against its administration to *sensitive subjects*. In the accompanying nuclei of the sentences, *no changes* in the GSH content of red blood cells is balanced against *an abrupt fall* in the GSH content. This is the two-pronged contrast that is typical of many 'but' structures in various parts of the world (cf. Longacre 1976:105–6).

In the Mexican travelogue text there is a paragraph, the first two sentences of which begin with concessive margins. Presumably, the occurrence of the concessive margins – initial in both sentences – and the similarity in content of the nuclei of the two sentences as well, establishes these two sentences as co-ordinate items in some sort of co-ordinate paragraph. There are no elements of contrast as in the above example. Rather, the first and second sentences simply assert that the caverns are believed to be as marvelous as Carlsbad Caverns, and that they are very large. What is germane to our present discussion, however, is the role of the preposed concessive clauses in establishing this balancing and co-ordination:

1 Although these caves have not yet been properly explored, many people believe that they are as marvelous as our own Carlsbad Caverns in the State of New Mexico.
2 Even though nobody can be sure of their size and quality, it is known that they are large, for they have been found to connect with another system of caves nearly twenty miles away.
3 They are the largest known caverns in all Mexico.

4.3 *Summary*
Before closing this subsection it needs to be emphasized that all the above constructions involving adverbial clauses in intraparagraph cohesion involve some sort of paraphrase relation of the adverbial clause with something else in the paragraph, i.e., they involve lexical overlap. Otherwise, an adverbial clause simply contributes local background to the sentence in which it occurs. In all the texts which we have been drawing examples from, there are numerous examples of adverbial clauses in such localized intrasentential function which have no relevance to any information outside the sentence itself. Thus, we have, for example, adverbial clauses which function as asides to the reader. In the medical text just cited the writer says in one place, *As the reader of this book undoubtedly knows* ... Similar to these asides are bibliographical references such as, *As X (date) has shown* or *As X and Y (date) have*

observed. It's hardly necessary to multiply examples on this point. We content ourselves with the following paragraph in the Mexican travelogue text:

1 It was Cortes who discovered the silver and started the mines going which made this village thrive and still keep it going.
2 While prospecting for tin and copper to use in making cannon, he made his rich discovery.
3 Later, when he thought that the King of Spain might come to visit him in Mexico, Cortes had a tunnel built through one of his mines near the plaza of the village so that the king might see for himself how rich the region was.
4 So that his visitor might be comfortable during his trip through the mines, Cortes had the tunnel made deep enough for a man to ride through it on horseback!

Notice that sentence 2 begins with an adverbial clause (in concurrent-time margin), *While prospecting for tin and copper to use in making cannon*. The rest of the sentence, i.e., *he made his rich discovery*, is a paraphrase of the first part of sentence 1. The initial adverbial clause of sentence 2 is, however, paraphrased nowhere in the paragraph; it brings in new and relevant information but serves no cohesive function. Notice also that sentence 3 has a preposed *when*-clause in concurrent-time margin and has a postponed *so that*-clause in the purpose margin. Both of these items have information of relevance mainly to the sentence itself. Likewise, the last sentence of the paragraph begins with a purpose clause *so that his visitor might be comfortable during his trip through the mines*. There is no other reference anywhere in the preceding sentences to Cortes' concern for the comfort of this royal visitor. Presumably, then, this purpose clause also is of relevance mainly to the sentence in which it occurs – although the last two sentences are united by references to the expected visit of the king of Spain.

4.4 *Lexical overlap as conjunction*
We have tried in the above section to establish the thesis that lexical overlap is the primary mode of intersentential connection. A corollary of that thesis is that a lexical overlap – especially when it is a back-reference – can become stylized and reduced until it becomes similar to a conjunction. Thus, instead of the specific repetition of a verb in back-reference the subsequent allusion may be by virtue of a verb of highly generic meaning such as 'do', 'be', or 'say'. In the parts of South America where this stylized conjunctival back-reference is encountered, the verb is often combined with a demonstrative stem. The verb is either uninflected or minimally inflected, resulting in what has sometimes been called a mini-clause.

Thus, in Cayapa (Wiebe 1977) narrative, forms consisting of a demonstrative plus 'be' plus a few inflectional elements form the most common conjunctival element: *Tsej-tu* (with *tu* indicating same subject in the verb of the preceding sentence as in the verb to follow in the sentence being introduced); *Tsen-nu* (with different subject indicated); *Tsen-nu-ren* (with *-ren* indicating that the main verb of the sentence will be an important event; and *Tsen-bala-n* (with *bala* 'when' and *-n* indicating role reversal or frustration). All these forms sum up a previous sentence 'So being then . . .' but contribute bits of information such as might be found in any dependent Cayapa verb. Often they are best translated simply as 'and then'.

Cayapa also uses forms of demonstrative plus 'do' as in *Tsangue'* (with -' marking same subject), 'having done this', or again simply 'and then', or 'next . . .' and forms of demonstrative plus 'say' as in *Tsandi'* (with -') meaning 'on so saying, then . . .'

The situation is not greatly different in several other Chibchan languages (Paez, Guambian, and Colorado) as well as in Tucanoan languages, where the 'mini-clause' is the commonest conjunctival element. As such, in its various forms the mini-clause is a reduction and stylization of the adverbial clause.

4.5 *Lexical overlap as particle*

As a second corollary of the main thesis of this half of this chapter, it remains to note that initial back-references to a preceding sentence, or a stylized and reduced reference, can be substituted for (in many languages) by a true conjunction, i.e., an element that is a particle or a particle complex.

Then picture a sentence such as *Tom mowed the grass* followed by another sentence *He put the lawnmower away*. The second sentence could begin with an explicit back-reference *After mowing the grass, he* . . . or with a stylized back-reference (much like Cayapa) *After doing that, he* . . . or simply with *Then he* . . . On this basis it could be argued that adverbial clauses exemplify the basic mood of intersentential cohesion, while such a reference can become stylized and conjunctival (as in Cayapa), or be simply substituted for by a conjunction.

This is true of other types of back-reference in English as well. Thus, consider the following four pairs of sentences:

(1)   He's sick. Since he's sick, I won't bother him
(2)   He's sick. Therefore/so, I won't bother him
(3)   He's sick. Even though he is sick, I've got to see him about this matter
(4)   He's sick. Nevertheless, I've got to see him about this matter

However, it was not from a consideration of English but from a germinal comment of Maryott's (1967) regarding Sangir (Philippines) that it first became clear that many if not all intersentential conjunctions could be considered to be substitutes for adverbial clauses in the same function. For example, Maryott posited three temporal margins: a prior-time margin with a conjunction meaning 'after', a concurrent-time margin with a conjunction meaning 'while', and a subsequent-time margin with a conjunction meaning 'until'. He then went on to observe that the Sangir conjunction *tangu* 'then' could substitute for any of the temporal margins. He also posited three margins in logical function: a cause margin with adverbial introducer 'because', a concurrent logical margin with an introducer meaning 'since', and a result margin with an introducer which means 'with the result that'. He then suggested that any of these margins can be substituted for simply by the word *diadi* meaning 'therefore'.

4.6 *Adverbial clauses as topics*
At the level of the individual sentence, we can say that an adverbial clause whose role is to maintain cohesion within the discourse as a whole is functioning as a *topic* with respect to the sentence to which it is attached.[11] Let us look briefly at some of the grammatical ramifications of the topicality of adverbial clauses which are serving this linkage function.

Some of the general characteristics of topics are (1) they appear in sentence-initial position, (2) they are discourse dependent, (3) they need not be arguments of the main prediction, (4) they are definite, and (5) they set a 'spatial, temporal or individual framework within which the main prediction holds' (Chafe 1976:50 and Li and Thompson 1976b).

Now, as we have seen in Part II of this chapter, it is extremely common to find adverbial clauses functioning as topics in every language. But in some, this function is explicitly marked.

In several languages, conditional clauses are marked as topics, and in some, the marking they share also appears on interrogatives. In Hua, a Papuan language, for example, conditionals, topics, and interrogatives can all be marked with *ve* (Haiman 1978):

(127)   a. E-si-*ve*   baigu-e
            come-3SG FUT-*ve* stay(FUT)-1SG

    (i) *Conditional*
       If he comes, I will stay

    (ii) *Interrogative*
       Will he come? I will stay

    b. *Topic*
      Dgai-mo-*ve*   baigu-e
      I-CONNECTOR-*ve* stay(FUT)-ISG
      'As for me, I will stay'

In Turkish the conditional suffix -*se* also marks topics (Eser Ergovanti, personal communication):

(128)   a. Istanbul-a   gid-er-*se*-n,   Topkapı
           Istanbul-DAT go-AORIST-COND-2SG Topkapi

           müze-sin-i   muhakkak gez
           museum-POSS-ACC for sure   visit
           'If you go to Istanbul, be sure to visit the Topkapi museum'

      b. *Topic*
         Ahmed-i-*se* cok mesgul
         Ahmed-be very busy
         'As for Ahmed, he's very busy'

The reason why conditionals, topics, and questions in many languages may share the same morphology is that conditional clauses, like topics, are presupposed parts of their sentences. Both of them may be thought of as establishing a framework within which to proceed with the discourse, much as a question might. Thus, (127a) is semantically similar to a 'mini-conversation' in (129a), and (128b) is similar to the 'mini-conversation' in (129b):

(129)   a. A: Is he coming?
         B: (Yes)
         A: Well, then, I'll stay
      b. A: You know Ahmed?
         B: (Yes)
         A: Well, he's very busy

(For further discussion, see Haiman 1978; Keenan and Schieffelin 1976a,b; and Li and Thompson 1976b.)

    But conditionals are not the only adverbial clauses which may be marked as topics: in many languages, a variety of clause types may be so marked.

    Chao (1968:81, 113) points out that clauses of concession, reason, time, and condition may all occur with the four topic/interrogative particles in Chinese. Here is just one example, showing a concessive clause, a question, and a topic sentence with the final particle *a*:

(130)   a. *Concessive*
          Suiran   wo xiang qu *a*, keshi ni   bu   rang wo
          although I   want go   but   you NEG allow I
          'Although I want to go, you won't let me'

       b. *Interrogative*
          Ta shi nali-de   ren   *a*?
          he is where-GEN person
          'Where is he from?'

       c. *Topic*
          Zheige ren   *a*, ta yiding   shi yige hao   ren
          this   person   he certainly is a   good person
          'This person, he must be a good person'

In Godié, the Kru language of the Ivory Coast which we looked at earlier, the 'non-final' morpheme *nʌ* occurs at the ends of adverbial clauses functioning as topics (Marchese 1977):

(131)   ʌ̄ tʌ   . nɔ kaa   nʉ ʌ̄ yi ɔ   'ni
         I look for(COMPL) him long time and I POT him see

         ʌ̄ *ni*   ɔ   *nʌ* nʉ   yii   kɷ bʉlʉ
         I *see*(COMPL) him   and he (POT)me up take
         'I looked for him until I found him . . . *When I had found him,
         he took me . . .*'

The italicized clause in the above section of a narrative is an example of what we discussed above as an 'absolutive clause'. Notice that it ends with the marker *nʌ*, and that it has all the characteristics of topics that we listed above: it occurs sentence initially and does not function as an argument of the main clause predicate; its discourse role is to link the preceding clause with the clause to which it is attached and, at the same time, it sets a temporal framework within which the following predication holds; finally, in recapitulating already-mentioned material, it is definite. Further evidence that *nʌ* is a topic marker comes from a dialect of Godié in which single nouns which function as topics may be followed by the *nʌ* marker:

(132)   Zozii *nʌ*, ɔ yʌmʌ guu   cɨcɨcɨ
         Jesus   he healed sickness of all kinds
         'Jesus, he healed all kinds of diseases'

In Isthmus Zapotec, adverbial clauses may take an optional final particle *la* (which one language consultant calls a 'comma'). It is found only on those clauses which are initial and definite:

(133)   Kumu wara be *la*, naa   uyaa'
         since sick he   (COMPL)go I
         'Since he was sick, I went'

(134)   Laga kayuni be nga *la*, bedanda   hnaa   be
         while (PROG)do he that   (COMPL)arrive mother his
         'While he was doing that, his mother arrived'

A clause which represents new information, such as the result clause in (135), cannot take *la*, then, because it is not the topic:

(135)   Dede ma ke ganda   saya' (*la), tantu   ja ndaane'
         till   I   not (POT)can walk   so much full my belly
         'I am so full I can't walk'

la can also be found with initial noun phrases which are functioning as topics, but, as expected, never with focused initial noun phrases:

(136)   Ngiiu-ke *la*, bigapa ba'du-ke
         man-that   hit   child-that
         'That man, he hit the child'

(137)   Tu   bi'ni ni? Betu (**la*) bi'ni ni
         'Who did it? Betu   did it'

In Lisu, a Tibeto-Burman language, adverbial clauses functioning as topics are marked with the same marker *nya* which is used for NP topics (see Hope 1974:64; and Li and Thompson 1976b):

(138)   Ame   thæ nwu patsɨ-a dye-ạ   ŋu bæ-ạ   *nya*
         yesterday TIME you plain-to go-DECLAR FACT say-DECLAR TOP

         nwu *nya* asa ma mu-a
         you TOP Asa not see-Q
         'When you went to the plain yesterday, didn't you see Asa?'
         ('Assuming that it is a fact that you went to the plain yesterday,
         ... didn't you see Asa?')

Thus, we see that in some languages, the discourse-cohesion role played by certain adverbial clauses is signaled explicitly by marking them as topics.

5 Conclusion

We've tried to show in this part of the chapter that adverbial clauses may be of relevance to a stretch greater than the sentence in which they find themselves, that they may provide cohesion for an entire discourse, or they may provide cohesion for some paragraph within it. The data and evidence that we have accumulated appear to be sufficient to suggest that the fundamental device of intersentential connection is lexical overlap which involves grammatically definable parts of the sentence. The thesis is that one grammatically definable part of a sentence (sentence margin or a clause within the nucleus of a sentence) refers in some way to all or part of another sentence in the surrounding context. Such references are systematic, can be codified, and be used to implement a theory of the structure of discourse and paragraph. Taking lexical overlap in grammatically definable parts of sentences as a fundamental device of intersentential cohesion, it can further be shown that in some languages conjunctions are essentially verbal and demonstrative elements that have developed from such an overlap. Finally, it can be shown that even in languages where such a development cannot be traced, conjunctions can often be shown to be a substitute for the use of such overlap. Adverbial clauses are a frequent grammatical codification of such overlap and are therefore crucial to the understanding of cohesion in discourse.

NOTES

1 *Denn*-clauses are exceptional: they appear to be subordinate, but they exhibit 'normal' verb-second word order. Compare:
   (i) Er musste bezahlen
       he had to pay

   a. ***denn***   er *war* da
      because he was there

   b. ***weil***   er da   *war*
      because he there was
      'He had to pay because he was there'

2 Adverbial clauses of comparison, degree, and extent form a topic worthy of cross-linguistic research. They are not treated in this chapter.

3 We are grateful to Matthew Dryer for his valuable help in clarifying this issue.

4 The distinctions below are adapted from J. Schachter's (1971) pioneering study on the syntax and semantics of conditional sentences in English.

5 Our thanks to Robert Hetzron for clarifying this point for us.

6 For some discussion, see Fraser (1969) and de Chene (1976).

7 The term 'absolutive' comes from traditional Latin grammar, *absolutus* meaning 'free' or 'unconnected'. In traditional Latin grammar, however, its usage is restricted to clauses of the second type described in this section, exemplified by (120), whose subject bears no grammatical or semantic

relation to the main verb. Our use of 'absolutive' here is more general. For a plea that absolute constructions in Indo-European be regarded as a type of subordinate clause, see Berent (1973).

8 *Qala* can only be used when the subjects of the main and subordinate clauses are different.

9 Overlap linkage may also be via a part of the sentence nucleus itself. Thus, the first part of a co-ordinate sentence may repeat or allude to part of a previous sentence, as in the following example:

With Eugene the first sign of trouble is usually smouldering resentment. He cherishes some real or imaginary hurt for several days, and then ...

Likewise, the first base of an antithetical sentence may embody a back-reference to the preceding sentence:

Johnnie has made some progress in social relations recently. He apparently is adjusting somewhat better to his peer group, but ...

The second base of a reason sentence (i.e., the part of the sentence introduced by *for*) may have a similar function:

Mac was tired, bone tired from the experiences of the past 48 hours. He slept the clock around for he was completely exhausted.

10 In previous work (Longacre 1968:1.56–63), Longacre has summarized some of the variety of grammatical linkage found in Philippine languages – devices which embody sequential back-reference of this sort.

11 This discussion owes much to input from Russell Schuh, Velma Pickett, Robert Hetzron, Lynell Marchese, and John Haiman. See also Marchese (1977), Haiman (1978).

5 Sentences as combinations of clauses

ROBERT E. LONGACRE

0 Introduction

In discourse, whether dialogue or monologue, simple predications combine into larger units. Clauses – the surface structure units which correspond most closely to individual predications – combine into clusters of clauses which are distinguished in most languages as sentences versus paragraphs. These sentences are tighter bundles than paragraphs. They commonly have more cross reference between their component parts (clauses) and more 'closure' (i.e., it is somewhat easier to tell where one stops and another starts) than is the case with combinations of sentences which we call paragraphs. Although paragraphs encode essentially the same relations (see section 2) as those found in sentence structures, they are looser and more diffuse. Paragraphs typically do not have as many overt grammatical ties between their component sentences as do the parts of the sentence itself. Nor do paragraphs usually have grammatical closure (cf., however, Foré in 4.1).

In this chapter I feature the sentence with only passing attention to the paragraph. The sentence is considered here not as a unit consisting of a predicate and nouns related to it (a simple clause), but rather as a combination of such units (clauses) into still larger structures of a sort here summarized. This chapter describes the notions encoded in these combinations of clauses and goes on to describe and illustrate the formal features of these sentences in languages around the world.

1.0 Definitions and distinctions

Before proceeding further, it is essential to define a few terms which are useful in describing sentence structures, and to posit a few distinctions.

1.1 *Nucleus, base and margin*
Three useful terms in distinguishing the parts of a sentence are: 'nucleus', 'base', and 'margin'. Take the following sentence: *When they*

heard the news, Mary was elated but John was sad and thoughtful. The stretch *Mary was elated but John was sad and thoughtful* sets off this sentence as typologically distinct from other sentences such as *Mary was elated and so was John* and *Mary was so elated that she danced a jig.* On the other hand, the stretch *When they heard the news* can attach indifferently to many divergent types of structures. For example, it can also attach to the latter two sentences above: *When they heard the news, Mary was elated and so was John* and *When they heard the news, Mary was so elated that she danced a jig.* In summary, these distributional observations could be correlated as in Table 5.1.

Table 5.1. *Sentence margin and sentence nuclei*

Part (a)	Part (b)
When they heard the news	Mary was elated but John was sad and thoughtful Mary was elated and so was John Mary was so elated that she danced a jig

In keeping with such observations as above, it is useful to consider that Part (a) is a 'sentence margin' and Part (b) illustrates three kinds of 'sentence nuclei'. The nucleus[1] of a sentence is its most characteristic part and is, furthermore, independent of the margin. The margin, on the contrary, goes with a variety of nuclei and is thus non-characteristic and, in addition, it is subordinated to the rest of the sentence (see section 1.2 below).

Many languages have a variety of 'sentence margins'; these are the adverbial clauses described in chapter II:4. Thus in English we have not only temporal margins as in the *when* clause above but margins of other sorts: conditional (introduced by *if*), concessive (introduced by *although*), purpose (introduced by *in order to*), and cause (introduced by *because*).

Sentence nuclei contain the distinctive features of sentence types as described below in further sections of this chapter. In the examples summarized in Table 5.1, sentences with medial *and*, *but*, and *so . . . that* illustrate some distinctive nuclei. The parts of a sentence nucleus consist of (a) a conjunction and (b) bases (although conjunctions are not present in all types). The term 'base' is here used to describe a functional subpart of a nucleus. Thus, in Table 5.1 the following are all bases: *Mary was elated, John was sad and thoughtful, so was John,* and *she danced a jig.* Bases may be elliptical or may contain substitutes. Thus *so was John* refers back to *elated,* with *so* acting as a substitute.

The term 'base' is needed because a functional part of a nucleus need not be a single clause. Note the following expansion of the first sentence referred to above: *When they heard the news Mary was elated and danced a jig, but John fell into a moody silence, paced the floor, and swore softly under his breath.* Here each base of the nucleus is filled by an embedded sentence of coordinate structure (with regular non-recurrence of identical subject in subsequent clauses). The *but* separates the two main parts of the nucleus; each subpart has its own sentential structure.

Such recursive occurrence of sentence within sentence is endemic in the sentence structure of most languages around the world. Note the following more extreme example: *Had they sent for him or in some way acknowledged his existence he probably would have summoned enough pride to reject their offer, but this endless waiting finally wore him down.* To begin with, this sentence is a bipartite structure hinging on the word *but*, each part being a base. In turn, however, the first base of this *but* sentence is itself complex: it is a contrafactual sentence: *Had they sent for him or in some way acknowledged his presence, he probably would have summoned enough pride to reject their offer*, whose first part is a conditional margin which is also complex: an *or* sentence.

So we see that not only may a nucleus be complex but a margin may be complex as well, i.e., we may in effect subordinate a sentence rather than simply a clause. The following example is relevant: *When Napoleon dominated the continent and only England held out against him, a child was born in an obscure village in northern Scotland.* Here the sentence *Napoleon dominated the continent and only England held out against him* functions as sentence margin when subordinated by the introducer *when*.

In this chapter I will try, however, to restrict examples of sentences to those of the simpler sort (with complex sentences in their bases).

1.2 *Coordinate and subordinate clauses*

The nucleus/margin distinction which is illustrated above ties into a broader concern of 'coordinate' versus 'subordinate' relationships of units. Subordinate clauses are clauses which function as noun phrases, as modifiers of nouns, and as modifiers of verb phrases or entire propositions. Clauses which function as noun phrases are found in nearly all languages as sentential expansions of subject/object slots. These are called complements in this book and are discussed in chapter II:2. Clauses which are modifiers of verbs and propositions are adverbial clauses which function as sentence margins (see chapter II:4). Finally, most (but not all) languages have subordinate clauses, called relative clauses, which serve to modify a noun phrase. The ways in which this function is realized is the topic of chapter II:3.

1.3 Co-ranking and chaining structures

Sentence structures around the world may be conveniently divided into two main types called 'co-ranking' structures and 'chaining' structures. These two structures are very distinct. In co-ranking structures, such as those found in a typical Indo-European language, it is possible to have several verbs of the same rank, commonly referred to as independent verbs. Thus, we can speak of a sentence as consisting of a coordination of independent clauses. In English the conjunctions *and*, *but*, and *or* plus a few others join such independent clauses into sentence units (Longacre 1970). In a chaining structure, on the other hand, it is simply not possible to combine two verbs of the same rank in the same sentence. A sentence typically ends in a dominating verb of fuller structure than any of the preceding verbs. These preceding verbs are commonly referred to as medial verbs while the dominating verb at the end is known as the final verb. Thus in a sentence such as *Kawa left and the patrol officer arrived*, in a co-ranking language the verbs *left* and *arrived* are of the same rank, and differ in no way inflectionally. In a chaining language *left* and *arrived* would be different types of verbs. *Arrived* would be a verb inflected for tense, mood, and aspect while the verb *left* would be not only somewhat deficient in certain of these inflectional categories but might also indicate in its verb morphology whether the subject of the following clause is the same as or different from the subject of its own clause. The following data from Selepet, a language of the Eastern Morobe district of Papua New Guinea (data from McElhanon), are illustrative: Firstly as simplex sentences we have

> Kawa ari-op
> Kawa left
> 'Kawa left'

and

> kiap   ya taka-op
> patrol officer that arrived
> 'That patrol officer arrived'

However, when put together in the same sentence we get

> Kawa ari-*mu* kiap ya taka-*op*
> 'Kawa left and that patrol officer arrived'

Here -*mu*, which indicates 'third person singular, subject switch', has replaced -*op*, which indicates 'third person singular, remote past tense'.

It is important to note that chaining structures consisting of one or more clauses with medial verbs followed by a clause with a final verb are not parallel to Indo-European sequences of one or more subordinate clauses followed by an independent clause. An Indo-European language (or, for that matter, co-ranking languages in general) offers an option between such alternative expressions as *After chopping the wood, John carried it to his house* and *John chopped the wood and carried it to his house*. A language completely of the chaining variety offers no such option; both the subordinate-independent and coordinate constructions of English would be rendered by a clause with medial verb followed by a clause with final verb. In brief, the subordinate/coordinate distinction is irrelevant (in that there is no choice between the two) and both are absorbed into the medial/final distinction.

Both co-ranking and chaining structures have a derivative type of structure in which stripped down or inflectionally reduced verbs are found. In co-ranking structures this inflectional reduction results in what I term a 'merged sentence', in which the reduced verb still has many characteristics of a main verb (cf. section 1.4). In some co-ranking structures neither verb is reduced (in a sequence) but the otherwise obligatory subject is omitted from one clause. By a corresponding device in chaining languages, non-final verbs are stripped to stems with minimal inflection although the medial/final distinction is still preserved in this further elaboration of the basic chaining patterns.

1.4 *Methods of cohesion*

Various degrees of cohesion between sentence bases are posited here. Cohesion effected by a sentence-medial conjunction is both explicit and loose. Thus *and, but, for,* and *so* in sentence-medial position in English explicitly mark differing relations. But, on occasion, at least *and, but* and *so* may occur in sentence-initial position where they serve to bind sentences into the less tightly knit connections of the paragraph. Furthermore, the decision to opt for one sentence or two when *and* and *but* are involved is sometimes delicate, if not arbitrary. For these reasons we may consider that cohesion via sentence-medial conjunction is somewhat loose.

Cohesion may also be via juxtaposition with a non-final pause in sentence-medial position and overall unifying phonology. Here also some lexical features (e.g. repetition and/or paraphrase) reinforce the unity. Probably the very absence of conjunction in sentences that employ juxtaposition necessitates a tighter unity—which is signaled by phonological and lexical means.

The tightest degree of cohesion between clauses is found in sentences in which the component clauses overlap each other and are mutually dependent, as in a 'merged sentence'. Take the following sentences: *I intend to tell her*, *They made John walk*, *They let him go*. The first part of each sentence is incomplete, *I intend...*, *They made ...*, and *They let ....* The second part of each sentence is not only incomplete but does not contain a finite verb. Furthermore, the status of *John* and *him* is somewhat uncertain in the last two sentences. Do *John walk* and *him go* make plausible groupings? Or is *John* object of *made* and *him* object of *let*? *They made John* is an intelligible stretch only if John is a robot or papier mâché statue. *They let him*, like *they made John*, is incomplete without something of the sort which follows here.

The answer to all these problems seems to lie in assuming the constructions to be composites in which two clauses are present but overlap. In sentence one *I* is subject of both the clause which expresses 'having an intention' and the clause which expresses 'going to tell her'. In the second sentence *they* is subject of the first clause while *John* is some sort of 'object' of the same; but *John* is also the logical subject of the second clause. Similarly, *him* can be construed as object of the first clause of the third sentence and subject of the next clause.

In spite of the composite nature of such sentences, they have very tight surface unity. Phonologically, they do not permit internal pause – no more than in a simple clause structure without embedding (or other complications), i.e., *I intend to tell her* is just as phonologically unified as *I told Mary the news*. Lexically, the whole unit is restricted in that when the merged sentences are properly sorted out as to types, the verbs which occur in the first clause are found to constitute a closed list.

In terms of dynamic language processes, merged sentences often develop into simple clauses which contain auxiliary plus main verb. Thus, *I will do it* is a development from something similar to *I intend to do it*, but *will* has been reduced from a main verb in the first clause of a merged sentence to an auxiliary – as it has been traditionally (and I believe, correctly) analyzed. Interestingly, although we tend to think of the first verb as dominant in English merged sentences, it is precisely this verb which is reduced diachronically to auxiliary status.

1.5 *More complex structures*
Many languages also have a few sentences which impress the analyst as essentially elaborations of clause structure into units whose complexity is such that they are better handled as sentence structures. Of relevance here are 'quotation' sentences, which are presented and discussed under 3.1.3.

2.0 Notions that encode within sentence structure

While an understanding of the formal devices of sentence structure is crucial to the understanding of a sentence, it is equally crucial to understand what notions are encoded within such structures.[2] To begin with, we note that apparently the sentence level exists for the purpose of encoding combinations of predications, i.e., relations within the domain of the propositional instead of the predicate calculus. Nevertheless, surface structure sentences are not necessarily confined to such elements. As we have seen above in treating juxtaposed sentences in certain languages, sometimes elements from the predicate calculus such as instrumentality or benefaction are encoded by means of a pair of clauses. Ignoring these complications which have been noted above in passing, I now proceed to give, in abbreviated form (cf. Longacre 1976:98–163), the notions which underlie sentence structure. It should be noted that the same notions also underlie paragraph structure in most languages – although the particular division of functional load between paragraph and sentence is often language-specific. It should also be noted that certain of these notions clearly underlie whole discourses, especially expository discourses. Furthermore, narrative discourse is built on the idea of temporal succession. I will not illustrate materials from paragraph and discourse structure in this section but will confine the examples to the encoding of the various notions here listed as sentence structures. In order of presentation I discuss (as basic to the structure of discourse) conjoining, alternation, temporality, and implication. Then (as elaborative devices in discourse) paraphrase, illustration, deixis, and attribution. Finally, I discuss frustration, which is a further relation imposed upon many of those already listed.

2.1 *Conjoining*

Under conjoining I distinguish coupling, contrast, and comparison.

2.1.1 *Coupling*

Coupling may be defined as a non-temporal underlying *and* relation. This is commonly expressed in the surface structure in some sort of coordinate or parallel sentence.

Coupling with the same first term is seen in *She's big and (she's) tall*. We also may have parallel coupling in such a sentence as, *I spit on your coat; I spit on your hat; and I spit on your dress*. In English it is not usual to repeat the full clause structure as in the above example. Presumably the preceding example has special motivation of emphasis (and spite) to account for its fullness of structure. In English it is more common in sentences in which the noun is varied from clause to clause to put the nouns into a coordinate noun phrase as in *The men, women, and children talk English*. Nevertheless, in some parts of the world, noticeably in the Philippines and New Guinea, a fuller structure such as 'The men talk English, the women talk English, the children talk English' is definitely preferred.

2.1.2 *Contrast*

We deal here with underlying *but* relations. While coupling involves varying activities and varying participants, the notion of contrast requires paired lexical oppositions. Contrast, in fact, must be two-pronged; i.e., there must be at least two opposed pairs of lexical items.

Contrast may be expressed by means of positive and negative values of the same predicate accompanied by differing participants: *I went downtown, but she didn't*. It is obvious, of course, that in such an example as the one above, one or the other predicate in positive or negative value can be substituted for by a synonym. Contrast may also proceed by means of antonyms: *I went downtown, but she stayed home*. Contrast may sometimes be entirely within the terms (with the predicate unchanged) as in *Bill works outside during the day and inside at night* where *outside* and *inside* are contrasted and so are *day* and *night*. The above varieties of contrast are very commonly expressed in English and in many languages in some kind of antithetical sentence.

A further variety of contrast is exception. Thus, we can have a sentence such as *Grandfather didn't go to sleep, but everybody else did*. Here the universal set minus *grandfather* is contrasted with *grandfather*, and *didn't go to sleep* is contrasted with 'going to sleep'. While this may be expressed as above in an antithetical sentence, it is expressed more commonly in English in a single clause with an *except* adjunct, i.e *Everybody went to sleep except grandfather*.

2.1.3 *Comparison*

We have here comparisons of equality and inequality as is common in Indo-European languages, i.e., *Bill is as big as John* and *Bill is bigger than John*. The number of participants expressed in this sentence does not materially alter the situation. Thus, we can have *John loves Mary less than Bill loves Jane*. It seems that such a notion is a useful construct in English whereas it is not useful in such an area as Papua New Guinea. Comparison in Papua New Guinea is not expressed within a single sentence, but by a pair of sentences within a paragraph. It is, furthermore, really not comparison, but contrast. In Safeyoka (a dialect of Wojokeso), for example, we find pairs of sentences such as 'The black man's boats are small. The white man's boats are huge'. There is no direct way of saying 'The black man's boats are smaller than the white man's boats' or 'The white man's boats are bigger than the black man's'.

2.2 *Alternation*

We deal here with underlying *or* relations of roughly two sorts. The first sort of statement of alternation involves only two possible alternatives, or at least the presuppositions of the sentence envision only two alternatives. Examples are *Either he did it or he didn't, Is he dead or alive?, Are you going to your village by plane or by canoe?* In the second sort of sentence expressing alternation we find that the number of alternatives is open or at least more than two: *Either John will come, or Mary will come, or Sue will come.* It is evident again that in a language such as English telescoping and deletion are preferred, as in *Either John will come, or Mary, or Sue.*

In some languages these two types of construction are distinguished better in their surface structure than in English. Thus, in the Ek-Nii language of Papua New Guinea (data from Stucky), the equivalent of 'or' occurs between the two bases of a sentence if only two alternatives are envisioned. If more than two alternatives are envisioned, there will also be an 'or' in sentence-final position, i.e., 'Either John will come, or Mary will come, *or*'; meaning 'John will come, Mary will come, or somebody else'.

2.3 *Temporality*

A variety of temporal relations are expressed in any language. These can be roughly grouped under overlap and succession.

2.3.1 *Overlap*

Overlap encodes underlying *meanwhile* and *at the same time* relations. Overlap may be to all practical purposes coterminous, i.e., two actions are considered to start and stop at roughly the same time, as in *As he walked along, he prayed.* Bases of such sentences are entirely reversible: *He prayed as he walked along.* Overlap may also be punctiliar–continuous or vice versa, that is, continuous–punctiliar. We can say *He glanced back as he walked on* or *While he was walking, he stumbled.* In either case there is a continuum of activity during which another activity takes place. Finally, overlap may be punctiliar–punctiliar, i.e., two punctiliar events may be reported as timed at the same instant: *As I brought up my head, she tossed the knife.*

2.3.2 *Succession*

Succession is an underlying *and then* relation. While the terms punctiliar and continuous are used above to refer to actions involved in overlap, the terms span and event are used here for actions involved in succession. The purpose of this terminological distinction is simply to keep track of whether we are involved in overlap or succession. A sentence may report span–span, for example *They played tennis for an hour, then swam for another hour.* It may also report event–span, for example *He put the wood on the stove and then sat there for an hour.* Likewise, it may report span–event: *He lived in Paris for seven years, then moved to Spain.* Finally, of course, succession may report event–event: *He sat down, took the book, and opened it.* The events reported may involve reciprocity on the part of the participants, such as *He gave her some water and she drank it* where the indirect object of the first clause is subject of the second clause.

Note that this summary of temporal relations is by no means complete. We find, for example, sentences in which there is a series of events taking place during a given span as in *While I was downtown, my nephew picked the lock on my study door, entered the room, and searched it.*

It is important to note that underlying temporal relations are themselves temporally ordered. This may lead to a surface structure restriction in some languages (e.g. those of Papua New Guinea) whereby clauses must be linearly ordered according to time succession. In most languages, however, there exist devices whereby the order of presentation in the sentence can be different from that of the temporal occurrence of events, in which case special surface features such as the use of 'before', 'after', and so forth are used to keep track of the chronology.

2.4 *Implication*

By this term is meant any *if . . . then* notions. I group under this heading conditionality, causation, counterfactuality, and warning. I will discuss the first three of these here.

2.4.1 *Conditionality*

The simplest sort of conditionality encountered in languages is hypotheticality, the unweighted *if* relation. Thus, in *If he comes, I'll go* or *If he doesn't go, I won't go either* there is nothing implied as to the outcome of the situation. In the first sentence the person may or may not go. All that is stated is that my going is contingent on his coming.

Sentences which involve a universal quantifier in the first base are a further type of conditional. Here, we have sentences such as *Wherever you go, I'll be thinking of you* which resolves itself into a condition such as *If you go any and all places, I'll be thinking of you*. The universal quantifier may go on any element in the first base, so we can have sentences such as: *Whomever we sent got lost*; *Whatever road you take, you won't get there*; *However you do it, I'm opposed*; etc. In English, such structures are expressed by an interrogative structure suffixed with *ever* or by such words as *everyone* in *Everyone who goes there gets lost*. In a typical Philippine language, such structures are expressed by a preposed concessive margin with an interrogative, i.e., 'Even if we sent whom, he gets lost' or 'Even if you go where, I'll be thinking of you'.

A further type of conditionality involves a temporal referent such as *You have to pay before you can occupy the room*. This can be called contingency.

2.4.2 *Causation*
Causation differs from conditionality in that in causation there is a given, which is the antecedent event. Coupled with the given is its consequent: something else is implied by the antecedent and that something else took place. Thus, in the sentence *You stayed home because you were afraid*, it is given that you were afraid and it is further asserted that fear resulted in your staying home.

Aristotle distinguished among his four types of causes efficient cause and final cause. Final cause is usually called 'purpose'. Nevertheless, there are certain advantages in calling both varieties 'cause', the chief advantage being that they are often expressed by very similar surface structures (see chapter II:4, part I, section 3.2.1 for discussion).

A further variety of causation is circumstance. This is a relation which means *in the circumstance that*. Many languages distinguish circumstance from cause in their surface structure. In English we have, as observed above, special adverbial introducers *since* or *in that* to mark circumstance: *In that he still is convalescing, let's leave him alone*.

2.4.3 *Counterfactuality*
Counterfactuality, like causality, involves a given. The sentence *Had he come, I would have come*, takes as its given, 'he didn't come'. It further expresses an implication, namely, 'My (possible) coming was conditional on his coming'. With these two we would have the meaning of causality rather than counterfactuality. The distinctive feature of counterfactuality is its double implication. Something further is implied in the above sentence, namely, 'He didn't come and because he didn't come, I didn't come either'. In the surface structures of the world's

languages counterfactual conditions may be very similar to other sorts of conditions or may be structurally very distinct (see chapter II:2).

2.5 *Paraphrase*
Communication flow in most situations and information distribution in discourse requires that certain elements of discourse be repeated. Typically, this repetition is not exact and information is gained or lost in the repetition. It is in this sense that 'paraphrase' is used here. I distinguish here two varieties of paraphrase in which there is very little noticeable loss or gain of information, then two varieties of paraphrase in which there is gain of information in the second base as opposed to the first base, and finally two varieties of paraphrase in which there is loss of information in the second base as opposed to the first base.

2.5.1 *Paraphrase without noticeable gain or loss of information*
Often a sentence will use two items which are very close synonyms in two successive clauses, such as *He's prejudiced; he's just plain bigoted* or *I went home; I went to the house* where *home* and *house* are all but indistinguishable in contemporary usage. A further variety of paraphrase that amounts to even closer lexical equivalence is 'negated antonym paraphrase'. With a pair of antonyms and negation of one of the two members, we get a very close paraphrase, as in *It's not black; it's white* or *He's not rich; he's poor*.

2.5.2 *Paraphrase in which there is gain of information in the second base*
This is done basically by two devices: either by using more specific lexical items in the second base, or by adding in the second base modifiers, further phrases, or qualifying clauses. The two are not necessarily exclusive in the same sentence. Thus, in the sentence *He cooked the bananas, he fried them* it appears that the device used is what could be called 'generic–specific paraphrase'. In the sentence *He sang, he sang two songs* (called recapitulation sentence in the surface structure of English above), a noun phrase is added in base two. In the following sentence translated from Ibaloi we have the causer specified in the second base, but not in the first: 'He was unconscious; Dabonay, a woman, had knocked him unconscious'. This sort of paraphrase may be called 'amplification paraphrase'. It needs to be underscored, however, that both generic–specific and amplification paraphrase may characterize a second base as opposed to the first. To go back to the first example above, we can say *He cooked the bananas, he fried them in vegetable oil* where both the more specific term *fry* in base two and the additional phrase *in vegetable oil* are used.

2.5.3 *Paraphrase in which there is loss of information in the second base*
This is accomplished by two devices, each of which is the converse of the two described just above under 2.5.2: firstly, by using more generic lexical terms in the second base, or secondly, by dropping in the second base items which occurred in the first base. The former may be termed 'specific–generic paraphrase' and the latter, 'contraction paraphrase'. Again, the two devices are not necessarily exclusive. Possibly some kind of summary is implied when either or both these devices are used. Thus, we can say *He fried the bananas in vegetable oil; he cooked them* – where not only is a more generic term found in the second clause, but also where *in vegetable oil* is dropped as well. Perhaps in both these sentences there is something summary in the use of *cook*. The thrust may be 'They didn't eat them raw'. Pure contraction paraphrase gives a somewhat implausible sentence: (?) *He fried the bananas in vegetable oil; he fried them*. Contraction paraphrase with use of a close synonym in the second base is more plausible: *I'm going home to see Mama, I'm going to the house*.

2.5.4 *Other kinds of paraphrase*
This is not meant to be an exhaustive summary of paraphrase. There are further kinds of paraphrase such as negated higher gradient paraphrase in *It's not hot, but it's warm*; negated extremes paraphrase in *It's neither hot nor cold, just warm*; and summary paraphrase as in *John works at the saw mill, Jim works at the repair shop – that's what they're all doing*. In the last example the clause after the dash serves as a summary paraphrase of the previous parts of the sentence.

2.6 Illustration
I assume here that the basic devices of illustration, which are very important in achieving clarity and appeal in discourse, are simile and exemplification.

2.6.1 *Simile*
Simile involves an explicit comparison. I believe this is a basic device behind most figures of speech and metaphor, but that there are surface structure devices whereby similes can be deleted and telescoped to form metaphors. Here again, however, languages differ radically. To express a comparison in Trique, a simile must be used, and the simile must be very explicit. It must involve the particle *ro?* 'like' between the two bases of the comparison and the verbs of both bases must be identical: for example 'Like does this, so does that'; 'Like goes this, so goes that'; 'Like is this, so is that'; 'Like appears this, so appears that'. Therefore,

if one were to compare a woman to a rose, one would have to say 'She is like a rose is'. English here characteristically uses *like* as a preposition: *She is like a rose*; *He acts like a baby*; *A pretty girl is like a melody*.

2.6.2 *Exemplification*

In this structure a set is mentioned, and one or more members are taken as exemplary of the set as in *Take any common garden vegetable, for example, spinach*.

2.7 *Deixis*

Under this heading are grouped various devices for introducing or identifying a participant or prop which figures in a sentence. Needless to say, such devices are of great importance in initiating discourses, where the structures here exemplified may stretch over several sentences or paragraphs. Such structures may start by introducing a participant or prop and making a statement about him or reporting an action in which he is involved. Alternatively, a structure may begin by reporting an event or situation involving a certain participant or prop and then may identify him later on in the sentence or paragraph; we will refer to this as an identification sentence.

Structures of this sort are very important in Ibaloi. The following sentences are translations from Ibaloi but make good English. The Ibaloi introduction sentence is exemplified by the Ibaloi equivalent of the following: 'There was an old cow that died from the cold; we boiled it and ate it'. The next example is a translation of an Ibaloi identification sentence: 'The Spanish picked him up on their way, and he was the one who showed the way up here'. This sentence is really saying: 'The Spanish picked up a certain person on their way and then that person in turn showed the Spanish the way for the rest of their journey', but in the second half of the Ibaloi sentence the construction is topicalized, i.e., 'he was the one who showed the way up here'. What this is doing in effect is taking a person picked up on a journey and then revealing what his role is to become in subsequent portions of the discourse. In the same way, the example 'Kimboy got a hammer and that was what they used' says more than just 'Kimboy got a hammer and they used the hammer'. It is saying that Kimboy got a hammer and the hammer became an important prop. The situation here is somewhat curious in that topicalization is evidently a surface structure and yet is well motivated in the underlying structure of the discourse. A further example of deixis occurs in the sentence: *There was a man called Peter, he was an electrician*. Here Peter is introduced by name and is further introduced by occupation. The first clause is existential; the second is equational. Yet another example is *Peter was an electrician, he worked for Thomas Smuthers* where the first clause is equational and the second is predicational.

2.8 *Attribution*

Attribution occurs in various ways: speech may be attributed to a person, or awareness may be attributed to him, or a term may be introduced and defined. Many of these work out as quotations in the surface structure of languages.

Speech attribution is considered to be the notional counterpart of surface structure quotation. The surface structure may, of course, be direct or indirect and it may be construed in various ways in different languages. In some languages a quotation is clearly construable as object of the verb 'say'. In other languages it is awkward to construe it as the object of the verb 'say' and it is much simpler to presume that we have some kind of quotation formula followed by a quotation (Elkins 1971, Longacre 1970). In the latter case we handle quotation on the sentence level, whereas in the former case, we handle it on the clause level.

There may be awareness attribution. The basic verb here is the verb 'know'. Other verbs can be used such as 'feel', 'see', 'understand', etc. Examples in English: *I knew that something was wrong; I saw that she was in a bad mood.*

Somewhere one must account for metalanguage and definition. Possibly it is not different in principle from quotation. Thus, we have sentences such as *This is called žaka in Trique.* Take also Bloomfield's rather well known definition of a morpheme: *A linguistic form which bears no partial phonetic–semantic resemblance to any other form is . . . a morpheme.*

2.9 *Frustration*

The key notion in frustration is expectancy reversal. There is an action, event, or state which implies or normally calls for another action, event, or state as its sequel or concomitant. This P⊃Q relation is, however, not followed through in this structure. Rather – whether stated or unstated – there is a blocking circumstance or consideration (R) which results in Q_β, that is, Q with the opposite positive/negative of the intended value. There may also be a stated surrogate (S) which is there resorted to as a substitute for the intended Q.

2.9.1 *Frustration involving temporal notions*

Frustration may involve overlap, as in *He drives down crowded streets, but doesn't look out for pedestrians*. Here it is expected that a man who drives down crowded streets (P) will look out for pedestrians (Q) but, in the case in point, this man does not (Q$_\beta$). One can go on to state the possible consequence (s). *He drives down crowded streets, but doesn't look out for pedestrians, so he struck a child the other day*. There may also be frustrated succession as in *They started out for Paris, but someone slipped a time bomb in their car, and/so they never arrived*. Here it is expected that normally setting out on a trip (P) is followed by arriving at the destination (Q). But here there is a blocking circumstance (R), the time bomb, and the opposite of the expected activity, namely, *they never arrived* (Q$_\beta$).

2.9.2 *Frustrated implication*

We may have here frustrated hypotheticality: *Even if she comes, I'm not going to go with her*. This sentence signifies that the expected implication, *If she comes, I'll go with her*, isn't going to carry through. There may be frustrated contingency: *Even when I have the money, I'm not going to marry her* – which is a denial of *When I have the money, I'm going to marry her*. Frustrated efficient cause is seen in such a sentence as *She was poisoned, but didn't die* where poison is expected to cause death. Frustrated final cause figures in *He came, but didn't get a meal* where it is presupposed that he came expecting to get a free meal.

2.9.3 *Frustrated modality*

Many varieties of frustration seem to amount to what might be called frustrated inertial guidance systems or (less grandiosely) frustrated modality. Thus, granted intent, obligation, and facility as modalities, frustration may be expressed in relation to any of the three. *I intended to go, but some friends dropped in, so I didn't*. Here the intent to go would normally be followed by going. Some friends dropping in is the blocking circumstance, and the opposite outcome, *so I didn't*, is indicated. There may be frustrated obligation as in *I should have gone, but I didn't* or *I shouldn't have gone, but I did*. There may be frustrated facility as in *I could have promoted him, but I didn't*.

2.10 *Organization of what follows*

Having finished looking at the various semantic notions that are encoded in sentence structure, in the following sections of this chapter I take the co-ranking versus chaining distinction as primary and discuss various systems of sentence structure under each. The five languages and language groups chosen for extended presentation reflect a variety of sentence-building strategies and illustrate the distinctions sketched in this section. English is described first, largely for the convenience of the reader in passing from relatively familiar to more 'exotic' materials.

3 Co-ranking structures

3.1 *English*

3.1.1

English sentence structure makes extensive use of medial conjunctions in building sentence nuclei. Thus, we have 'coordinate' sentences with a medial *and*, an open-ended number of sentence bases, and certain possibilities for omitting repeated elements. Among the latter is the well-known omission of the identical subject in non-initial clauses as in *I went downtown, walked around the streets for a while, and went into a bakery shop*. We also find omission of the repeated verb: *Mary bought a hamburger, Susan a hot dog, and Anthony fish and chips*. The 'antithetical' sentence is different not only by virtue of having a medial *but*, but also by being strictly binary in structure. The 'alternative' sentence with a medial *or* may be binary (in the case of antonymic structures which indicate excluded middle) or open. Thus, we can say *Is he dead or alive?* but we can also say *He's going to the store, or to the theater, or to the office, or who knows where*.

Granted that *and*, *but*, and *or* are coordinators (medial links) *par excellence* in English, there are other conjunctions which also seem to set up nuclear patterns within the sentence (rather than introducing adverbial clauses in sentence margins). Thus, the conjunction *for* seems to function as the medial link in a 'reason' sentence while the conjunction *so* functions similarly in a 'result' sentence. In the former the element encoding efficient cause is last; in the latter the element encoding efficient cause is first.

3.1.2

Certain regular patterns of juxtaposition characterize English sentences. Thus, we have a recapitulation sentence, the purpose of which is apparently to create a certain mild suspense and emphasis in such sentences as *I went home, I went to see what was really going on* or *Fred was the one, Fred was the one who stole the officer's badge*. We also use juxtaposed sentences to express paraphrase in English: *He's a monster, he's a brute*. In both these sentence types there is rejection of any medial conjunction. Instead we find a phonological feature, i.e., (non-final) pause. English also occasionally omits the medial conjunction in coordinate and antithetical sentences, giving such structures as *I came, I saw, I conquered* and *It's not black, it's white*. We can compare the latter structure with such sentences as *It's not black but, on the contrary, it's white*, and *It's not black, but white*. Certain common proverbs built on antithesis also omit the medial conjunction: *Old men for council; young men for war* and *Man proposes, God disposes*.

3.1.3

English also contains 'direct quotation' sentences which consist essentially of a quotation formula plus a quote. In spite of the superficial similarity of such structures to clauses with object complements, the quote part of a quotation sentence does not plausibly construe as the object. Take, for example, the following three sentences:

(a)   McDougall replied 'On the contrary, Mary doesn't resemble Jane'

(b)   'On the contrary', replied McDougall, 'Mary doesn't resemble Jane'

(c)   'On the contrary, Mary doesn't resemble Jane', replied McDougall

It might with some plausibility be argued that the quote patterns as an object complement if all quotations were structured like (a) above. But, unfortunately, (b) and (c) also occur. In (c) the order object–verb–subject occurs, and in (b) the so-called 'object' is split by the verb + subject sequence. Furthermore, the subject + verb or verb + subject moves as a cohesive block in the above permutations. As such, it is not a normal immediate constituent grouping for English where verb plus object forms more of a unit than subject plus verb. In brief, the quote as 'object' complement acts very differently from other non-suspect objects in the language. A further consideration is that the quote may be of almost any length, so that 'John said . . .' can introduce a long and involved discourse.

It seems plausible, therefore, that the quotation sentence re-works the structure of the English clause on a higher level of structure (the sentence). At this higher level a bipartite structure, the quotation formula plus the quote, appears with certain possibilities of linear permutation and accordion-like expansion of the material in the quote slot.

3.2 *Ibaloi (Philippines)*[3]

The range and variety of Ibaloi (Ballard *et al.* 1971a, 1971b) sentence types are at least as great if not greater than what we encounter in English – both in respect to sentence types which employ medial conjunction and in respect to sentence types which are built upon juxtaposition. Ibaloi thus offers a fruitful comparison with English. Ibaloi also has a system of sentence margins which are not, however, strikingly different from those found in English and are not presented here.

3.2.1

Ibaloi has a wealth of sentence-medial conjunctive links which determine a considerable variety of sentence types. Not only are there 'and', 'but' and 'or' sentences but there are further sentence-medial conjunctions which express simultaneous actions, actions in sequence, 'tacking on' a further idea, result, and surprise: there is also a pair of conjunctions which expresses temporal contingency.

The Ibaloi coordinate sentence couples two or three sentence bases by means of *tan* 'and' between each pair of bases. This sentence type is semantically non-committal and does not imply temporal relations, paraphrase, or contrast. The clauses that are linked with *tan* typically are from the same lexical domain. This often results in a certain parallelism of content which is sometimes reinforced with *eshom* . . . *eshom* 'some . . . others' in the two bases.

> Enshi'y kenen ko *tan* ayshi'y panbaljan   ko
> none   eat   I   and none   place to live my
> 'I have nothing to eat and no place to live'

> Etoling i eshom *tan* ediyag   i eshom
> dark   some and cross-eyed some
> 'Some were dark-skinned and some were cross-eyed'

It is evident that the Ibaloi coordinate sentence is somewhat more restricted in use than the English coordinate sentence. The Ibaloi addition sentence which 'tacks on' something further by means of the conjunction *jet* 'and' absorbs some of the functions of the English coordinate sentence. The wide range of this sentence type semantically is seen in its encoding of the following notions (described in section 2 of this chapter): succession, efficient cause, paraphrase, coupling, and introduction. While most of these can be expressed in an 'and' sentence in English, it is of interest that the encoding of a paraphrase relationship in English rejects any medial conjunction while Ibaloi can use *jet* 'and' in an addition sentence or a paraphrase sentence.

> Binoshasan sha sota kapi *jet* indaw sha'd   San Fernando
> harvested   they the coffee and took they to San Fernando
> 'They harvested the coffee and took it to San Fernando'
>
>   (succession)

> Ka di   pangotkot ni dokto   shima despag shima inon-an
> you here dig   camote at that below at that saw
>
> tayo *jet* mengan kito *jet* on-oli kito'n emin
> we   and eat   we   and return we   all
> 'Go dig camote down below at that (place) we saw, and we will
> eat, and we will all return (home)'   (succession)
>
> Inandabos kono   *jet* ingkal   to'n emin i baro   to
> naked   hearsay and removed she all   clothes her
> 'She was naked (they say); she had removed all her clothes'
>   (paraphrase)

The Ibaloi antithetical sentence is quite parallel to the English sentence type of the same name. In both languages this sentence type encodes (in terms of the categories in section 2) contrast, frustration, and negated antonym paraphrase.

The most characteristic conjunction in the Ibaloi antithetical sentence is *nem* 'but'. A further conjunction *jey* 'while, but' is also used here and there is occasional absence of conjunction (juxtaposition). The choice of *nem*/*jey*/ϕ depends on the notional structures (varieties of contrast, varieties of frustration, and varieties of negated antonym paraphrase). All the examples below are chosen from situations in which *nem* is used, since this is the most characteristic of this sentence type.

> Ekakmet   ninemanemat i baliw   niyay ja shanom *nem*
> not I(EMPH) try   crossing of the   river   but
>
> si-kato'y kaonbaliw ni olay kaonsabi son si-kak
> she   crossed   always reach   me
> 'I never once tried to cross the river, but she was the one who
> always crossed to come to me'   (contrast)
>
> Kinedked ko'y bokdew ko, *nem* keak etey
> cut   I   throat   my but not I die
> 'I cut my throat but I didn't die'   (frustration)
>
> Jet eg kono   inanpiging ni inkaysepa to shima bajisbisan,
> and not hearsay tilted   landing   its at the under caves
>
> *nem* inandeteg kono
> but straight   hearsay
> 'It was not tilted when it landed under the eaves, but it was
> straight'   (negated antonym paraphrase)

The Ibaloi alternative sentence is also much like its English counterpart. It may encode alternation with only two possible alternatives, or more open situations where several choices are possible. There is frequent ellipsis in the second base. The alternative conjunction is *ono*.

Jet kaon-an   to nem binediw ni daki *ono* binediw ni bii
and way to-see   if   crossed the boy or   crossed the girl
'And we will see if the boy crossed the river or the girl'

Mayrodoy, *ono* enshi?
continue   or   not
'Shall we continue or not?'

There is also an Ibaloi result sentence which is broadly parallel to the English sentence of the same name. The conjunctive link 'therefore' may be (*jet*) *isonga*, (*jet*) *nakol ni* or ∅. When (*jet*) *nakol ni* occurs the sentence refers to some sort of difficulty.

Etey emola   ira, *isonga*   eg ali   sha on-ondaw
died probably they therefore not here they come
'They probably died, that is why they've never come back here'

Taka kapanngi-ngii ni ayshi'y asawam; nakol ni si-kam i
I you laughing-at   none   wife your therefore you

emengiloto ni moka kena
cooking   you   eat
'I am laughing at your not having a wife; as a result you are the one cooking your own food'

While the above Ibaloi sentence types are as a whole parallel to English except for the occurrence of two types to express coordination, there are other Ibaloi types that are less parallel. Several of these express temporal relations, which are structurally highlighted in Ibaloi to a degree not characteristic of English. The simultaneous sentence encodes overlap (with occasional use to express close temporal succession 'about as soon as A, then B' and close logical connection). In the simultaneous sentence *jey* 'at the same time, while, meanwhile' is a genuine coordinate link, not a subordinator. It does not travel with the clause that it precedes but is simply a medial link:

Eg metakwaban *jey*   nandabos kita
not be opened   while naked   we
'No one opens (the door) when we're naked'

Kaonnanginangis *jey*   kaontiyetiyed ja ondaw da nodta
kept crying   while climbing   go   to
baley shi Bayojok
house of Bayojok
'He kept on crying as he was climbing up to the house of Bayojok's family'

There are two conjunctive sentence types which express temporal succession. The first type with a medial *asan* 'and then' link is limited to sentences in which the bases have the same subject. Furthermore, *asan* attracts to itself any subject pronoun in the following base. Tense is usually progressive in the following base and special morphophonemic rules apply. Sentences with *asan* are open-ended – although in actual text the longest example found has five bases with four intervening *asan* links.

> Esolokan tedo'n polo'n akew *asan*   shaka ibka
> more   three tens   days and then they   bury
> '(The mummifying) would go more than thirty days, and then they would bury him'

> Menongpitak nin *asan*   naka kaleta'y kemkemti
> whistle I   first and then I   bite   firefly
> 'I'll whistle first and then I'll sting the firefly'

Another sentence expresses temporal contingency rather than simply succession, i.e., the second event is conditioned on prior occurrence of the first. This sentence also employs a medial *asan* but has a sentence–initial *ampet* 'unless, until'.

> *Ampet* edagboan ka   *asan* ka   masi-met
> unless paid   you then you enthusiastic
> 'You have to be paid before you are enthusiastic'

> *Ampet* memshit ka   *asan* moka olopa
> unless feast   you then you   take along
> 'First you must celebrate *peshit*, and then you can take her along with you'

Ibaloi also has a surprise sentence regularly marked by medial link *ngaran ni* 'what do you know!' It has no regular structural counterpart in English. The second base always expresses some unexpected and rather unpredictable development.

> Kowan ko nem pampamaayan i bagto; *ngaran ni*
> say   I that soft touch   trial   what do you know!

> agpayso gayam
> true   after all
> 'I thought that the trial (by ordeal) was something easily deceived; what do you know, it really works!'

> Jet kimawak ja kowan ko ey nak iarew iya saleng ko;
> and went I   say   I   I   light this torch

ngaran ni   apil   gayam – botatew
what do you know different after all botatew
'And I went to light my torch; but what do you know, it was
different; (it was) a botatew (spirit)'

Ibaloi also has a wealth of sentence types that employ juxtaposition. I
will illustrate quickly these types with one sentence each. The parallel
sentence is a juxtaposed type in which no conjunction is employed when
the bases are very parallel structurally. While English can do something
like this in various situations including succession (*I came, I saw, I
conquered*), Ibaloi employs this parallel structure not for temporal
succession but for listing ('coupling' in section 2.1.1):

Wara'd tan   i apag, wara'd tan   i dokto, wara'd tan   i
is   there meat is   there camote is   there

inepoy, wara'd tan   i kankanen
rice   is   there dessert
'There is meat, there is camote, there is rice, there is dessert'

The paraphrase sentence is a juxtaposed type not unlike its English
counterpart:

Dimaw i solsharo; shakel i Japan   na dimaw
went   soldiers many Japanese went
'The soldiers went; many Japanese went' (in this example the
soldiers are Japanese)

Ibaloi has a juxtaposed sentence type that expresses temporal
sequence – without the special feature of parallelism which characterizes
the parallel sentence:

Sikmaten nen Governor Gaelan itan na solat; binasa to;
catch   Governor Gaelan that   letter read   he

in-oli   to di   sotan na solat
brought back he here that   letter
'Governor Gaelan received the letter; he read it; he returned it
personally here'

The introduction sentence is a juxtaposed sentence the first base of
which is an existential clause; the second base predicates something
about the person or thing whose existence is affirmed in the first base:

Wara'y Kristiano'n Japan;   si-kara'y maronong
were   Christian Japanese they   well behaved
'There were Christian Japanese (soldiers); they were the ones
who were not cruel'

There is also an identification sentence which contains a topicalization device (strongly deictic) in its second base. This sentence may have a *jet* 'and' instead of juxtaposition but I present the latter here (the deictic element is italicized):

> Angken odopen   sha's iyay; *si-kato'y* singa maybejad
> okay   take along they this   he   like   used to pay
>
> shita otang
> on   debt
> 'It's okay if they take this fellow; he will be what (we) will use to pay the debt'

Ibaloi has a somewhat more complex system of quotation sentences than English. The direct quote, which is as a whole parallel to English can have up to two quotation formulae (the second of which must be the verb *kowan* 'say'). Unlike English, direct quotations have a quotative word, *ey*.

> Binistigar toak; kowan to *ey* Kaspangariganey kapture-en
> quizzed he me me say   he   supposing   capture
>
> sha koyo ni guerilla niman, ngantoy pesing mo'n
> they you   guerillas   now what do   you
>
> jay solat?
> this letter
> 'He quizzed me; he said to me "Supposing they capture you, what will you do with this letter?"'

The Ibaloi indirect quotation sentence has some uses parallel to English (indirect speech and awareness) and others that are less parallel (intent, naming, mistaken idea). I illustrate only the latter three here.

> Kowan to *ey*   shi Kabayan i pengibotan   to ni kabajo
> said   he (that)   Kabayan place to steal he   horse
> 'His intent was that Kabayan be the place for him to steal a horse'   (intent)
>
> [Sota kabisiljana ma'n] kowan sha *ey* si Agajap
> the leader their then   say   they that   Agajap
>
> [ebadeg ga too]
> big   man
> '[Their leader], whom they call Agajap, [he was a big man]'
>   (naming)
>
> Kowan ko *nem* wara'y toka adibja mango
> say   I   that is   she visits mango
> 'I thought (wrongly) that she had someone to play with'
>   (mistaken idea)

Notice in this last example that *nem* (associated with contrast and frustration; cf. antithetical sentence above) occurs as the quotative word rather than *ey*.

3.3 *Chicahuaxtla Trique (Mexico)*

Trique is an example of a language that makes extensive use of juxtaposition as a sentence-building device. The Trique[4] conjunctions *sa³ni⁴* 'but', *da³di³⁴ʔ si³* 'because' and *ni⁴* 'and' (except as members of pairs of conjunctions) mark onset of a new sentence; they do not occur as sentence-medial links.

Quotations in Trique may be direct or indirect. The quotation formulae of direct quotations are usually postposed, while the formula of quotation is itself one of the juxtaposed sentence patterns which are described below:

> 'Ga̱⁴ʔa̱⁴h re⁵ʔ' ga³ta³⁴h si³ gu³ni²¹
> go   you said   he heard I
> '"Go" he said to me'

The indirect quotations employ *si³si⁴* 'that'; the quotation formula is invariably preposed:

> Ga̱³ta³⁴h re⁵ʔ gu³ni̱²¹ si³si⁴ ga̱⁵ʔa̱⁵
> said   you heard I that should go I
> 'You told me to go'

In Trique we do not find such sentence types as coordinate and antithetical which we encounter in Indo-European languages and in the Philippines. These relations are expressed in a sequence which involves two or more sentences; i.e., they are expressed in paragraph structures. Rather, on the sentence level we find contrasting patterns of juxtaposition with many subtle features which are structurally contrastive from type to type. In this respect Trique reflects a situation that is typical of the Otomanguean languages of Mesoamerica. Chatino (Pride 1965) is another such typical language, as is also Mesquital Otomi (Lanier 1968). In the latter, however, Spanish loan conjunctions are being borrowed and inserted at the seams of juxtaposed bases in many sentence types. Often the old juxtaposed construction exists along with a parallel construction which contains the Spanish loan conjunction.

In Trique there occur patterns of juxtaposition in which we find some of the relations that we encounter in languages that have sentence-medial conjunctions. We also find, however, pairs of clauses which, in effect, are doing the work of single clauses in a typical Indo-European language. We also occasionally find combinations of clauses that appear to express something almost modal or aspectual in thrust. Furthermore, some of these patterns of juxtaposition – most of which are tightly bound phonologically – involve an ambivalent noun at the seam of the two clauses. In this respect certain of the juxtaposed sentences discussed in the three languages under consideration are similar to what are called merged sentences in English and Philippine languages (see chapter II:2). Let us look at some examples.

Two of the juxtaposed sentences in Trique are parallel in many respects to the juxtaposed sentences of English. There is a paraphrase sentence and there is a recapitulation sentence. For the former we have examples such as:

> Na^{4}či^{3}ni^{4}ta^3 žu^{3}ku^3 (,) zi^4 ga^{3}ʔah^{34} ni^{ʔ4}ya^4 žu^3
> will turn up animal   not gone   lost   it
> 'The animal will turn up, it's not really lost'

The recapitulation sentence in Trique, as opposed to English, is a device for avoiding hanging too many nouns on the same verb. Thus, rather than saying, 'That woman went to the mountains to see her cattle and horses', it is more natural in Trique to say:

> Ga^{3}ʔah^{34} zi^3 ža^{5}na^5 dah^3 kïhi^3 (,) ga^{3}ʔah^{34} ni^{ʔ4}ya^3
> went   woman that mountain   went   see
>
> dah^3 tro^2 nga^4 dah^3 gwa^{2}yu^3
> animal her cattle with animal her horse
> 'That woman went to the mountains, she went to see her cattle and horses'

It is noteworthy that these two sentence types in Trique, which are the most parallel to juxtaposed sentences in English, permit internal pause (,) at the seam of the two bases when they have complicated internal structure. This is not true of the other juxtaposed sentence types where, if anything, one picks up speed at the seam of the two bases and pauses somewhere internally within one base rather than at the seam of the two bases.

Temporal succession and temporal overlap are expressed in two further juxtaposed sentences of Trique, the sequence sentence and the simultaneous sentence. They are binary structures; even in the sequence sentence one cannot express a long sequence of actions, rather one combines in such a sentence two actions which are typically associated as parts of the same process or as part of an expectancy chain. Thus, we have a sequence sentence such as:

>Gi³ri³⁵ʔ ni³   ži³lu²¹ li³h   ža²³ ni³
>found   they worms little ate they
>'They found some little worms and ate them'

The noun phrase *ži³lu²¹ li³h* 'little worms' at the seam of the two clauses is object of the verbs which both precede and follow it. The simultaneous sentence requires that the predicate of the first clause be continuative in aspect. This gives the feeling of 'as they ...' Thus, we have a sentence:

>A³gą³⁴ʔ ni³   ya²h n·ih³/a³di³yą³⁴ ni³   ri³ą³⁴   ni²ma³
>beat   they drum   precede they before corpse
>'They beat a drum as they walk before the corpse' (where /
>separates the two clauses)

The simultaneous sentence is used to express the lexical concepts 'bring' and 'take'. Thus, we have sentences such as:

>Ni³ka³⁴h ni³ ča³   / ga³ʔna³⁵ʔ ni³   yu³h ną³h
>had   they tortillas came   they place here
>'They brought tortillas'

>Ni³ka³⁴h ni³ ča³   / ga³ą³⁴h ni³   yu³h mą³h
>had   they tortillas went they place here
>'They took tortillas over there'

Final cause (purpose), which is usually expressed within a purpose margin of Indo-European languages, Philippine languages, and some other languages of Mesoamerica, is expressed in Trique in a juxtaposed purpose sentence. The second base of such a sentence must have a verb in the anticipatory mood.[5] The second base may occur twice: i.e., there may be two purpose constructions in the same sentence. Thus, we have sentences such as:

>Ri³ki²³ si³ ča³   /ža⁵h
>gave   he tortilla will eat I
>'He gave me a tortilla for me to eat'

Purpose occurring twice in a sentence is seen in such an example as:

>Ni³ko³⁵ʔ ne³h po³li³sya²³/gi⁴da³ʔa³⁴ ni³ /ga⁴či⁴   ni³
>followed the police   will seize they will put they
>du³gwa²gaʔa³
>jail
>'The police followed him in order to seize him and put him in
>jail'

When such a purpose sentence occurs with both verbs in the anticipatory mood, it is impossible to distinguish it from a sequence sentence with both verbs in the anticipatory mood: i.e., a sentence such as, 'He will-grab it he will-eat' can be either 'He'll grab it in order to eat it' or 'He'll grab it and eat it'.

The suggestion sentence in Trique is weakly conditional in thrust and mildly hortatory. It has some rather specialized constraints: namely, the first clause must have a verb in second person, and the second clause must have a verb in first person plural inclusive of second person. Thus, we have sentences such as:

> Ga⁴di³ą³⁴ re⁵ʔ / gy⁴ʔ
> go ahead you   will go we
> 'You go first and we'll go'
>
> Du⁴gu³ʔni²ʔ re⁵ʔ / du⁴gwa³či²ʔ go³če²³ da³h
> hurry   you   will pass we car   that
> 'You hurry up and we'll pass that car'

The identification sentence in Trique is a deictic device. A statement is made in the first clause and a participant indicated in that statement is identified in the second clause. This gives us a sentence such as:

> Ne³⁴ʔ ne⁵h mą³h gi³nga³h ngo⁴ žu³mą?ą⁴³
> over side there lay   a   village
> / gu⁴ʔna³ 'ži³-ri³ʔni³'   zi³-nu⁴gwą⁴ʔ my³ʔy²ʔ
>   called it foot-of ash tree language-of us
> 'Over there there was a village which was called "the foot of the ash tree" in our language'

Most of the remaining juxtaposed sentence types in Trique can be considered to be essentially a predication spread over two clauses. Thus, a cause sentence brings in a causer, i.e., a further participant, in the second clause. The first clause is often a meteorological expression, but it can be an intransitive or equative clause as well. In a Trique meteorological clause such as *gą³mą³⁵ʔ* 'rained', there is no expressed subject; rather the construction is considered to be complete without a subject. When put into a cause sentence, we get a sentence such as:

> Gą³mą³⁵ʔ / gi³ʔya³h yą³ʔąhą⁴³
> rained   made   God
> 'God caused it to rain'

We also see the same construction in a non-meteorological expression such as 'God baptized the baby in the church caused the priest' or more freely, 'The priest baptized the baby in the church'. The 'audition' sentence in Trique is a device for expressing the addressee; i.e., the construction which is usually handled as an indirect object in an Indo-European language. Thus, instead of saying, 'John said to Mary', Trique says:

> Ga³ta³⁴h Juan / gu³nï³ Maria
> said   John   heard Mary

The direction sentence expresses the object of a verb of emotion by resorting to the verb 'see'. Consequently, instead of saying, 'I'm angry at you', Trique says:

> A³ʔmą³ ru³wa²h / ni³ʔi²¹ re⁵ʔ
> angry I   see-I you

The emphatic sentence in Trique is a way of achieving focus on some participant within the next clause, but the emphatic word is itself a verb in Trique. There is a class of verbs *we²*, *se²*, *ni³ta⁴h* and *gi³zi²h* which can be translated 'Lo, it is', 'Lo, it isn't', 'There is/are none', and 'Tallies up to' respectively. Thus, we have sentences such as:

> Se²   gwi³⁵⁴ /wˑi³
> lo not person was he
> 'He really wasn't a person'

> Gi³zi²h gą⁵ʔą³h zna²du³ / gu³žu³ma²³
> tallied four   soldiers arrived
> 'All told, four soldiers arrived'

   The remaining Trique juxtaposed sentence type, the conative type, may be compared with such English sentences as *He attempted to learn how to swim*; *He struggled to be good*; and *He's learning to ice skate*. Thus, we have Trique sentences such as:

> Ču³⁴   ni³ a³ʔmi³⁴ ni³ na³⁴   zdi²la³
> learned they talk   they language Castilian
> 'They know how to talk Spanish'

> Gu³nu⁴kwa³h zi³ gu³či³⁵ʔ zi³ du³kwa² zi³
> managed   he arrived he house his
> 'He managed to arrive at his house'

4.0 Chaining structures

I now want to discuss a type of language that is radically different in surface structure. We shall see, however, that, in spite of the striking differences in surface structure between co-ranking languages and chaining languages (James 1970), the same relations–coupling, etc.– can be, and usually are, marked.

What is the geographical distribution of chaining structures of the sort here described? I believe the portion of the world in which they are the most fully and, one might say, remorselessly developed is the island of New Guinea – including Papua New Guinea and Irian Jaya (part of Indonesia) – and a few immediately surrounding islands. But chaining structures also occur in South America, specifically in Colombia, Ecuador, and Peru. Just how far they extend through the rest of the South American continent I do not know. Chaining structures also occur in the continental United States; it seems clear that northern Pomo (data from J. Ravenhill) and Crow (data from R. Gordon) are characterized by structures of this sort. All chaining languages which have been reported to date are those in which the predicate comes clause finally. Just as subject, object, location, and other elements precede the predicate in their own clause, so also subordinate clauses of various sorts may precede the main clause and be 'chained' to it.[6]

In this section of this chapter we confine ourselves to the consideration of structures from Papua New Guinea and from South America.

4.1 The distinctive features of clause chaining

The features which make chaining distinct from co-ranking structures, such as are found in Indo-European languages, the Philippines and Mesoamerica, are as follows. (a) There is a clause (characteristically final in a chain of clauses) that has a verb of distinctive structure that occurs but once in the entire chain while other (typically non-final) clauses have verbs of different structure (Elson 1964). This final clause is like an engine that pulls a string of cars. (b) Each non-final clause is marked so as to indicate whether the following clause has same subject or different subject from itself. This is sometimes carried so far as to indicate in the dependent verb form of a preceding clause the person and number of the subject in the clause which is to follow; that is, a verb may be dually marked, once for its own subject, and once for the subject of the following clause as well–if it is not the final distinctive verb of its chain. In some languages of South America, the marking of same or different subject is relative to the final verb in the final clause rather than to the verb of the immediately following clause. (c) A further feature of chaining is considerable attention to temporal relations such as chronological overlap ('while', 'at the same time') versus chronological succession ('and then') which shade off into logical relations such as cause and effect, result, and so forth. Temporal relations appear to be central in these languages and are extended metaphorically in other directions.

But although I am here discussing chaining in relation to sentence structure, it is necessary to proceed with caution at this point. In fact, the pronounced surface features of chaining can lead to two fallacious assumptions regarding such languages: firstly, that such a chain is necessarily a simple linear sequence; secondly, that such a chain is necessarily a sentence.

In regard to the first assumption it is only necessary to remember again that recursion is the rule rather than the exception in both sentence and paragraph structure around the world. Commonly, a sentence base may be expounded not only by a single clause, but also by a clause which is itself complex, containing an embedded sentence within it. For this reason we will probably find that certain chains are not simple linear sequences, but are recursive nestings of chain within chain. The chains may be on separate structural layers and even separate structural levels (sentence versus paragraph).

The second assumption requires more extended comment. The assumption that a chain is necessarily a sentence simply proves unfruitful in certain instances. Thus, in the Foré language in New Guinea (Scott 1973, Longacre 1972), there are chains on two levels. The most inclusive chain has its final verb marked for mood and occurs at the end of a sizeable stretch of discourse which can be as long as two or three pages. Within this larger chain, shorter chains occur which are (except for certain special devices) limited to same-subject chains. Such a chain runs on until there is a different subject introduced in the following clause, at which point a different-subject verb is used. A different-subject verb, which is very distinct morphologically from the sorts of medial verbs which precede it, may be considered to end a sentence (while the final verb ends the paragraph). If one wishes to end a sentence even though the next clause has the same subject (I would argue that there is some feeling for sentence length in languages), then one is able to use a special suffix which terminates the sentence. Thus, we have chains of medium length and chains of maximum length. It seems that the chain of maximum length compares well in distribution and length with a typical paragraph in an Indo-European language while the chain of medium length corresponds more to the sentence. This puts us in the rather unusual situation (by Indo-European standards) of having grammatical closure (that is, devices signaling the end of a unit) both on the sentence and on the paragraph levels. It must be emphasized, however, that while this is true of Foré, Kanite, and certain other languages in New Guinea, by no means are all the languages of the area structured in this way. In some languages, such as Wojokeso, the medial–final chain corresponds well to the sentence itself; i.e., it is the sentence which is marked with grammatical (as well as phonological) closure. The paragraph then becomes a cluster of such chains.

The following example of a Kanite (Papua New Guinea) sentence (Longacre 1972:5–6) should serve to illustrate some of the points made in this section (DS = different subject):

(1)   his-u′a-ke-′ka
        do-we-DS-you

(2)   naki a′nemo-ka hoya   ali-′ka
        so   women-you garden work-you

(3)   naki ali   ha′noma hu-ne′atale-′ka
        so   work finish   do-COMPL-you

(4)   inuna kae-′ka
        weeds burn-you

(5)   popo hu-′ka
        hoe do-you

(6)   inuna kae-′ka
        weeds burn-you

(7)   naki ha′no hu-talete-ke-ta′a
        so   finish do-COMPL-DS-we

(8)   naki viemoka-ta′a keki′yamo′ma ha′noma nehis-i-ana
        so   men-we   fence   finish   do-it-CONJ
        'If we do this, you women work the garden, when it is finished
        hoe and burn the weeds, when that is finished we men will finish
        making the fence'

This sentence is a series of eight clauses, of which the verbs are the most important structure in each clause. The last clause, (8), ends with a conjunctive marker -ana, which binds it into the broader framework of the paragraph, even though it ends in a final verb. The subject of the first clause is -u′a 'we'. This morpheme is followed by ke, a transition marker which tells us that there will be a different subject in the clause which is to follow. The final morpheme of the first form, -′ka, tells us that there will be a second person subject in the following clause. This second person subject is the subject of clauses (2–6); in each verb the suffix -′ka tells us that the next clause will also have a second person subject. In (7), again we have an occurrence of the transition morpheme

-ke which tells us that there will be a different subject in the following clause, and the person and number of this subject is indicated in the final morpheme *ta'a* 'we' of the verb form in (7). So we find that in clause (8), 'we men' is the subject of the clause. It is important to note, however, that even in this example the eight clauses do not compose a simple linear string, in spite of the chaining of clause to clause by means of the indication of same (unmarked) versus different subject in the following clause: (i) it is evident that there is a cluster of clauses (4–6); (ii) that (6) is a repetition of (4); and (iii) that base I is probably something of special structural importance (cf. English conditional margin). There is only one final verb in this sentence, i.e., *nehis-i-ana*. All other verbs are medials. Furthermore, even the final verb is morphologically modified (*-ana*) to fit into the longer chain which is the paragraph.

4.2 The germinal notions and their development (in Papua New Guinea)

I return now to the two considerations of marking of same versus different subject and marking of temporal succession ('and then') versus temporal overlap ('while', 'at the same time'). These notions are elaborated with considerable range and variety in Papua New Guinea. The two parameters, each with two values, give us a two-by-two scheme with four possible values. This is the ideal scheme. Although it is rarely found in such stark simplicity, it does characterize a few languages, for example Kanite, Ek-Nii and Kate, as sketched below in Table 5.2.

Table 5.2. *Kanite, Eki-Nii, and Kate*

	Overlap	Succession
Same subject	(a)	(b)
Different subject	(c)	(d)

The following Kate forms, in which ss and DS represent same subject and different subject respectively, illustrate (a), (b), (c) and (d) (SIM = simultaneous, SEQ = sequential):

a. Fisi-*huk*　　　　na-wek
   arrived-he(SIM) ate-he
   'As he arrived, he was eating'

b. Fisi-*rạ*　　　　na-wek
   arrived-he(SEQ) ate-he
   'He arrived, then he ate'

c. Mu-*ha*-pie　　　　kio-wek
   spoke-DS-they(SIM) wept-he
   'As they spoke he wept'

d. mu-∅-pie   kio-wek
spoke-DS-they(SEQ) wept-he
'After they spoke he wept'

Characteristically the verb morphology cuts up the semantic space in all sorts of arbitrary ways so that scarcely two languages in highland New Guinea show us precisely the same structure in regard to the implementation of these two parameters. Thus, for example, in the Managalasi language, while the main structural distinctions are still correlated with same subject versus different subject and with overlap versus succession, different subject in both overlap and succession is marked by distinct suffixes which also indicate tense. There are suffixes which mark future, past, and present different-subject overlap, and further suffixes for future, past, and present different-subject succession. Same-subject overlap is indicated by but one suffix -i?i, while same-subject succession has four morphemes. Future, past, and present, when marked for same-subject succession, indicate what might be termed delayed succession (i.e., there is a bit of an interval between the two events referred to in this fashion) while -Na marks same-subject succession in normal undelayed sequence; cf. Table 5.3:

Table 5.3. *Managalasi*

		Overlap			Succession		
					fut	past	pres	Delayed
Same subject			-i?i			-Na sequence		Undelayed
Different subject	fut	past	pres	fut	past	pres	

But this is only the beginning. Gahuku, still another language, has two kinds of medial verbs. The regular medial verbs reflect the ideal scheme in respect to same-subject/different-subject overlap and succession, but there are reduced medial verbs in which only same subject is indicated, but overlap and succession are distinguished. Something of this sort in more complicated form is also found in Kunimaipa. In Yessan-Mayo there is a similar division of loose sentences and tight sentences. The loose sentences distinguish two kinds of overlap with same subject and three kinds of succession with same subject, but distinguish three kinds of overlap with different subject and three kinds of succession with different subject. The tight sentences, which indicate only same subject, have two kinds of overlap and two kinds of succession. Foré brings in a type of structure in which overlap, succession, and association (as parts of the same process) are marked within the same-subject chain (which corresponds to the sentence). Different-subject chains cross sentence boundaries and do not distinguish overlap versus succession versus association. Instead, the morphology of the different-subject verb marks different subject in the next clause, along with the person, number, and tense of the chain that it closes. This is quite the opposite of the Safeyoka dialect of Wojokeso (called simply Wojokeso below). In Wojokeso there is a same-subject series sentence which does not distinguish overlap from succession, while different-subject sentences, and they only, make this temporal distinction. In Golin there is same-subject overlap encoded within what is called the simultaneous sentence and there is a sequence sentence which can be marked for same subject or different subject. Finally, Kosena has a simultaneous sentence in which same subject and different subject are not distinguished, and it has a same-subject sentence which marks only succession, while different-subject succession must cross sentence boundaries as in Foré. Kosena is somewhat similar to Foré in that the larger of two levels of chaining corresponds to the paragraph.

I have indicated here only a few of the many bewildering and varied possibilities. In brief, starting with the two parameters – same versus different subject and temporal overlap versus temporal succession – from language to language and from dialect to dialect within Papua New Guinea these are developed as a sort of 'theme with variations' (cf. Longacre 1972:16–25).[7]

4.3 *Relations superimposed over chaining (Wojokeso, Papua New Guinea)*

To illustrate how in even such languages as these there is an overlay of structure which marks most of the (by now familiar) sentence relations which are described above for co-ranking languages, I present here the sentence system of Wojokeso (West 1973).

It is impossible to understand the nature of the Wojokeso sentence without first of all knowing a few things about the verb morphology. While many of the details cannot be traced out here, the following should suffice.

Medial verbs have first order suffixes which indicate temporal relations and same versus different subject in reference to the clause which follows. The medial verb also has second order suffixes which are tense–person–number markers which correlate somewhat with the same subject versus different subject distinction. Specifically: if a medial verb has no first order suffix following its stem, it occurs in a same-subject series sentence which makes no distinction between overlap and succession. In the following Wojokeso series sentence temporal succession is expressed. Medial verbs end in a second order suffix – (*o*)*ntae* 'first person dual series non-future', while the last and longest word of the sentence is the final verb (past tense, indicative). Medial verbs are marked only for future versus non-future and are not marked for mood; final verbs are marked according to a wide range of tense and mood.

Uhwono*ntae* nowentae sosyo ife'no*ntae* sɨkunofo lo*ntae*
see we   go we   sosyo pick we   dark   speak we

toho yohojo*ntae* toho hiyamno sofo*ntae* nopontae nowe*ntae*
wood gather we   wood carry   carry we come we go we

toho nomo'no*ntae*   yafe lo'mo po*ntae*
wood carry we (with rope from head) incline in   come we

mijo lomo wekapmmalohwoyofoho
water in   crossed we(INDIC)

'We looked and we went and picked some sosyo and we said "It's getting dark", and we gathered firewood and carried the firewood and came and went and carried the firewood by a rope hanging from our head and came down the incline and crossed the stream'

On the other hand, one of two long first order suffixes may occur on the medial verb: -(*a*)*honingk* which indicates different-subject succession, or -(*o*)*ntaningk* which indicates different-subject overlap. These markers (and their absence) distinguish the sequence sentence from the simultaneous sentence from the series sentence. Notice that the same-subject chain must perforce be a series sentence, and that different-subject chains must perforce be distinguished for succession versus overlap.

An example of a Wojokeso sequence sentence follows:

sɨkuno   nome-*honingk-i* sukwo'miyomo hofantiso   toho
darkness came-SEQ-3SG(DS) night in   mosquitoes bite

nelof-*ahoningk-i* *kokoko*   u   nakwo mempo saho
us bit-SEQ-3SG(DS) INTENSIFIER EXCL we   outside sleep

mafosyawosofo
not sleep

'Darkness came and at night mosquitoes bit us an awful lot so (being) outside we couldn't sleep'

This example is composed of three clauses. The long suffix (*a*)*honingk* is here followed by the third person suffix -*i* (marking the clause's own subject, not anticipating the subject of the next clause). The long suffix signals chronological succession and subject change. Thus, while 'dark-ness' is the subject of the first clause, 'mosquitoes' is the subject of the second clause, and 'we' is the subject of the third clause.

An example of a Wojokeso simultaneous sentence follows; there is an embedded series sentence in the first base:

> Nakwo ango yokino y-ø-ontone   wantojo iku'yo sohwo
> we   house bones do-SER-1PL(SS) wantojo leaf   those
>
> lohm'meemo lohof-ø-ontone hwofe momof-ø-onotone ole
> laid on   do-SER-1PL(SS) kunai put on-SER-1PL(SS) this
>
> hume-*ntaningk*-uhwone musopee'u siko toho
> to be-SIM-1PL(DS)   girls two   they fire
>
> yohoj-*ontaningk*-i   nakwo sɨwope humofohntof-uhwone
> brought-SIM-3DU(DS) we   tobacco smoked-1PL
> 'We did the frame of the house and put *wantojo* leaves on and put *kunai* on and while we were there and while the two girls brought firewood we smoked'

Here the long suffix (*o*)*ntaningk* indicates different-subject overlap. In its first occurrence the suffix is followed by -*uhwone*, first person plural; in its second occurrence it is followed by -*i*, third person singular. The whole first part of the sentence from *Nakwo* 'we' to and including *humentaningkuhwone* 'while we were there' is an embedded series sentence which functions as first base of the simultaneous sentence. The whole sentence might be paraphrased: 'We built the frame of the house and put *wantojo* leaves on it, and put *kunai* on it and were there; meanwhile the two girls brought us firewood; meanwhile we smoked'.

This three-way structural difference is reinforced further by the distribution of three series of tense–person–number markers. The three series are asymmetrically distributed relative to the absence of suffix, presence of different-subject succession suffix, and presence of different-subject overlap suffix.[8]

Thus, there is a different-subject non-future set of tense–person–number markers. This goes with either the sequence or the simultaneous sentence. There is also a same-subject non-future set of tense–person–number markers. This goes with the series sentence provided that it is non-future. Finally, there is a third set of tense–person–number markers which are future whether the subject be the same or different between the two clauses. Thus, whether we are in a sequence sentence, simultaneous sentence, or series sentence, if the tense indicated is future, then it will take the third set of markers; cf. Table 5.4.

Table 5.4 *Wojokeso medial verbs*

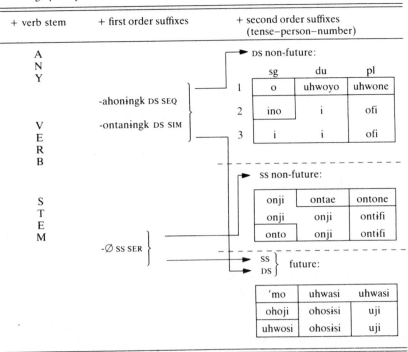

Note: In this table, sg, du and pl stand for singular, dual and plural numbers; while 1, 2 and 3 symbolize 1st, 2nd and 3rd persons.

In summary, medial Wojokeso verbs tell us whether the clause following will have the same or different subject and whether the relationship with the following clause will be one of sequence, simultaneity or neutrally marked (series). The medial verb further loosely indicates tense as non-future versus future relative to the fuller marking of tense in the final verb of the following structure. As already stated, these morphological features indicate three sentence types: series sentence, simultaneous sentence and sequence sentence, all of which are open ended or n-ary. Interesting varieties and subvarieties of these various sentences occur, but this is not the place to mention them.

A fourth sentence type, called the coordinate sentence, has the verb of its non-final base filled by what is essentially a modified indicative form rather than a medial form. To this degree, therefore, the Wojokeso coordinate sentence is more like a co-ranking structure. When, however, the future is called for, then the verb of the non-final base is a special medial verb form with a special set of future coordinate person–number markers. See Table 5.5.

Table 5.5. *Future coordinate person–number markers in Wojokeso*

	sg	du	pl
1	-me	-aso	
2	-iso	-fijoso	
3	-oso		

The hallmark of the coordinate sentence is the presence of a suffix *-so* (coordinator, roughly translatable as 'and'). This suffix goes on the non-final verb whether non-future (modified final) or future (medial form). The following example is non-future:

> Wojokesohwa mpe imentohof-*o-so* nakwo syoho'no
> (clan-name)   buy do-they-and   we   work for
> umentihwonefoho
> go we (INDIC)
> 'The Wojokeso bought (pigs) and we went to get work'

The next example is a future coordinate; it is embedded within a series sentence (the balance of which is not given here):

> Humanti-*fijo-so* uhwoni-*fijo-so* mekino sikwo'mno nto
> be-3PL-and   see-3PL-and   bow   black   already
> umo'naso uhwoningk-ø-uji . . .
> become   see-SER-3PL(FUT)
> 'They will wait and they will look and when they see that the bow has become black . . .'

The coordinate sentence is a very elastic structure. While its essential idea seems to be to indicate coupling without regard to chronological considerations, it can encode hypotheticality and temporal succession as well. Apparently, when the latter two notional structures are encoded in this sentence pattern, they are somewhat de-emphasized. Thus, 'I will go and they will be cross with me' is a non-emphatic way of saying 'If I go, they will be cross with me'.

Any of the four basic sentence types described above may be made an antithetical (ANTI) sentence by addition of the prefix *ko-* to the medial verb. The resulting construction is binary, and encodes frustration (i.e., expectancy reversal) of some variety, for example 'They worked hard but not much money was given them'. All the morphological features of the four basic sentence types are retained, even the suffix -*so* of the coordinate.

The following antithetical sentence is an overlay on a sequence sentence. It is, therefore, an antithetical sequence sentence:

> Ko-nejapowo'ningk-*ahoningk*-i   nakwo jomo mujo'njo
> ANTI-always gives us-SEQ-3SG(DS) we   ask not speak to him
> 'He always gives us but we don't pray to him'

The next example is an overlay on a coordinate (non-future) sentence. It is, therefore, an antithetical coordinate sentence.[9]

> Syoho yakumpohn'nyo *ko*-imalog-*o-so*   hamnoyoho engo
> work strong   ANTI-do-they-and money   much
>
> muyofoho
> not give
> 'They worked hard but not much money was given to them'

The four basic sentence types may be further modified by the suffix -'*manji* to the medial verb. The result is a (binary) conditional sentence which explicitly encodes hypotheticality, for example 'If I see him, I will tell him'. The morphological features of the medial verbs upon which this structure is built are retained except for the suffix -*so* of the coordinate sentence which is deleted on addition of -'*manji*.[10] The two examples which follow illustrate a conditional simultaneous sentence and a conditional series sentence respectively:

> Nop*ontaningk*-uji-'*manji* fisyusyi'nitumayo
> come(SIM)-3PL(FUT)-if   go find them
> 'If they will be coming, you go and find them'

> Kako uhwoningk-uhwosi-'*manji* wakumasyono
> he   see it(SER)-3SG(FUT)-if   intent you get(BEN 3SG)
> 'If he sees it he will get it for you'

Finally, the four basic sentence types may be modified once more by the insertion of a free conjunction *kalohi* which expresses cause–result between the two clauses. Again the structure is binary, and again the coordinate suffix -*so* is deleted on addition of the cause–result conjunction.

The result sentence with medial *kalohi* can be rendered in various ways in English. Thus,

> Jeko   honta *kalohi*   wohumantono'maho
> sunny time   because/so will stay we not

can be freely rendered as an English cause margin plus nucleus: 'Because it's not sunny we won't stay' or as a result sentence: 'It's not sunny so we won't stay' or even as a reason sentence: 'We won't stay for it's not sunny'. Wojokeso, like New Guinea chaining languages in general, does not have a subordinate–coordinate contrast as in English. Furthermore, where English has two nuclear and coordinate patterns, the result sentence with *so* and the reason sentence with *for*, Wojokeso has here but one pattern. This pattern is the more 'natural' one in which cause precedes result.

In the following examples, since addition of *kalohi* is compatible with the retention of all the morphological distinctions between various sorts of medials, we have result series sentence, result simultaneous sentence, and result sequence sentence.

> Nop-ø-onto   *kalohi* imasofoho
> came-SER-3SG(SS) so   did he it(INDIC)
> 'He came, so he did it'

> Nop-*ontangingk*-ofi *kalohi* imalefoho
> came-SIM-3PL(DS)   so   did I it(INDIC)
> 'They were coming so I did it'

> Nop-*anhoningk*-ofi *kalohi* imalefoho
> came-SEQ-3PL(DS)   so   did I it(INDIC)
> 'They came so I did it'

It is important to remember that none of the typical morphological features of chaining are removed – even when the various affixes which indicate the above relations are superimposed. We still have (except for the non-future coordinate) a clear chaining structure in which the medial–final contrast in verb morphology is preserved along with (partial) marking of same versus different subject in successive clauses, along with interest in distinguishing succession from overlap. These features remain basic in spite of the affixal overlay. Perhaps nothing more clearly illustrates the difference between chaining and co-ranking structures than such resort to overlay devices as here described. At the same time the persistence of certain notional categories such as are discussed in section 2 can be observed as well.

Relationships of a sort we are accustomed to seeing in co-ranking languages – relations usually expressed by free conjunctions – are expressed here largely by means of verb morphology. Only one free conjunction[11] occurs in the entire language.

Besides the structures mentioned, there is, of course, a simple sentence, that is, a one-clause structure in which the only verb in the sentence is a final verb. There is also some evidence that while no extensive system of sentence margins exists in such a language as Wojokeso, there is nevertheless a time margin. This is seen in that the base of a sentence often serves as a back-reference to the previous sentence and functions, therefore, as a time margin, as in '. . . and he came to our town. He came and . . .' That in quite a few languages such time margins, when accompanying main clauses, are skipped in the reckoning of same-subject versus different-subject concord provides evidence for time margins in New Guinea languages (Longacre 1972:10–14).

There also exists a counterfactual sentence structure of a very peculiar sort. There is a special set of counterfactual person–number markers. These are long suffixes running up to thirteen phonemes in length and not neatly analyzable into component suffixes. This can be seen in Table 5.6.

Table 5.6. *Counterfactual person–number markers in Wojokeso*

	sg	du	pl
1	-ontɨ'mtentesi	-ontentasi	
2	-ontentesi		-ontifitentesi
3			

The presence of one of these counterfactual(CF) person–number markers on the verb of a non-final clause, when followed by a clause whose verb is an unrealized subjunctive (suffix -*sohi*), marks the whole construction as a counterfactual sentence. It is very striking that in language after language throughout New Guinea there is a considerable specialization of verb morphology to mark one or both clauses of counterfactual conditions. An example of a Wojokeso counterfactual sentence follows:

N-*ontentesi* hwolaho mjohosɨhnne*sohi*lo
eat-2SG CF vomit   you would have thrown up
'If you had eaten, you would have vomited'

4.4 *Clause chaining in South America*

I confine myself here to a consideration of clause chaining in Chibchan languages (Colombia and Ecuador) and in the Tucanoan languages (of the Valpes region in Colombia). But chaining in South America is much more extensive geographically than this. We know that it also characterizes Quechua, as well as Aguaruna and Cashinahua in Peru.

Clause chaining in South America has points of comparison and contrast with clause chaining in New Guinea. Like clause chaining in Papua New Guinea there is a verb of distinctive structure that occurs but once in the entire sentence. Unlike New Guinea nothing quite as characteristic as medial verbs occurs. In Paez (Gerdel and Slocum 1976) the medial verb is a rather stripped-down structure whose chief characteristic is that it contains a morpheme which indicates same subject (*-rra*) or different subject (*-te'*) relative to the following clause. In the following example, the Paez suffixes just indicated serve to keep track of three participants in a confused situation:

Pal   case'j*rra*   nasaty uyiits*te'*,   new'weya' u'*tje'*,
father coming out(ss) people slapping (DS) to defend going(DS)

fyrūu yac*rra*,   angya's pecueya' yuj*te'*,   fytū'sa' teech
stick carrying me   to hit   coming(DS) stick   one

señora e'su   newe*rra*,   wenzh*te'*,   pala' iiwete uc
woman from behind deterring(ss) pulling(DS) father fell   he
'Father came out and was slapping people; as I went to defend them, he came carrying a stick to hit me; but a woman grabbed the stick from behind and she pulled, and he fell down'

Of interest here is (a) the unmarked participant (i.e., the narrator) versus the two named participants; and (b) a constituent grouping which gives major breaks at indication of oncoming different subject, and minor breaks at indication of oncoming same subject (as indicated clearly by the distribution of non-final pauses which follow different-subject verbs but do not follow same-subject verbs). The sentence is not, therefore, a linear string; rather same-subject sentences are embedded within the different-subject sentence (cf. Foré above, section 3.1).

Paez also has some co-ranking sentence structures – that is, coordinate, antithetical, and alternation sentences – where independent clauses with independent verbs are combined into sentence units. Of interest here is that the feature indicating same subject versus different subject is found in the coordinate sentence where the particles *sa'* 'and' (same subject) and *atsa'* 'and' (different subject) occur. I regard this as an extension of a feature normal in chaining structures to a co-ranking structure.

Guambiano of Colombia (data from Branks) and Cayapa of Ecuador (Wiebe 1977) are also languages which have chaining structures similar to those illustrated for Paez.

In Tucanoan languages we typically find two sorts of chaining structures which can be called the implicit chain and the explicit chain, where 'implicit' and 'explicit' refer to identification of participants. In the implicit chain, the medial verbs are bare stems (or minimally affixed in some languages); same versus different subject is understood according to certain tacit speaker–hearer assumptions which are stated below. In explicit chain, there are overt markers to keep these matters straight. The matter of temporal overlap versus temporal succession is a concern intertwined with the matter of subject reference – much as in chaining languages of Papua New Guinea.

Guanano (N. Waltz 1976), a typical Tucanoan language, illustrates these two chaining structures quite aptly.

The implicit chain is a sentence structure which has essentially three slots: an initial link slot, a medial base slot which may occur several times, and a final base slot. The initial link slot, which may occur twice, consists of conjunctions or certain types of dependent clauses which recapitulate and refer back to a previous sentence. In effect, they could be considered to fill a temporal margin in a chaining structure much as in New Guinea. The medial base has a verb with no suffix at all while the final base has a regularly inflected verb. This surface structure can encode temporal succession or temporal overlap. In the former case the sentence is n-ary and can be considered to be a sequence sentence. In the latter case the sentence is binary and can be considered to be a simultaneous sentence. There are no surface structure clues to distinguish the one from the other, but there is a constraint that the n-ary sequence sentence is (except for its use in reporting dialogue; see below) a same subject string, while the binary simultaneous sentence is invariably a different subject string.

When the implicit chain functions as a sequence sentence which encodes temporal succession, it is assumed that it is a same-subject string, as in the following example:

Wesepɨ sɨ   cjoha   cjohatini   tjuata, cjɨ   duha
field to arrive clean up clean up going return manioc pull

tjuhsɨ wɨja tjua   wihi, dahrechɨ, dahrechɨ tjuhsɨ, wipe,
finish scrape return arrive make food make food finish   strain

wipe tjuhsɨchɨ   ñɨco   co   waco
strain when finish(DS) when see I(SS) water to get(I)

buhahi
went to river
'Arriving at the field, cleaning (it) up, going around cleaning (it) up, returning, pulling up manioc, finishing scraping (it), returning (home), making food, finished making food, straining, when I saw that the straining was finished, I went to the river to get water'

In the above example *buhahi* '(I) went-to-river' is the final verb. Actually, the whole last stretch *wipe tjuhsʉchʉ ñʉco co waco buhahi*, which is the last base of the sequence sentence, is itself an embedded explicit chain sentence (as witnessed by different-subject marker *chʉ* on 'finish' and same-subject marker *co* 'first person singular feminine' on 'see'). See immediately below for a description of explicit chain sentences.

Dialogue (Carolyn Waltz 1977), however, may also encode within the sequence sentence: i.e., we may have something of the sort: (He) *said* [medial verb] 'Hello', (she) *said* [medial verb] 'Hello', (he) *said* [medial verb] 'How are you?' (she) *said* [medial verb] 'Fine, won't you come in', *he-came-in* [final verb]. Here again, however, aside from the occasional occurrence of a pronoun or noun in the chain, the subjects, in this case the speakers, are unmarked. Furthermore, it is assumed that since dialogue is being encoded in the sentence, there will be alternation of speakers (as previously identified). Therefore, when dialogue encodes within the implicit chain, the sequence sentence is assumed to be a different-subject chain.

The sequence sentence is a very important structure in a Tucanoan language. It backgrounds information by putting it into the medial bases and foregrounds important actions and/or events, by putting them into the final base of such sentences. When dialogue is worked into discourse, dialogue may be put almost entirely into the medial bases – thus at the same time adding vividness to the discourse while continuing an unbroken event line through the final bases of a series of sentences.

When this surface structure encodes temporal overlap (1) it is binary; and (2) it is assumed that it is a different-subject string: *Pjiha ta, chʉa niha*. 'From-jungle came, eating were (they)', i.e. 'When he came from the jungle, they were eating'. Here, the different participants need not be overtly identified if they are well established in the context. Obviously, of course, the probability that two actions are simultaneous (and hence involve different subjects) rather than sequential (and hence same subject) is itself a contextual inference. In daily conversation, and at a given point of a monologue discourse, if contextual clues are insufficient, there is resort to the explicit chain, whose description follows.

The explicit chain has four functional slots: link, medial base, final base, and post-final base. The initial slot (link) is as described for the sequence sentence and is not specific to this sentence type. The medial base slot contains three formally distinct medial structures: the contingency dependent clause ('if/when/since'), the concessive dependent clause ('although'), and the concurrent dependent clause ('while'), respectively. These are not, however, three sentence margins which occur in pre-nuclear position. The concept of sentence margin is better reserved for adverbial clauses which can occur with an inventory of differing sentence types and which are relatively detachable. The three structures here described are, however, specific to this sentence type. Furthermore, all contain the chaining feature (same- or different-subject marker) which cross-references to the other part of the nucleus. They act, therefore, like medial bases of a chaining structure rather than like sentence margins in a co-ranking structure.

One common filler of the medial base is the contingency dependent clause. It has verbs which are marked for same versus different subject. Same-subject markers distinguish first, second, third person; singular versus plural; and masculine versus feminine. The different-subject marker is but one suffix. These markers are: (a) same subject: -cʉ, 1/2SG MASC, -co 1/2SG FEM, -ro 3SG MASC/FEM; -na 1/2PL, -a/-ga 3PL; (b) different subject: -chʉ. Here a nuclear base with a medial verb absorbs, in effect, the functions of temporal, conditional, and circumstantial margins in a co-ranking language, as in the following Guanano sentence:

Tiro   waha-ro,   tjuatasi
he when/if/since goes he(ss) (he) won't return
'If he goes, he won't return'

A second structure found in the medial base slot, the concessive dependent clause, has a verb form like that in the contingency dependent clause with the following modification: namely, the verb stem is followed by the suffix -pa (concessive) plus the dependent contingency verb suffixes (same- or different-subject markers) plus the suffix -ta (specifier clitic). We get structures like:

To waha-pa-chʉ-ta,   tina tjuasi
he even though he goes(DS), they won't stay
'Even if he goes, they won't stay'

Yuhu waha-pa-cʉ-ta   tjuasi
I   even though I go(ss) (I) won't return
'Even though I go, I won't stay'

The third structure, the concurrent dependent clause, expresses temporal overlap relative to the following sentence nucleus. It begins with *pʉ* 'until' or with the time–locative introducer *te* 'until' followed by the dependency contingency verb in the regular position in its clause:

> Pʉ   ti   tǫho   to piihtichʉ,   ǫta pisanocha
> until that bunch it finished when just perched (he)
> 'Until that bunch (of palmfruit) was finished he just perched there'

In looking at the above structures in the first medial base of this sentence type it is interesting to note that same or different subject is very carefully marked, as opposed to the implicit marking which we found characterizing the structure which is common to the sequence and simultaneous sentence. It is evident, therefore, that if a speaker wants to be explicit in Guanano as to same- versus different-subject sequence, he resorts to the explicit chain sentence, not to the implicit chain (sequence or simultaneous). This is necessary whenever we have a sequence involving different actors rather than the same actor, or when we have simultaneity involving the same person doing two actions at the same time.

In summary, in regard to the medial and post-final bases which occur with the final base of the explicit chain, it is interesting that there are but four formally distinguishable structures (as fillers in two slots) and between them they cover the ground which is covered by the fillers of temporal margin, conditional margin, circumstance margin, concessive margin, and concurrent temporal margin, in Indo-European or Philippine languages.

It is evident that we have here two interestingly contrastive structures. The implicit chain sentence (which encodes sequence and simultaneity) has uninflected verbs in its non-final bases and a regularly inflected verb in its final base. It proceeds by certain implicit conventions concerning whether we are to reckon same subject or different subject from base to base. The other structure, the explicit chain sentence, is even more a chaining structure than the former. It has special dependent verb structures which occur in slots preposed (and postposed) to the final base of the sentence. Furthermore, these dependent verb structures indicate same or different subject relative to the verb of the final base. Between them, these two sentence structures account for most of what is happening on the sentence level in a typical Tucanoan language.

Guanano also has a counterfactual sentence. A counterfactual sentence has three slots: a link, a protasis slot, and an apodosis slot. It is a specialized version of the explicit chain. The link slot is as previously described for the other two sentences. The protasis slot is like the medial base. It contains a contingency dependent clause, or a concessive dependent clause. The apodosis has a hypothetical verb in the past tense plus a suffix -*boa* which expresses frustration; it is a modified final base. In Guanano not only is counterfactuality expressed in this surface structure, but also frustrated hypotheticality. Thus, we have sentences such as:

> Tiro waha-chɨ tina tjuataera-boa
> he   if-goes   they might not have returned
> 'If he had gone, they wouldn't have returned'

which are counterfactual in past time; and sentences such as

> Tiro waha-pa-chɨ-ta, tina tjuataera-boa
> he   even if goes   they might not have returned
> 'Even if he had gone, they still would not have returned'

which expresses frustrated hypotheticality. The two sentences differ simply in the inflection of the first verb. In the first example the protasis has a contingency dependent clause and in the second it has a concessive dependent clause.

Aside from these, there is a quotative sentence. It is a run-of-the-mill structure with a quotation and a postposed quotation formula, and it is not illustrated here. As in some other languages (e.g. Trique) there are no such structures as coordinate ('and') and antithetical ('but') sentences. Instead these relations are expressed as paragraph structures.

Tunebo (a Chibchan language, Headland and Levinsohn 1977) has a system of mutual expectancies in regard to marking same or different subject in the sentence that is similar to what has been indicated for Guanano. There is a suffix -*r* which indicates temporal succession and implies that the subject of the following verb is the same as that of the dependent verb or connector which ends in -*r*. There is another suffix -*yat* or -*t* which indicates temporal overlap and implies that the subject of the following verb will differ from the subject of the element marked with the suffix. While, however, the same subject is expected with -*r* and different subject with -*yat*/*t*, these constructions may be used to indicate temporal succession and temporal overlap respectively with other than the anticipated subject, if the subject is clearly marked by a noun in the sentence.

4.5 *The problem of the 'endless' sentence*
In respect to Foré and certain other languages of New Guinea we noted above that the medial–final chain is equivalent to the paragraph

rather than to the sentence and that shorter levels of chaining characterize sentences within the paragraph. We also challenged the assumption that the medial–final chain is necessarily a sentence in structure. It is a shock to realize, however, that in some languages, both in New Guinea and South America, we sometimes find chaining carried to such (by our standards) excessive lengths that the chain is plausibly neither a sentence nor a paragraph – unless we consider that the body of a discourse consists of but one sentence or one paragraph. While the latter is not impossible and, in fact, characterizes some shorter discourses, it is hard to believe that a text of seven or eight pages reduces to the structure of one sentence or even that the body of a text is simply one sentence.[12] It seems here that we must take stock and realize again that chaining is a surface-structure phenomenon which is capable of being plugged into various functions. As such, we can expect it to confine itself neither to the sentence nor to the paragraph in all languages.

Thus, Millie Larson (1978) presents an Aguaruna discourse in which, while the aperture of the discourse, closure, and finis are discrete and consist of smaller chains, the entire intervening body of the discourse which contains the episodes of the story is one long run-on chain of over sixty clauses. Furthermore, this chain is very evidently not a simple linear sequence. It may itself be divided into paragraphs and sentences by various defensible criteria. In such an instance, very plainly the surface structure of chaining is no longer marking sentence or paragraph, but is really co-extensive with the entire body of the discourse.

A similar situation probably exists for Waffa in New Guinea. In Waffa, in at least one discourse type (the legend narrative discourse), Hotz and Stringer (1970) report that there are long chains which clearly can be broken up into weakly delineated paragraphs and weakly delineated sentences.[13] Furthermore, there obviously are groups of paragraphs distinguished from each other within such a long chain. These groups seem to correspond to weakly delineated embedded discourses.

5 Where sentence is not a separate level

There are languages in which it appears that the four levels – clause, sentence, paragraph, and discourse – are not needed to describe the structures involved, but that only three such levels are necessary. Thus, for certain aboriginal Australian languages (Mantjiltjara, Walmatjari, Wik-Munkan),[14] we apparently have a situation something like the following: there is a simple (or complex) sentence which has a one-clause base and may have a rather full gamut of sentence margins attached to it. Beyond that there is not much point in distinguishing, for example, coordinate sentence from coordinate paragraph or antithetical sentence from antithetical paragraph; i.e., sentence and paragraph in effect collapse. There is, however, some evidence that sentence and paragraph should possibly be retained as thematization units (Kilham 1977). This evidence may call for fresh evaluation of the whole question of structural levels in these languages.

6 Conclusion

An understanding of sentence structure around the world requires that we have some idea both of the sentence forming devices and also of the various notions that are expressed through these devices. We also would hope to attain some idea as to which devices most commonly express which notions. The present chapter is meant to be a step in these directions.

NOTES

1 Besides the sentence nucleus and its margins there is also a sentence periphery, which consists of such functional elements as exclamations, vocatives, and sentence adverbs.
2 This is a summary of more detailed material which has been presented elsewhere (Ballard, Conrad, Longacre 1971a, 1971b; Longacre 1972:51–92; Longacre 1976:98–163). Furthermore, various people besides myself have endeavoured to give such summaries and the varying notional catalogues make an interesting comparison. Of special interest is Beekman's catalogue (Beekman and Callow 1974) in that he attempts to classify notions of the sort that I present here according to those which are main-line to discourses and those which are supportive propositions. This seems to me to be an especially fruitful line of inquiry. Grimes (1975) also forms an interesting comparison with the catalogue of notions given here, as does Hollenbach (1975: Appendix). All the latter are to varying degrees influenced by Fuller (1959). Somewhat divergent is the work of Halliday and Hasan (1976) which attempts to classify interclausal relations in English according to surface structure conjunctions.
3 Sources of information about Philippine languages other than Ibaloi are papers (published and unpublished) by Ruth Lusted (Atta Negrito, unpublished), Roy Mayfield (Agta, 1972), Janice Walton (Itneg, submitted), Stewart Hussey (Aborlan Tagbanwa, unpublished), Jean Shand (Ilianen Manobo, submitted), Seymour Ashley (Tausug, unpublished), William Hall (Siocon Subanon, 1973), Lawrence Reid (Central Bontoc, 1970), Gordon and Thelma Svelmoe (Mansaka, 1974), Richard Elkins (Western Bukidnon

Manobo, 1971). The data here referred to are summarized in Longacre (1968 ii), along with data from a number of other Philippine languages.

4 Trique has an intricate tonal structure in which five tone levels (with 1 the highest, and 5 the lowest) occur either isolated or in combination ('glides').

5 The anticipatory mood is marked by a complicated pattern of tone lowering which differs according to the tone class to which a verb belongs. It combines the functions of a future tense, a subjunctive, and a command form. Thus $ga^3\,{}^{2}na^{35}\,{}^{2}$, 'came', in the anticipatory mood is $ga^5\,{}^{2}na^5\,{}^{2}$ which, according to context, can be variously translated 'will come', 'would have come' and 'come'.

6 One might speculate that chaining structures could occur in which: (a) languages are vso (verb–subject–object); (b) there is a special sentence-initial verb; and (c) all other verbs in the sentence are some sort of (morphologically distinct) 'consecutive' verb. Classical Hebrew almost achieves this in that it can have sequences consisting of a so-called perfect tense followed by a string of 'waw-consecutives' (*w-* 'and' plus the imperfect with vowel changes). Unfortunately, however, the initial perfect is not obligatory and may in many cases be circumstantial in function. At any rate, one snag in the development of such structures as are here speculatively posited is the fact that the initial clause of a sentence is the position where back-reference to a previous sentence may occur in connected discourse. In that the sentence-initial position is customarily pre-empted for this function it is not available for regular occurrence of a distinctive chain-initial verb.

7 While my immediate reference in this section has been to my own summary of 1972, I acknowledge as sources of data (besides where otherwise noted): Gibson, McCarthy, and Harris (Kanite, unpublished); Graham Scott (Foré, 1973); Alfred and Dellene Stucky (Ek-Nii, unpublished); James Parlier (Managalasi, unpublished); Ellis Deibler (Gahuku, University of Michigan dissertation); Elaine Geary (Kunimaipa, unpublished); Velma Foreman (Yessan-Mayo, 1974); Doreen Marks (Kosena, unpublished); Ken McElhanon (Selepet, Kate – personal communication). The Deibler and Foreman studies which were available to me when I wrote my summary were preliminary drafts.

8 The three sets of tense–person–number suffixes are a study in themselves. No two cut up semantic space in the same way. Basically the sets involve singular, dual, plural versus first person, second person, third person. But all sets of tense–person–number markers in Wojokeso involve some collapsing of person–number categories together. Furthermore, the suffixes which mark tense–person–number in the counterfactual and in the future coordinate constitute two further sets which indicate two further ways of cutting up semantic space. Consequently, if we lay out in front of us these five sets of tense–person–number markers, no two of the five cut up semantic space in the same way, although the scheme of two parameters with three values underlies all five of them.

9 In any co-ranking structure with which I am familiar, 'antithetical' and 'coordinate' are opposed sentence types. Here, however, the two are seen

conflated. This is interesting in view of Halliday and Hasan's (1976) contention that the English 'but' includes the notion 'and'.

10 Note that *'manji* is added to medial verbs and overlays all the apparatus inherent in this distinction. Therefore, although 'if' clauses are sentence margins in some languages, this does not seem applicable here. Indeed, the co-ranking structure of margin–nucleus gives way in a chaining language to a distinct apparatus, medial base (repeated) + final base.

11 There are other New Guinea languages, for example Telefol, which have a considerable inventory of such conjunctions, along with typical New Guinea verb morphology.

12 Obviously in a long so-called 'one-sentence' text, the narrator breathes several times in the course of delivering it. The phonology is not marked differently in this respect from an English discourse split into various sentences with intervening pauses. Clearly, then, at least a number of *phonological sentences* occur within the large chain.

13 By 'weakly delineated' I simply mean that, while there is some overt formal marking, it is not plentiful nor readily obvious.

14 For data here I am indebted to: James Marsh (Mantjiltjara, unpublished); Joyce Hudson (Walmatjari, unpublished); Barbara Sayers (Wik-Munkan, 1976).

Bibliography

Abaev, V. I. 1964. *Grammatical sketch of Ossetic*. Bloomington, Indiana University Press

Adler, E. 1966. Vodskij jazyk. In Vinogradov 1966:118–37

Aissen, J. and D. Perlmutter. 1976. Clause reduction in Spanish. *Berkeley Linguistics Society* 2:1–30

Allen, R. 1966. *The verb system of present-day American English*. The Hague, Mouton

Anderson, J. M. 1971 *The grammar of case: towards a localistic theory*. Cambridge, Cambridge University Press. (Cambridge Studies in Lingustics, 4)

Andersson, L. G. 1975. *Form and function of subordinate clauses*. Gothenburg, University of Göteborg, Department of Linguistics. (Gothenburg Monographs in Linguistics, 1)

Andrews, A. 1975. Studies in the syntax of relative and comparative clauses. Unpublished Ph.D. dissertation, M.I.T.

Aronson, H. 1972. Some notes on relative clauses in Georgian. In Peranteau *et al.* 1972:136–43

Bach, E. and R. T. Harms, eds. 1968. *Universals in linguistic theory*. New York, Holt, Rinehart and Winston

Bagari, D. 1976. Subordinate adverbial clauses in Hausa. Unpublished Ph.D. dissertation, University of California, Los Angeles

Bailey, T. G. 1924. *Grammar of the Shina languages*. London, Royal Asiatic Society

Bailey, T. G. 1956. *Urdu*. London, English Universities Press. (Teach Yourself Books)

Ballard, D. L., R. J. Conrad and R. E. Longacre. 1971a. The deep and surface grammar of interclausal relations. *Foundations of Language* 7:70-118

Ballard, D. L., R. J. Conrad and R. E. Longacre. 1971b. More on the deep and surface grammar of interclausal relations. Ukarumpa, New Guinea, Summer Institute of Linguistics. (Language Data, Asian-Pacific Series, 1)

Bamgboṣe, A. 1974. On serial verbs and verbal status. *Journal of West African Languages* 9:17–48

Bartholomew, D. 1973. Otomi dependent clauses. In Corum *et al.* 1973:1–8

Baskakov, N. A. 1940. *Nogajskoj jazyk i ego dialekty*. Moscow, Nauka

Beaubien, F., M. F. Sabourin and M. St-Amour. 1976. *Faire*-attraction: déplacement du sujet. *Recherches Linguistiques à Montréal* 7:21–39

Beekman, J. and J. Callow. 1974. *Translating the word of God*. Grand Rapids, Zondervan

Berenstein, A. 1977. Antipassive in K'ekchi. Unpublished manuscript, Department of Linguistics, University of California, Los Angeles

Berent, G. P. 1973. Absolute constructions as 'subordinate clauses'. In Corum *et al.* 1973:147–54

Beythan, J. 1943. *Praktische Grammatik der Tamilsprache*. Leipzig

Bird, C. 1968. Relative clauses in Bambara. *Journal of West African Languages* 5:35–47

Bloomfield, L. 1933. *Language*. New York, Holt

Bolinger, D. 1972. *That's that*. The Hague, Mouton

Boyle, D. 1973. *Ach* and *agus* as coordinate and subordinate conjunctions in Gaelic. In Corum *et al.* 1973:220–8

Brecht, R. D. 1974. Tense and infinitive complements in Russian, Latin, and English. In R. D. Brecht and C. V. Chvany, eds. *Slavic transformational syntax*. Ann Arbor, University of Michigan Press: 193–218

Browne, W. 1973. Relative pronoun = relative + pronoun? Evidence from Serbo-Croatian. Paper presented to Department of Linguistics, Cambridge University

Buck, C. D. 1933. *Comparative grammar of Greek and Latin*. Chicago, The University of Chicago Press

Buechel, E. 1939. *A grammar of Lakota*. Saint Francis, S. Dakota, Rosebud Educational Society

Byarushengo, E. R., A. Duranti and L. M. Hyman, eds. 1977. *Haya grammatical structures*. Southern California Occasional Papers in Linguistics, 6

Castillo, Carlos, 1939. *Mexico*. Ed. by Burton Holmes. Chicago, Wheeler

Chafe, W. L. 1976. Givenness, contrastiveness, definiteness, subjects, topics, and point of view. In Li 1976:25–55

Chao, Y-R. 1968. *A grammar of spoken Chinese*. Berkeley, University of California Press

Chomsky, N. 1981. *Lectures on government and binding*. Dordrecht, Foris

Churchward, C. M. 1941. *Fijian grammar*. Sydney, Australian Medical Publishing Co.

Clark, R. 1973. Case markers and complementizers: a Maori example. *Stanford Working Papers on Language Universals* 12

Cole, P. and J. M. Sadock, eds. 1977. *Syntax and semantics 8: Grammatical relations*. New York, Academic Press

Comrie, B. 1976. The syntax of causative constructions: cross-language similarities and differences. In Shibatani 1976:261–312

Corum, C., T. C. Smith-Stark and A. Weiser, eds. 1973. *You take the high node and I'll take the low node*. Chicago, Chicago Linguistic Society

Craig, C. G. 1977. *The structure of Jacaltec*. Austin, University of Texas Press

Crazzolara, J. 1960. *A study of the Logbara (Ma'di) language*. London, Dawson

Creider, C. 1974. Notes on Luo syntax. Unpublished manuscript, University of Western Ontario

Creider, C. 1976. A typological sketch of Nandi. Unpublished manuscript, Department of Anthropology, University of Western Ontario

Creider, C. 1977. The syntax and semantics of relative clauses in Inuktitut. Unpublished manuscript, Department of Anthropology, University of Western Ontario.

Darden, B. J. 1973. Indirect speech and reported speech in Lithuanian and Bulgarian. In Corum *et al.* 1973:326–32

Davis, J. F. 1973. A partial grammar of simplex and complex sentences in Luiseño. Unpublished Ph.D. dissertation, University of California, Los Angeles

de Chene, B. 1976. 'Even' and the meaning of conditionals. Unpublished manuscript, University of California, Los Angeles

Dik, S. C. 1972. *Coordination*. Amsterdam, North-Holland

Dixon, R. M. W. 1972. *The Dyirbal language of North Queensland*. Cambridge, Cambridge University Press

Dixon, R. M. W. 1977. The syntactic development of Australian languages. In C. N. Li, ed. *Mechanisms of syntactic change*. Austin, University of Texas Press: 365–415

Döhmann, K. 1974. Die sprachliche Darstellung logischer Funktoren. In Menne and Frey 1974:28–56

Dougherty, R. C. 1970. A grammar of coordinate conjoined structures I. *Language* 46:850-98

Downing, B. 1973. Corelative relative clauses in universal grammar. *Minnesota Working Papers in Linguistics and Philosophy of Language* 2:1–17

Dunn, C. J. and S. Yanada. 1958. *Japanese*. London, English Universities Press. (Teach Yourself Books)

Duranti, A. 1977. Haya relative clauses. In Byarushengo *et al.* 1977:119–132

Ebert, R. P. 1973. On the notion 'subordinate clause' in standard German. In Corum *et al.* 1973:164–77

Elkins, R. 1971. Western Bukidnon Manobo sentence structure. *Lingua* 27:216–62

Elson, B. F., ed. 1964. *Verb studies in five New Guinea languages*. Norman, University of Oklahoma, Summer Institute of Linguistics

Fillmore, C. J. 1968. The case for case. In Bach and Harms 1968:1–88

Fillmore, C. J. and D. T. Langendoen, eds. 1971. *Studies in linguistic semantics*. New York, Holt, Rinehart and Winston

Foreman, V. 1974. *Grammar of Yessan-Mayo*. Santa Ana, Calif., Summer Institute of Linguistics. (Language Data, Asian-Pacific Series, 4)

Forester, C. S. 1964. *The ship*. London, Reader's Digest Association (Reader's Digest Condensed Books)

Fraser, B. 1969. An analysis of concessive conditions. *Chicago Linguistic Society* 5:66–75

Fuller, D. P. 1959. The inductive method of Bible study. 3rd edn. Pasadena, Fuller Theological Seminary, Mimeo

Furbee, N. L. 1973. Subordinate clauses in Tojolabal-Maya. In Corum *et al.* 1973:9–22

Gardiner, A. 1973. *Egyptian grammar*. 3rd edn. Oxford, Oxford University Press

Garn, S. M. 1961, *Human races*. Springfield, Ill., Bannerstone House

Gary, J. O. and E. Keenan. 1977. On collapsing grammatical relations in universal grammar. In Cole and Sadock 1977:83–120

George, I. 1975. A grammar of Kwa-type verb serialization: its nature and significance in current generative theory. Unpublished Ph.D. dissertation, University of California, Los Angeles

George, I. 1976. Verb serialization and lexical decomposition. In L. M. Hyman, L. C. Jacobson and R. G. Schuh, eds. Papers in African Linguistics in honor of Wm. E. Welmers. *Studies in African Linguistics*, Supplement 6:63–72

Gerdel, F. and M. Slocum. 1976. Paez discourse, paragraph and sentence structure. In Longacre and Woods 1976, Vol. 1:259–443

Givón, T. 1971. Dependent modals, performatives, factivity, Bantu subjunctives, and what not. *Studies in African Linguistics* 2:61–81

Givón, T. 1972. Studies in ChiBemba and Bantu grammar. *Studies in African Linguistics*, Supplement 3:1–247

Givón, T. 1973. Pronoun attraction and subject postposing in Bantu. Unpublished manuscript, Department of Linguistics, University of California, Los Angeles

Givón, T. and A. Kimenyi. 1974. Truth, belief and doubt in Kinya-Rwanda. *Studies in African Linguistics*, Supplement 5:95–113

Gleitman, L. 1965. Coordinating conjunctions in English. *Language* 41:260–93

Gonda, J. 1966. *Concise elementary grammar of the Sanskrit language*. Montgomery, University of Alabama Press

Goodwin, W. 1892. *Greek grammar*. Boston, Ginn

Gorbet, L. 1972. How to tell a head when you see one: disambiguation in Diegueño relative clauses. Unpublished manuscript, Department of Linguistics, University of California, San Diego

Greenough, G. B. *et al.*, eds. 1903. *Allen and Greenough's new Latin grammar*. Boston, Ginn

Grimes, J. 1975. *The thread of discourse*. The Hague, Mouton

Grosu, A. and S. Thompson. 1977. Constraints on the distribution of NP clauses. *Language* 53:104–51

Guitart, J. 1978. On the pragmatics of Spanish mood in so-called semi-factive predicates. Unpublished manuscript, State University of New York, Buffalo

Haiman, J. 1974. Concessives, conditionals, and verbs of volition. *Foundations of Language* 11:341–59

Haiman, J. 1978. Conditionals are topics. *Language* 54:564–89

Hale, K. L. 1976. The adjoined relative clause in Australia. In R. M. W. Dixon, ed. *Grammatical categories in Australian languages*. Canberra, Australian Institute of Aboriginal Studies: 78–105

Hale, K. L. and P. Platero. n.d. Aspects of Navajo anaphora: relativization and pronominalization. Unpublished manuscript, Department of Linguistics, M.I.T.

Hall, W. C. 1973. An outline of Siocon Subanon sentence structure. *Philippine Journal of Linguistics* 4/5:1–22

Halliday, M. A. K. and R. Hasan. 1976. *Cohesion in English*. London, Longmans

Hardy, H. K. 1977. Temporality, conditionality, counterfactuality, and contrast. Unpublished manuscript, University of California, Los Angeles

Headland, P. and S. Levinsohn. 1977. Prominence and cohesion in Tunebo discourse. In Longacre and Woods 1977, Vol. 2:133–58

Healey, P. M. 1966. *Levels and chaining in Telefol sentences*. Canberra, Australian National University, Research School of Pacific Studies, Department of Linguistics. (Pacific Linguistics, B.5)

Hetzron, R. 1969. *The verbal system of Southern Agaw*. Berkeley, University of California Press

Hetzron, R. 1977. *The Gunnan-Gurage languages*. Naples, Istituto Orientale di Napoli

Hoffman, C. 1963. *A grammar of the Margi language*. Oxford, Oxford University Press

Hollenbach, B. 1975. Discourse structure, interpropositional relations, and translation. *Notes on Translation* 56

Hooper, J. B. 1975. On assertive predicates. In J. Kimball, ed. *Syntax and Semantics 4*. New York, Academic Press: 91–124

Hooper, J. B. and S. A. Thompson. 1973. On the applicability of root transformations. *Linguistic Inquiry* 4:465–97

Hope, E. R. 1974. *The deep syntax of Lisu sentences: a transformational case grammar*. Canberra, Australian National University, Research School of Pacific Studies, Department of Linguistics. (Pacific Linguistics, B.34)

Hopper, P. J. 1979. Aspect and foregrounding in discourse. In T. Givón, ed. *Syntax and semantics 12: Discourse and syntax*. New York, Academic Press: 213–42

Horn, L. 1978. Remarks on Neg-raising. In P. Cole, ed. *Syntax and semantics 9: Pragmatics*. New York, Academic Press: 129–220

Hotz, J. and M. Stringer. 1970. Waffa sentence, paragraph and discourse. Unpublished manuscript, Ukarumpa, New Guinea, Summer Institute of Linguistics

Huddleston, R. 1971. *The sentence in written English*. Cambridge, Cambridge University Press

Hutchison, J. P. 1976. Aspects of Kanuri syntax. Unpublished Ph.D. dissertation, Indiana University

Hyman, L. 1971. Consecutivization in Feʔfeʔ. *Journal of African Languages* 10:29–43

Hyman, L. and D. J. Magaji. 1970. *Essentials of Gwari grammar*. University of Ibadan, Institute of African Studies. (Occasional Publications, 27)

Jackendoff, R. 1971. On some questionable arguments about quantifiers and negation. *Language* 47:282–97

Jakobson, R. 1957. Shifters, verbal categories, and the Russian verb. In his *Selected writings* (1971), Vol. 2. The Hague, Mouton: 130–47

James, D. J. 1970. Embedding and coordinating transforms in Siane. In S. A. Wurm and D. C. Laycock, eds. *Pacific linguistic studies in honour of Arthur Capell*. Canberra, Australian National University, Research School of Pacific Studies, Department of Linguistics: 1095–125. (Pacific Linguistics, C.13)

Jeffers, R. 1975. Remarks on Indo-European infinitives. *Language* 51: 133–48

Jenkins, L. 1972. *Modality in English syntax*. Bloomington, Indiana University Linguistics Club

Jenkins, M. 1959. *A Welsh tutor*. Cardiff

Jespersen, O. 1964. *Essentials of English grammar*. Montgomery, University of Alabama Press

Johnson, D. 1977. On relational constraints on grammars. In Cole and Sadock 1977:151–78

Justus, C. 1977. Syntactic change: toward a definition of the units of a system subject to historical change. Unpublished manuscript, Department of Linguistics, University of California, Berkeley

Kac, M. B. 1972. Clauses of saying and the interpretation of *because*. *Language* 48:626–32

Karlsson, F. 1972. Relative clauses in Finnish. In Peranteau *et al.* 1972:106–14

Karttunen, L. 1971a. Implicative verbs. *Language* 47:340–58

Karttunen, L. 1971b. Some observations on factivity. *Papers in Linguistics* 4:55–70

Kayne, R. 1975. *French syntax*. Cambridge, Mass., M.I.T. Press

Keenan, E. L. 1972. Relative clause formation in Malagasy (and some related and some not so related languages). In Peranteau *et al.* 1972:169–89

Keenan, E. L. 1975. Logical expressive power and syntactic variation in natural languages. In his *Formal semantics of natural language*. Cambridge, Cambridge University Press: 406–21

Keenan, E. L. and K. Bimson. 1975. Perceptual complexity and the cross-language distribution of relative clause and NP-question types. In R. E. Grossman, L. J. San and T. J. Vance, eds. *Functionalism*. Chicago, Chicago Linguistic Society: 253–59

Keenan, E. L. and B. Comrie. 1977. NP accessibility and universal grammar. *Linguistic Inquiry* 8:63–100

Keenan, E. O. and B. Schieffelin. 1976a. Foregrounding referents, a reconsideration of left dislocation in discourse. *Berkeley Linguistics Society* 2:240–57

Keenan, E. O and B. Schieffelin. 1976b. Topic as a discourse notion: a study of topics in the conversations of children and adults. In Li 1976:335–84

Kempson, R. 1975. *Presupposition and the delimitation of semantics*. Cambridge, Cambridge University Press

Kilham, C. A. 1977. Thematic organization of Wik-Munkan discourse. Unpublished Ph.D. thesis, Australian National University

Kimenyi, A. 1976. Topics in the relational grammar of Kinyarwanda. Ph.D. dissertation, University of California, Los Angeles. (Published in 1980 as *A relational grammar of Kinyarwanda*. Berkeley, University of California Press. University of California Publications in Linguistics, 91)

Kiparsky, P. and C. Kiparsky. 1970. Fact. In M. Bierwisch and K. E. Heidolph, eds. *Progress in linguistics*. The Hague, Mouton: 143–73. (Janua linguarum, Series major, 43)

Kirsner, R. and S. A. Thompson. 1976. The role of pragmatic inference in semantics: a study of sensory verb complements in English. *Glossa* 10:200–40

Klein, P. W. 1977. Semantic factors in Spanish mood. *Glossa* 11:3–19

Klima, E. 1964. Negation in English. In J. A. Fodor and J. J. Katz, eds. *The structure of languages*. Englewood Cliffs, N.J., Prentice-Hall: 246–323

Kühner, R. and C. Stegmann. 1955. *Ausfürliche Grammatik der lateinischen Sprache: Satzlehre*, Vol. 2. Leverkusen, Gottschalk

Kuipers, A. H. 1967. *The Squamish language*. The Hague, Mouton

Kuipers, A. H. 1974. *The Shuswap language*. The Hague, Mouton

Kuno, S. 1973. *The structure of the Japanese language*. Cambridge, Mass., M.I.T. Press

Lafont, R. 1967. *La phrase occitane*. Paris, Presses Universitaires de France

Lakoff, G. 1974. Syntactic amalgams. *Berkeley Studies in Syntax and Semantics* 1(9):1–24

Lakoff, G. and S. Peters. 1969. Phrasal conjunction and symmetric predicates. In Reibel and Schane 1969:113–44

Lakoff, R. 1969. A syntactic argument for negative transportation. *Chicago Linguistic Society* 5:140–7

Lakoff, R. 1970. Tense and its relation to participants. *Language* 46:838–49

Lakoff, R. 1971. If's, and's and but's about conjunction. In Fillmore and Langendoen 1971:114–49

Langdon, M. 1970. *Grammar of Diegueño*. Berkeley, University of California Press

Langdon, S. 1911. *A Sumerian grammar and chrestomathy*. Paris

Lanier, N. 1968. Three structural layers in Mezquital Otomi clauses. *Linguistics* 43:32–85

Larson, M. 1978. *The functions of reported speech in discourse*. Dallas, Summer Institute of Linguistics. (Publications in Linguistics, 59)

Lehmann, C. 1979. Der Relativsatz von Indogermanischen bis zum Italienischen: Eine Etüde in diachroner syntaktischer Typologie. *Sprache* 25:1–25

Lehmann, W. 1974. *Proto-Indo-European syntax*. Austin, University of Texas Press

Lewis, G. L. 1967. *Turkish grammar*. Oxford, Clarendon Press

Li, C. N. ed. 1976. *Subject and topic*. New York, Academic Press

Li, C. N. and S. A. Thompson. 1976a. Strategies for signaling grammatical relations in Wappo. *Chicago Linguistic Society* 12:450–8

Li, C. N. and S. A. Thompson. 1976b. Subject and topic: a new typology of language. In Li 1976:457–89

Li, C. N. and S. A. Thompson. 1977. Relativization strategies in Wappo. Unpublished manuscript, Department of Linguistics, University of California, Los Angeles. (Published in 1978 in *Berkeley Linguistics Society* 4:106–13)

Li, C. N., S. A. Thompson and J. O. Sawyer. 1977. Subject and word order in Wappo. *International Journal of American Linguistics* 43:85–100

Lindenfeld, J. 1973. *Yaqui syntax*. Berkeley, University of California Press

Lockwood, W. B. 1968. *Historical German syntax*. Oxford, Oxford University Press

Longacre, R. E. 1966. Trique clause and sentence: a study in contrast, variation, and distribution. *International Journal of American Linguistics* 32:242–52

Longacre, R. E. 1968. *Philippine languages: discourse, paragraph and sentence structure*. Santa Ana, Calif., Summer Institute of Linguistics. (Publications in Linguistics and Related Fields, 21)

Longacre, R. E. 1970. Sentence structure as a statement calculus. *Language* 46:783–815

Longacre, R. E. 1972. *Hierarchy and universality of discourse constituents in New Guinea languages: discussion*. Washington, Georgetown University Press

Longacre, R. E. 1976. *An anatomy of speech notions*. Lisse, Peter de Ridder

Longacre, R. E. and F. Woods, eds. 1976–7. *Discourse grammar: studies in languages of Colombia, Panama and Ecuador*. 3 vols. Dallas, Summer Institute of Linguistics. (Publications in Linguistics and Related Fields, 52)

Lord, C. 1973. Serial verbs in transition. *Studies in African Linguistics* 4:269–96

Lukas, J. 1967. *Study of the Kanuri language*. International African Institute

Lyons, J. 1977. *Semantics*. Cambridge, Cambridge University Press

MacDonell, A. A. 1927. *A Sanskrit grammar for students*. Oxford, Oxford University Press

Majtinskaja, K. E. 1960. *Vengerskij jazyk III: Sintaksis*. Moscow, Nauka

Manley, T. 1972. *Outline of Sre structure*. Honolulu, University of Hawaii Press

Marchese, L. 1976. Subordination in Godié. Unpublished M.A. thesis, University of California, Los Angeles

Marchese, L. 1977. Subordinate clauses as topics in Godié. In M. Mould and T. J. Hinnebusch, eds. Papers from the 8th Conference on African Linguistics. *Studies in African Linguistics*, Supplement 7:157–64

Martin, S. E. and Y.-S. Lee. 1969. *Beginning Korean*. New Haven, Conn., Yale University Press

Maryott, K. 1967. Sangir sentence structure. Unpublished manuscript, Summer Institute of Linguistics

Mathias, J. 1978. Voir, faire, laisser: grammatical relations in clause merger. Unpublished manuscript, State University of New York, Buffalo

Matisoff, J. 1973. *Grammar of Lahu*. Berkeley, University of California Press

Mayfield, R. 1972. Agta sentence structure. *Linguistics* 85:22–66

Mazaudon, M. 1976. La formation des propositions relatives en tibétain. *Bulletin de la Société de Linguistique de Paris* 73:401–14

McCarthy, J. 1965. Clause chaining in Kanite. *Anthropological Linguistics* 7:59–70

McCawley, J. 1972. Japanese relative clauses. In Peranteau *et al.* 1972:205–14

Menne, A. and G. Frey, eds. 1974. *Logik und Sprache*. Bern, Francke. (Exempla Logica, 1)

Meyer-Lübke, W. 1900. *Grammaire des langues romanes*. Paris

Miller, J. 1971. Some types of 'phrasal conjunction' in Russian. *Journal of Linguistics* 7:55–69

Milner, G. B. 1967. *Fijian grammar*. Suva, Fiji Government Press
Moravcsik, E. 1971. On disjunctive connectives. *Language Sciences* April 1971:27–34
Morgan, J. L. 1969. On the treatment of presupposition in transformational grammar. *Chicago Linguistic Society* 5:167–77
Murane, E. 1974. *Daga grammar*. Norman, University of Oklahoma, Summer Institute of Linguistics
Newmeyer, F. 1969. *English aspectual verbs*. Studies in Linguistics and Language Learning VI
Noonan, M. 1977. On subjects and topics. *Berkeley Linguistics Society* 3:372–85
Noonan, M. and E. Bavin Woock. 1978a. The semantic basis of complementation in Lango. *Buffalo Working Papers in Linguistics* 1:107–18
Noonan, M. and E. Bavin Woock. 1978b. The passive analog in Lango. *Berkeley Linguistics Society* 4:128–39
Noonan, M. and E. Bavin. 1981. Parataxis in Lango. *Studies in African Linguistics* 12: 45–69.
Olli, J. B. 1958. *Fundamentals of Finnish grammar*. New York
Olson, M. L. 1973. *Barai sentence structure and embedding*. Santa Ana, Calif., Summer Institute of Linguistics. (Language Data, Asian-Pacific Series, 3)
Oranskij, I. M. 1963, *Iranskie jazyki*. Moscow, Nauka
Päll, E., E. Totsel and G. Tukumtsev. 1962. *Eesti ja vene keela Kõrvutav grammatika*. Tallinn
Palmer, F. R. 1968. *A linguistic study of the English verb*. London, Longmans
Payne, J. 1974. Some relative-clause constructions in Old Russian. Unpublished manuscript, Department of Linguistics, Cambridge University
Pedersen, H. 1908. *Vergleichende Grammatik der Keltischen Sprachen I*. Göttingen, Vandenhoek and Ruprecht. (Göttinger Sammlung indogermanischer Grammatiken)
Pekmezi, G. 1908. *Grammatik der albenischen Sprache*. Vienna
Peranteau, P. M., J. N. Levi and G. C. Phares, eds. 1972. *The Chicago which hunt*. Chicago, Chicago Linguistic Society
Pickett, V. 1960. *The grammatical hierarchy of Isthmus Zapotec*. Baltimore, Linguistic Society of America. (Language Dissertation, 56)
Poebel, A. 1923. *Grundzüge der sumerischen Grammatik*. Rostock
Postal, P. 1974. *On raising*. Cambridge, Mass., M.I.T. Press
Pride, K. 1965. *Chatino syntax*. Norman, University of Oklahoma, Summer Institute of Linguistics. (Publications in Linguistics and Related Fields, 12)
Prokof'eva, E. D. 1966. Sel'kupskij jazyk. In Vinogradov 1966:396–415
Quirk, R. *et al.* 1972. *A grammar of contemporary English*. London, Longmans
Rajemisa-Raolison, R. 1966. *Grammaire malgache*. Fianarantsoa
Redden, J. A. 1966. Walapai II, morphology. *International Journal of American Linguistics* 32:141–63
Reibel, D. A. and S. E. Schane. 1969. *Modern studies in English*. Englewood Cliffs, N.J., Prentice-Hall
Reid, L. A. 1970. *Central Bontoc: sentence, paragraph, and discourse*. Norman,

University of Oklahoma, Summer Institute of Linguistics. (Publications in Linguistics and Related Fields, 27)

Riddle, E. 1975a. Some pragmatic conditions on complementizer choice. *Chicago Linguistic Society* 11:467–74

Riddle, E. 1975b. A new look at sequence of tenses. Paper given at Linguistics Society of America annual meeting

Rosenberg, M. 1975. Factives that aren't so. *Chicago Linguistic Society* 11:475–86

Rosenthal, J. 1972. On the relative clauses of classical Nahuatl. In Peranteau *et al.* 1972:246–55

Ross, J. R. 1967. Constraints on variables in syntax. Unpublished Ph.D. dissertation, M.I.T. (Also circulated by Indiana University Linguistics Club)

Rost, R. 1887. *Grammaire albanaise*. London

Rutherford, W. E. 1970. Some observations concerning subordinate clauses in English. *Language* 46:96–115

Saloné, S. 1977. Conditionals. In Byarushengo *et al.* 1977:149–60

Sayers, B. J. 1976. The sentence in Wik-Munkan; a description of propositional relationships. Canberra, Australian National University, Research School of Pacific Studies, Department of Linguistics. (Pacific Linguistics, B. 44)

Schachter, J. 1971. Presupposition and counterfactual sentences. Unpublished Ph.D. dissertation, University of California, Los Angeles

Schachter, P. 1974. A non-transformational account of serial verbs. *Studies in African Linguistics*, Supplement 5:253–70

Schachter, P. 1976. The subject in Philippine languages: topic, actor, actor–topic, or none of the above. In Li 1976:491–518

Schachter, P. and F. T. Otanes. 1972. *Tagalog reference grammar*. Berkeley, University of California Press

Schaeffer, F. A. 1968. *The God who is there*. Downers Grove, Ill., Inter-Varsity Press

Schaeffer, F. A. 1969. *Death in the city*. Downers Grove, Ill., Inter-Varsity Press

Schuh, R. G. 1972. Aspects of Ngizim syntax. Unpublished Ph.D. dissertation, University of California, Los Angeles

Schwartz, A. 1971. General aspects of relative clause formation. *Stanford Working Papers on Language Universals* 6:139–71

Scott, G. 1973. *Higher levels of Foré grammar*. Canberra, Australian National University, Research School of Pacific Studies, Department of Linguistics. (Pacific Linguistics, B.23)

Seaver, P. 1978. Interclausal relations in Spanish. Unpublished manuscript, State University of New York, Buffalo

Shackle, C. 1972. *Punjabi*. London, English Universities Press. (Teach Yourself Books)

Shibatani, M., ed. 1976. *Syntax and semantics 6: The grammar of causative constructions*. New York, Academic Press

Sjoberg, A. 1963. *Uzbek structural grammar*. Bloomington, Indiana University Press

Smith, C. 1969. Ambiguous sentences. In Reibel and Schane 1969:75–9

Smyth, H. 1920. *Greek grammar*. Cambridge, Mass., Harvard University Press

Spears, A. 1973. Complements of *significant*-class predicates: a study in the semantics of complementation. *Chicago Linguistic Society* 9:627–38

Stahlke, H. 1970. Serial verbs. *Studies in African Linguistics* 1:60–99

Stark, D. S. 1962. Boundary markers in Dakota. *International Journal of American Linguistics* 28:19–35

Steever, S. 1977. Raising, meaning, and conversational implicature. *Chicago Linguistic Society* 13:590–602

Švendova, N. J. 1970. *Grammatika sovremennogo Russkogo literaturnogo jazyka*. Moscow, Nauka

Svelmoe, G. and T. Svelmoe. 1974. *Notes on Mansaka grammar*. Huntington Beach, Calif., Summer Institute of Linguistics. (Language Data, Asian-Pacific Series, 6)

Tereščenko, N. M. 1966a. Neneckij jazyk. In Vinogradov 1966:376–95

Tereščenko, N. M. 1966b. Èneckij jazyk. In Vinogradov 1966:437–57

Tereščenko, N. M. 1973. *Sintaksis samodijskix jazykov*. Leningrad, Nauka

Terrell, T. and J. B. Hooper. 1974. A semantically based analysis of mood in Spanish. *Hispania* 57:484–94

Thompson, L. C. 1965. *A Vietnamese grammar*. Seattle, University of Washington Press.

Thompson, S. A. 1972. *Instead of* and *rather than* clauses in English. *Journal of Linguistics* 8:237–49

Thord-Gray, I. 1955. *Tarahumara dictionary*. Miami, University of Miami Press

Thurman, R. 1975. Chauve medial verbs. *Anthropological Linguistics* 17:342-52

Tolkien, J. R. R. 1969. *Smith of Wootton Major*. New York, Ballantine

Tryon, D. T. 1970. *Conversational Tahitian*. Berkeley, University of California Press

Urmson, J. 1963. Parenthetical verbs. In C. Caton, ed. *Philosophy and ordinary language*. Urbana, University of Illinois Press: 220–40

Vincent, A. 1973. Tairora verb structure. In H. McKaughan, ed. *The Languages of the Eastern family of the East New Guinea Highland stock*. Seattle, University of Washington Press: 561–87

Vinogradov, V. V., ed. 1966. *Jazyki narodov S.S.S.R*, Vol. 3. Moscow, Nauka

Visser, F. 1973. *An historical syntax of the English language*, Vol. 3. Leiden, Brill

Vogt, H. 1971. *Grammaire de la langue géorgienne*. Oslo, Universitetsforlaget

Waltz, C. 1977. Some observations on Guanano dialogue. In Longacre and Woods 1976-7, Vol. 3:67–110

Waltz, N. 1976. Discourse functions of Guanano sentence and paragraph. In Longacre and Woods 1976-7, Vol. 1:21–145

Washabaugh, W. 1975. On the development of complementizers in creolization. *Stanford Working Papers on Language Universals* 17

Watson, R. 1966. Clause to sentence gradations in Pacoh. *Lingua* 16:166–88

Weber. D. 1978. Relativization in Huallage (Huánuco) Quechua. Unpublished M.A. thesis, University of California, Los Angeles

Welmers, W. E. 1973. *African language structures*. Berkeley, University of California Press

Welmers, W. E. 1976. *A grammar of Vai*. Berkeley, University of California Press

West, D. 1973. *Wojokeso sentence, paragraph and discourse analysis*. Canberra, Australian National University, Research School of Pacific Studies, Department of Linguistics. (Pacific Linguistics, B.28)

Wheelock, F. 1963. *Latin*. London, Barnes and Noble

Wiebe, N. 1977. The structure of events and participants in Cayapa narrative discourse. In Longacre and Woods 1977, Vol. 2:191–227

Williams, J. M. 1967. Some grammatical characteristics of continuous discourse. Unpublished Ph.D. dissertation, University of Wisconsin

Wilson, C. 1975. *Presupposition and non-truth-conditional semantics*. New York, Academic Press

Wittgenstein, L. 1953. *Philosophical investigations*. London, Macmillan

Xromov, A. L. 1972. *Jagnobskij jazyk*. Moscow, Nauka

Yates, A. 1975. *Catalan*. London, English Universities Press. (Teach Yourself Books)

Yokoyama, O. T. 1981. On sentence-coordination in Russian: a functional approach. In R. A. Hendrick, C. S. Masek and M. F. Miller, eds. *Papers from the Seventeenth Regional Meeting, Chicago Linguistic Society*. Chicago: 431–8

Zakijev, M. A. and R. X. Kurbatov. 1971. *Sovremennyj tatarskij literaturnyj jazyk*. Moscow, Nauka

Index

Note: References in this index are to all three volumes of *Language typology and syntactic description*. For ease of reference volume numbers are shown in bold type.